The Peavey Revolution

Hartley Peavey
the Gear,
the Company,
and the All-American
Success Story

By Ken Achard

Backbeat Books
San Francisco

Published by Backbeat Books
600 Harrison Street, San Francisco, CA 94107
www.backbeatbooks.com
email: books@musicplayer.com

An imprint of CMP Information
Publishers of *Guitar Player, Bass Player, Keyboard,* and *EQ* magazines

CMP
United Business Media

Copyright © 2005 by Ken Achard. All rights reserved. No part of this book covered by copyrights hereon may be reproduced or copied in any manner whatsoever without written permission, except in the case of brief quotations embodied in articles and reviews. For information, contact the publishers.

Distributed to the book trade in the US and Canada by
Publishers Group West, 1700 Fourth Street, Berkeley, CA 94710

Distributed to the music trade in the US and Canada by
Hal Leonard Publishing, P.O. Box 13819, Milwaukee, WI 53213

Interior Design and Composition by Richard Leeds – BigWigDesign.com
Cover Design by Richard Leeds – BigWigDesign.com

Library of Congress Cataloging-in-Publication Data

Achard, Ken.
  The Peavey revolution : Hartley Peavey : the gear, the company, and the
  all-American success story / Ken Achard.
    p. cm.
  Includes index.
  ISBN 0-87930-849-4 (alk. paper)
  1. Peavey Electronics—History. 2. Peavey, Hartley, 1941– I. Title.

ML424.P43A65 2005
786.7'1973—dc22
                    2005013768

Printed in China
05 06 07 08 09 5 4 3 2 1

Trademarks: To prevent this book being cluttered with ® and ™ marks, this paragraph serves to acknowledge all trademarks used in the text. PEAVEY® is a registered trademark of Peavey Electronics Corporation. All Peavey product names and logos are trademarks or registered trademarks of Peavey Electronics Corporation. 5150® is a registered trademark of E.L.V.H. Inc. AMX® is a registered trademark of AMX Corporation. Bigsby® is a registered trademark of Fred Gretsch Enterprises Inc. CobraNet™ is a trademark of Peak Audio Inc. Crestron® is a registered trademark of Crestron Electronics Inc. D-Tuna® is a registered trademark of E.L.V.H. Inc. EVH® is a registered trademark of E.L.V.H. Inc. Floyd Rose® is a registered trademark of Floyd Rose Marketing Inc. HipShot™ is a trademark of Hipshot Products Inc. Jack Daniel's® is a registered trademark of the Jack Daniel Distillery. Jazzmaster® and Telecaster® are registered trademarks of Fender Musical Instruments Corporation. Kahler® is a registered trademark of American Precision Metal Works Inc. Modulus® is a registered trademark of Modulus Guitars. Motorola® is a registered trademark of Motorola Inc. Quadrajust™ is a trademark of Hipshot Products Inc. THX® is a registered trademark of THX Ltd. Windows® is a registered trademark of Microsoft Corporation. Wolfgang® is a registered trademark of E.L.V.H. Inc.

CONTENTS

Foreword by Steve Cropper v

Introduction vi

PART ONE — Formative Years 1
Chapter 1: Right Place, Right Time 2
Chapter 2: Family Ties 5
Chapter 3: Epiphany 11
Chapter 4: Cancel the Interview! 14

PART TWO — From Dream to Reality 19
Chapter 5: Vertical Integration — 1967 20
Chapter 6: A Real Factory — 1968–69 27
Chapter 7: Liftoff — 1969–71 33

PART THREE — Acceleration 37
Chapter 8: On the Gas — 1972 38
Chapter 9: Breaking Waves — 1975–77 50

PART FOUR — Clear Water 65
Chapter 10: Taking Center Stage — 1979–84 66
Chapter 11: New Directions — 1985–89 84

PART FIVE — Triumph and Tragedy 105
Chapter 12: Flying High — 1990–94 106
Chapter 13: Letting Go — 1995–98 130

PART SIX — After Melia 147
Chapter 14: Turbulence — 1998–2001 148
Chapter 15: Renaissance — 2001–04 157
Chapter 16: A Maverick Looks to the Future — 2005 167

Appendix A: Product Chronology 174

Acknowledgments 182

Index 183

This book is dedicated to the employees of Peavey Electronics, whose talents have helped make the company a global success, and to everyone who shares Hartley Peavey's vision.

FOREWORD

By Steve Cropper

Hartley Peavey and I both grew up around gospel and blues music, and he started the same way I did, trying to play guitar. He developed a stronger desire to build amplifiers, so in 1965 he started a company in his dad's garage. It's been a long, hard road for him to convince musicians he makes some of the best instruments on the planet, but he eventually achieved worldwide success by maintaining the high quality of his products—and by respecting the musicians who play them. When we were working on the Cropper Classic guitar, Hartley said, "I trust your ears," and everybody at Peavey bent over backwards for me. I think the guitar turned out pretty good. I have several, and Hartley's always been very good about sending me guitars to auction for charity. Thanks to him we're able to raise a lot of money for the kids.

A few years ago I attended Peavey's annual golf tournament. While heading to the event, someone pointed out Hartley's house, which was right next to the golf course. I thought, "Cool—I'm going to be working with someone who not only likes music but must really love golf, since he lives on a golf course." After leaving the locker room I ran into Hartley. He was dressed much like he does when he goes to work, in his street shoes and a Hawaiian shirt. I asked him if he was going to get ready to tee up, and he replied, "I don't play golf." I said, "But you live on the course." "Yes," he said. "And I'm not very far from the dining room." That day Hartley was all about entertaining his guests, who had traveled from all over to attend the event. I didn't see anyone not having a good time—especially Hartley Peavey. He was with his people, and that makes him happy.

▲ *Steve Cropper with his Cropper Classic*

Steve Cropper defined soul guitar in his work with artists such as Booker T. and the MGs, Wilson Pickett, and Sam & Dave. He gained global renown through his work with the Blues Brothers, and he continues a busy schedule of touring and recording.

INTRODUCTION

Hartley D. Peavey, Founder, Chairman, and CEO of Peavey Electronics Corporation

We live in a world of instant fame and equally instant oblivion. Celebrities seem to come and go with the change of the seasons, and their accomplishments are forgotten even more quickly than they were lauded. The same holds true for brand names—with a few notable exceptions. The brands that endure over decades do so because they have a strong identity and are associated with products of exceptional value that evolve in direct response to customer needs. The story traced through the pages of this book is of one such brand. It is the story of a unique company and the founder who gave that company its name—a name that has cut a wide swath through the world's music and sound industry.

The term "living legend" is too often assigned to individuals whose influence proves to be ephemeral, but it is not a term that should be used lightly. Politicians rarely deserve it, because history is their judge. Explorers, artists, and scientists sometimes qualify, but often it is only after death that their achievements are fully measured. The world of business occasionally offers up individuals who, within their own industry, become legendary; in many cases, their products carry their names—Ford automobiles and Gillette razors are two examples that come to mind.

That Hartley Peavey is a living legend few in the music industry would dispute. Many biographies have been written about famous entrepreneurs, and many have tried to find the alchemy for business success by analyzing their methods and behavior. Hartley delights in telling you that he is just "a country boy who has always liked to tinker," but behind that humble self-image lurks a complex visionary driven by passionately held principles, overwhelming persistence, and a voraciously inquisitive mind. He is outspoken, stubborn, and fair—but never suffers fools gladly. He is restless and energetic, a man to whom the word "defeat" is anathema. He is a natural and captivating orator who can evoke the intensity of a Southern Baptist preacher.

To Hartley, business is war: only the fit will survive and only the strong will prevail. It is not surprising that he is a student of military strategy who has analyzed the major wars of the 20th century. He believes in careful planning and good tactical decisions, and his decisive management style is driven by clear objectivity. Constantly seeking out the weaknesses in his adversaries and finding ways to capitalize on them made his company great—and made it a force in the industry well before many of his "friendly competitors" realized what had happened.

Within these pages I have set out to document the life of Hartley Peavey, the growth of his company, and the development of its products—and, in doing so, to recognize and pay tribute to those who have played a part in this extraordinary commercial enterprise. Melia Peavey, in a 1988 interview with the Jackson Journal of Business, referred to Hartley's dream of establishing an "Industrial Camelot," a place where everyone would live and work in an environment where they could be or do anything of which they were capable. Many have subsequently come to that Camelot and developed acumen, skills, drives, and ambitions they might never have realized without their time there.

The story of Peavey Electronics—from its days as a one-man operation in an attic workshop to its current position as a world-class corporation employing more than 2,000 workers and occupying over 2 million square feet of space under roof at its peak—is a remarkable tale by any measure.

INTRODUCTION

> *"Far better it is to dare mighty things, to win glorious triumphs, even though checkered with failure, than to take rank with those poor spirits who neither enjoy much nor suffer much, because they live in the gray twilight that knows not victory nor defeat."*
>
> — THEODORE ROOSEVELT

That much of its growth has been self-financed makes it even more impressive. Today, the company's products are distributed around the world and it holds more than 130 patents, yet innovation continues to be its lifeblood. Like its founder, Peavey is never content to rest on its laurels.

I first met Hartley Peavey in 1972, became part of the extended Peavey family in 1973, and worked with or for him for 30 years—three of the four decades through which he has nurtured and grown Peavey Electronics. It is a company he still owns and a company he still manages—every day. If, as you read these pages, you detect a hint of awe in my tone, please forgive me for expressing the great respect I have for this man.

An entire room at the Peavey Museum is devoted to the collection of awards and accolades that have been bestowed on Peavey over the years by governments, industry associations, the trade and consumer press, and other sources—far too many to catalogue in this book. Suffice it to say that they demonstrate the esteem with which Hartley and his enterprise have been, and are, held. It is said, though, that success does not come without failure, and Peavey Electronics has had its share of failures and disappointments. Research and development can only thrive if mistakes are allowed to be the impetus for greater effort. Some great products have failed inexplicably to capture a market, or simply been ahead of their time. Such experiences leave scars, and as I explored the past for this book, it was plain that some of the 11,000 or so good folks who have at one time or another held a Peavey employee ID badge have painful memories. The heat in the Peavey kitchen—where the quest for excellence, growth, and profit is inexorable—can be hard to bear. It is, however, out of this environment that the brand has acquired its strength. Peavey is a brand that is synonymous with value—the balanced compound of price, performance, and quality—and value is a prize that is hard won.

Peavey is an industrial autocracy, which makes it a particularly interesting business to study. Few enterprises of its size can lay claim to 40 years of continual sole ownership. It is an environment where ruthlessness is often confused with personal conviction or even self-preservation. Hartley has said that he wakes up each day scared, knowing that he will be challenged to "lean further out of the window" to continue his success. Fame, wealth, and notoriety can profoundly change an individual, and I am often asked: "What is Hartley Peavey really like?" He can be deadly serious, but he can also be great fun—and his infectious laugh bears witness to a wonderful sense of humor that puts people at ease. The first time I stepped into his office, he waved me to a seat, opened two cans of beer, put his feet on the desk, and started talking. His conversation was casual and engaging, but also thoughtful and enlightening. An inquisitive thread ran through it as he probed for market intelligence. Thirty years on, he is likely to do the same. With Hartley Peavey, what you see is what you get.

Hartley is a master of pithy statements, and throughout this book I have dropped in quotes that provide a glimpse of what goes on inside his mind. There are also some quotes from others that he uses often to illustrate his philosophy. He is quick to pay tribute to the efforts of those who have helped to build the company, and of himself he says, "I am the catalyst. A catalyst is that which enhances or speeds up a reaction without itself being changed."

—*Ken Achard*

PART ONE

Formative Years

Right Place, Right Time

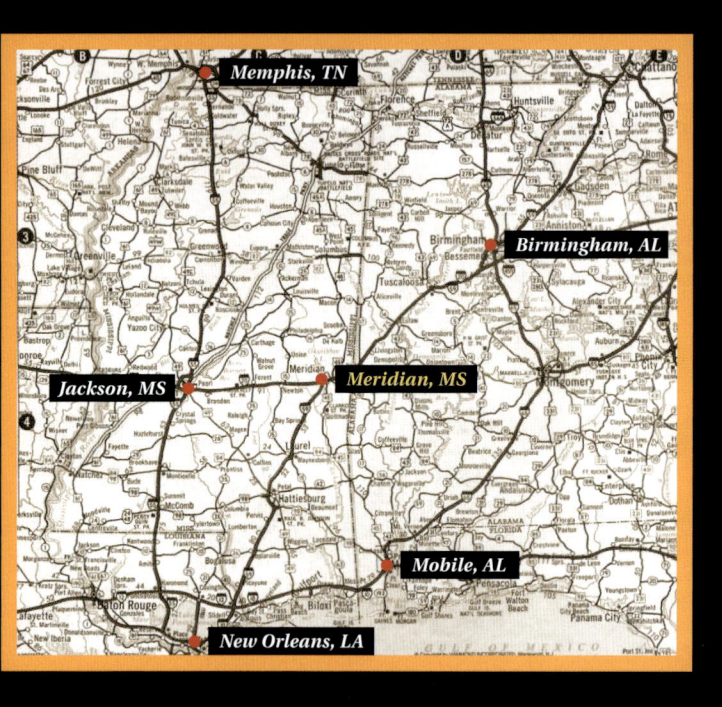

Peavey International Headquarters in Meridian, MS

Meridian, Mississippi, lies at a crossroads. Incorporated in 1860, it sprang up where the route north from New Orleans to Nashville met the westbound road from the Carolinas to Texas. Today, interstate highways 20 and 59 intersect in Meridian.

During the Civil War, Meridian paid a heavy price for its central location. In February 1864, after Grant had taken Vicksburg, the victorious Union commander sent Sherman's forces east to Meridian, where they tore up the railroad tracks and laid waste to much of surrounding Lauderdale County, leaving, as Sherman put it, "a swath of desolation 50 miles broad." It would be well into the following century before Meridian recovered, and it was in this setting that Hartley Peavey's grandparents and parents grew up—a time and a place where struggle, determination, and respect for the value of a dollar were the stuff of everyday life.

Meridian also lies at a musical crossroads. It was the birthplace of Jimmie Rodgers—the man who has been called the Father of Country Music. Born in 1897, "The

● *Hartley as a child*

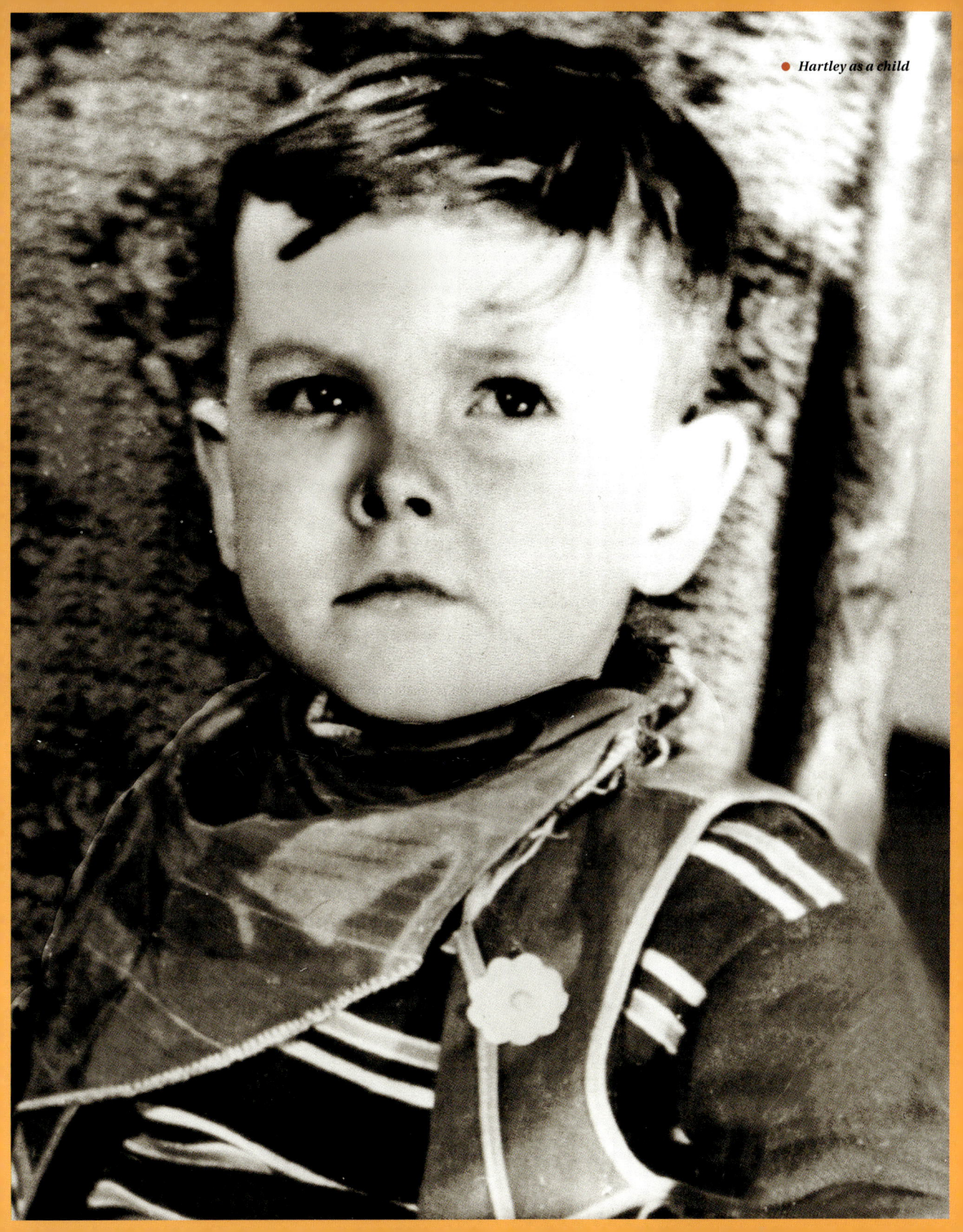

Singing Brakeman" is widely credited as the progenitor of this important genre of American music, which took root in his unique blend of yodeling, blues, and rural folk styles. Meridian is home of the Jimmie Rodgers Museum and hosts an annual Jimmie Rodgers Festival.

Meridian is also close to the Mississippi Delta, the cradle of the blues. This second great strain of American music emerged in the late 19th century, born out of the toil and deprivation of the African Americans who were bound in slavery on the cotton plantations of Louisiana, Mississippi, and Alabama. The abolition of slavery changed the agriculture and economics of the region, but it did little to relieve the deprivation. The misery of this hard life gave birth to the blues, a musical style that channeled poverty and hopelessness into the sound of redemption.

For many in the Delta, the mighty Mississippi River offered a way out. Seeking a better life, they followed it north to Memphis and St. Louis and, eventually, Chicago, taking their music with them. In the process, the blues shaped and influenced and mingled with other types of music, giving birth to new styles like jazz and forming the basis of modern popular music.

The roster of blues greats born and raised in Mississippi is overwhelming: Robert Johnson, Son House, Muddy Waters, B.B. King, Sonny Boy Williamson, Big Bill Broonzy, Elmore James, Mississippi John Hurt, Albert King, Willie Dixon, Otis Rush, Jimmy Reed—the list goes on and on. And, of course, there was that young man born in Tupelo on January 8, 1935, who would go on to merge the two great strains of music from his native state into a whole new kind of American music. His name was Elvis Presley.

It was into this extraordinary musical environment that J.B. Peavey would be born in 1912. He would play saxophone in the Meridian High School band and eventually found a music store where his son Hartley would explore his interest in music and musical gear—a true child of the music business.

Hartley would grow up during a crucial time, too, for the children of the early 1940s became the teenagers of the '50s. It was a time when post-war utilitarianism began to give way to innovation and "feeling good." As the American economy began to boom again, there was strong belief in the promise of a better tomorrow. Young people felt emancipated—they had a little money in their pockets, and they expressed themselves more freely and openly than any generation that had preceded them.

Nothing distilled this revolution more than the incredible amalgam of musical styles and influences that became rock 'n' roll. Hartley Peavey will tell you that his epiphany came in 1957, at a Bo Diddley concert in Laurel, Mississippi. Transfixed by the performance, he vowed to become a world-class rock 'n' roll star—and he did, although not quite in the way he first imagined it.

Those who know him well will tell you that Hartley would have been successful wherever and whenever he was born. But being born where he was and when he was undoubtedly provided a powerful impetus to his future influence on American music.

Family Ties

On the 30th of December 1941, Hartley Davis Peavey was born in Meridian, Mississippi, the first child of J.B. "Mutt" Peavey and his wife, Sarah. Hartley—a name the young boy hated—was the last name of his grandfather's best friend. Davis was his mother's maiden name, and it was fashionable at the time to use the maternal family name for a child's christening.

J.B. owned the local music store, Peavey's Melody Music Company, which he had founded in 1938. He handled the sales duties while Sarah answered the phone and tended to the accounts. Their young son could often be found asleep behind the counter in his bassinet.

▲ *Some say Hartley was a wild child!*

▶ *The young scientist*

Iliad when he was in the fifth grade and got spankings for not playing baseball, which he thought was a stupid pursuit. He collected comic books, and he loved to read fantasy, adventure, and science fiction tales. Fascinated by aircraft and rockets, he would draw them in his notebooks at school. His family lived a simple, down-to-earth life—but Hartley's mother had aspirations for her son, which included the proper way to dress. Hartley recalls:

> My mother had watched all these movies from back in the '30s, and she had this idea of what little boys should wear. And it was not at all what little boys in Mississippi wore! She made me go to school in the first grade wearing these damn knickers—corduroy pants with elastic around the calf. We lived in a section of town called East End, which was not exactly where the elite lived. One of the reasons why East End was not particularly "cool" was because there was a big old cotton mill, and I went to Witherspoon School where they had a lot of "cotton mill kids." They came to school with what we call "coveralls" and tennis shoes. All the kids wore blue jeans or coveralls, and me and one other guy came in knickers!
>
> My best friend in school was Richard "Bunky" Pryor. His mother made him come to school in knickers, too, and he and I became good friends because both of us had to walk down the hall fighting almost every guy in the first and second grade. I was doing pretty good until I hit a third-grader, and then I got my butt

beaten—whereupon I decided fighting was not my thing. Fact is, I'll never forget my first black eye. I jumped on this big old boy who was giving me crap for some reason and *bam!* . . . he hit me in the eye. I didn't realize he had blackened my eye, but I had a big shiner. My dad said, "Son, what happened to you?' I said, "I had been watching this worm crawl across this tree root and somebody bumped into me and I fell down and hit my eye." That's when I discovered I was a lover and not a fighter.

The Peaveys had a second son, Robert, who was born when Hartley was eight years old. Because of the age difference, the brothers grew up doing their own things. Their personalities could not have been more different: Bob was a quiet, reserved kid who took piano lessons and earned high marks in school, while Hartley was a rebel who liked to build things and bend the rules. Dixie Wiggins—the daughter of one of Hartley's future teachers—was a friend of little brother Bob and remembers visiting the Peavey home as a child. "Hartley's bedroom," she says, "had a workbench where he made balsa wood aircraft models, which he would paint and hang from the ceiling with fishing line." She remembers a veritable squadron of models flying from the ceiling.

◀ *Joseph Lane "Pop" Peavey (right) pictured driving the first car in Meridian*

CHAPTER 2 • FAMILY TIES

Young Hartley was enthralled with machines and science. "When I was in the seventh grade," he recalls, "I started entering science fairs. Most of the other kids' projects were primitive, but mine were pretty slick because I was good with my hands. In the eighth or ninth grade, I got all the way up to the state level. I had a big display—I had about ten rockets that I had turned on a wood lathe; for a kid, it was pretty damned complex. I had solid fuel, liquid fuel—all the different types of rockets they had back in the '50s. It looked great. But some little girl had a molasses can with a Bunsen burner under it with a little pinwheel. Turn on the gas, light the fire, the water heats up, and steam comes out the hole she'd put in the lid and the little pinwheel turns. Well, she won the science fair because her display actually moved. So I said, 'That's it, screw it—I'm never going to enter another science fair.'"

> *"I didn't have any money and couldn't afford to buy the things I wanted, like a stereo system or a guitar, so I ended up building my own."* —HARTLEY PEAVEY

Hartley cites his grandfather, Joseph Lane Peavey, as his biggest childhood influence. J.L., whom he affectionately called "Pop," was born on March 2, 1870. He went to work for the telephone and telegraph company at the turn of the century, and because he spoke a little French was transferred to Louisiana to run telegraph wires. Many of the residents there were Cajuns, descended from the French settlers removed from Acadia in eastern Canada by the British during the French and Indian War. The Cajuns didn't understand electricity and thought the telegraph wires would damage their crops, requiring some careful explanations by J.L.

Pop met Hartley's grandmother, Anna Burleson, in Lake Charles, Louisiana. She was born on October 11, 1875. After they were married, Pop and Anna returned to Meridian and he went to work for the A. Gresset Music House in the early 1900s. He worked there until he retired in the prewar years. Although he was not a musician himself, Pop became a successful piano salesman and was prosperous enough to buy one of the first automobiles in the state.

"Pop" Peavey was also an amateur inventor. His nephew Dick Wiggins Jr. remembers that he invented a night-vision visor for drivers and an indoor tornado shelter that was granted a U.S. patent. Pop liked to talk about his inventions and spin tall tales for young Hartley, who credits his grandfather for both his love of science and his own talent for telling stories.

Pop had a workshop with lots of tools and old telephone equipment where his grandson loved to hang out. "After school I used to go down to Pop's house and help him," says Hartley. "He was always working on something. He had mostly hand tools; I don't recall a single electric tool in the place. He'd give me a paintbrush or a hammer, and I just loved it. My grandfather was not a musician, but he was a tinkerer. My dad, on the other hand, was a great musician, but he had no mechanical ability. Somehow I got my grandfather's mechanical ability but not my dad's musical ability."

J.L. Peavey died of a heart attack on September 14, 1955, when Hartley was in the seventh grade. "When my grandfather died," Hartley says, "I inherited his tools because my dad cared absolutely nothing about them. We had a basement in our house, and that basement became my workshop—at least that's what I called it."

Pop's half-brother, Dick Wiggins, was a master machinist; he was born on October 13, 1880, and died on July 12, 1957, when Hartley was fifteen. Like Pop, Dick had a workshop where he would let Hartley help out with projects. Both Pop and Dick liked to tinker with radios, and one of Hartley's first projects was to build his own, which he used to listen to his favorite adventure programs, such as "Space Patrol," "Suspense," "Escape," "Inner Sanctum," and other sci-fi and adventure shows.

Hartley's father, Joseph Burleson Peavey, was born on August 20, 1912. He was known as "Mutt," although no one can recall why. ("He didn't know, either!" says Hartley.) Blessed with musical talent, he mastered the saxophone and joined a touring band after graduating from high school. In 1938, Mr. Mutt returned home to Meridian to settle down, opening a music store with $50 and a second-hand piano that his father had given to him. Soon after, he met Sarah Davis, a 23-year-old country girl from Clarke County, south of Meridian, who was working as a secretary. They fell in love and were married in the winter of 1938.

Mr. Mutt and Sarah were living in an apartment when Hartley was born; a year later, they purchased a house at 1220 16th Avenue—the house where Peavey, hunkered down in the basement, would build his first amplifier. During World War II new instruments were not being made, so Mr. Mutt (who was too old for the draft) bought old pianos, restored them, and sold them in his store. His business did well, and in 1946 he bought the downtown building that would be known as Peavey's Melody Music.

In the summer before Hartley entered seventh grade, his great uncle, Dick Wiggins, persuaded him to attend the Ross Collins Vocational School. Dick taught machine shop at the Collins School; the minimum entry age there was 14, but Dick was able to obtain special dispensation for his nephew. Although Hartley was the youngest student ever to enroll, he threw himself into mastering the metal lathe, the milling machine, and the other machines in the shop. His aptitude was apparent after Dick gave him his test for new students: he handed Hartley a metal rod and a micrometer, and instructed him to turn the rod to a size that had to be accurate within 3/1000s of an inch. Hartley got it right on the first try.

▲ *Hartley presents his father, J.B. "Mutt" Peavey, with a commemorative record for 30 years of service to the company*

Hartley rode to school each morning with Uncle Dick, who was a renowned local character. He drove a 1929 Plymouth that had ancient mechanical brakes, and he would cuss when anyone crossed his path, because it was unlikely he would be able to stop the car. Hartley admits that his own tendency to sometimes use "colorful language" is something he probably learned from Uncle Dick.

Hartley took courses in machine shop, basic electricity, radio shop, sheet metal, and mechanical drawing. Dick Wiggins Jr.—"Little Dick"—was his instructor in electricity, and he recalls young Hartley's sharp, inquisitive mind (and his love for his uncle's *Popular Mechanics*, *Popular Science*, and *National Geographic* magazines). He says that Hartley quickly became a fine machinist.

Hartley says that his time at the Collins School was crucially important to his later success. "The thought then—and probably now as well—is that anyone who works with his hands is somehow

Hartley as a teenager

a second-class citizen," he says. "I never subscribed to that, because I'm good with my hands. That's my talent—I can build things. I didn't have any money and couldn't afford to buy the things I wanted, like a stereo system or a guitar, so I ended up building my own."

When he wasn't immersed in his schoolwork, which was most of the time, Hartley helped out at the music store. He remembers going to his first National Association of Music Merchants (NAMM) trade show in Chicago in 1955. Staying at the swanky Palmer House Hotel, looking at all of the musical instruments, and seeing Bill Haley & the Comets perform made a big impression on him.

Mr. Mutt was determined that his son should be a musician, and he encouraged Hartley from an early age. "When I was in the fourth grade, he made me start playing the clarinet," Hartley says. "I hated it—I didn't want to play a musical instrument, and I sure as hell didn't want to play the clarinet. But he insisted. Later, when I went to junior high school, I switched over to trumpet. Dad said, 'Son, if you will get into the school band, I will buy you a car.' I would have done almost anything to get a car. Anything! I would have drunk a bucket of buzzard puke to get a car. I really wasn't interested in playing in the band, though. I'd fake it when everyone else was playing. I didn't practice. The band leader would be on my butt all the time, and he'd go tell my dad there wasn't anything he could do with me. But eventually I did get into the band. I was last chair, the worst trumpet player in the band. And sure enough, on September 8, 1957, Dad took me down to the Chevrolet place and bought me a car—a 1957 Chevrolet. It was red with a white top, and it was the love of my life."

Epiphany

"You are today where your thoughts have brought you; you will be tomorrow where your thoughts take you."

—JAMES LANE ALLEN

Late in 1957, Hartley drove his Chevy down to Laurel, Mississippi, to see a Bo Diddley concert. All night he stood riveted in front of the bandstand, totally captivated by the music.

The next day, Hartley asked his father if he could have a guitar. Mr. Mutt didn't think much of the idea. He was a traditional big-band musician, and most of the guitar players he dealt with at the store had poor work habits and weren't good about paying their bills. Eventually, though, Hartley got his father to agree to the idea—provided he took lessons.

Hartley was loaned an old Stella acoustic guitar and sent to Carl Fitzgerald, a local D.J. and country singer, for instruction. "The guitar I got had a damn cowboy

▲ *Hartley's original workshop and tools from his parents'*

like a 2x4. Carl wanted me to play 'Twinkle Twinkle Little Star' and learn all this theory and stuff, but I just wanted to play rock 'n' roll."

Hartley chafed at both the lessons and his substandard instrument. He kept pestering his father for a better guitar. "Finally he gave me the first Japanese guitar I had ever seen," he says. "It was a Suzuki classical with nylon strings. I didn't know anything about guitars, but I did know I didn't want nylon strings, so I got a set of steel strings and put them on the guitar. I began to tune them up and *crack!* . . . there went the bridge. That was my introduction to guitar repair. I got a piece of plywood from a piano crate and glued and bolted it to the soundboard so the strings would tune up to pitch. Then I wanted a pickup. In those days, the only aftermarket pickup you could buy was a DeArmond, and the thing cost $39. It might as well have been $39,000, so I asked Dad for a pickup. He said 'Son, when you learn how to play that guitar, I'll think about it.' That wasn't good enough for me, so I ordered six magnets from the classified ads in *Popular Science* magazine and then went down to the electronics parts house to get some wire. The smallest gauge they had was #38. I sat down at our dining table and wound a pickup by hand. It weighed a pound, but you know what? It worked!"

▲ *Hartley with Sam Phillips of Sun Records*

Hartley then fashioned a metal bracket for mounting the pickup in the guitar's soundhole and showed it to his father. "I was pretty proud of myself that I had gotten this thing to work, and I said, 'Dad, now I need an amplifier.' He said, 'Son, when you learn to play that thing . . .'"

Hartley acknowledges that his father's reluctance to support his desire to play electric guitar was probably crucial to his career direction. "I've often wondered what would have happened if he had given me a guitar and given me an amplifier. These days, that's probably what a father would do. But my dad was a product of the Depression—he didn't have it, so he didn't think I should have it." (Years later, J.B. Peavey told an interviewer from Mississippi educational TV that "if I had gone on and bought him a $1,000 outfit, what would have happened? I just believe he'd have picked on it for a few days and that would have been the end of it. He wanted an amplifier but I wouldn't give it to him, so he just decided to make one.")

"It's been said that necessity is the mother of invention," Hartley says, "so I modified the guitar to take steel strings, I made the pickup, and then I made an amplifier. I had been influenced by my Bo Diddley experience, and he had an amplifier that looked to be about six feet wide! It was big, so I decided I wanted a big amplifier with four 12" speakers in it. I built it over the Christmas holiday. I copied the schematic out of a tube manual, but it had an RIAA equalization circuit in it." (That is, the circuit was designed for playing LPs—Hartley was using a design intended for a record player, not a musical instrument amplifier.)

Hartley had made the first Peavey amp. "It didn't sound great," he admits, "but it was okay—and it was big! For that era, it was pretty loud too. I built it out of old junk parts that I got out of trash cans. In those days we had jukebox operators in town, and they used speakers mainly made by Utah. The 'spider' was mounted on a little platform that was attached with screws, and you could adjust it and move the voice coil around to keep it from rubbing. The dummies at the jukebox places didn't know that, so they'd sell me the speakers that were rattling for $2. I'd take them home and cut the caps off with an X-acto knife and stick in shims. I'd use photo negatives to center the voice coils, tighten the screws back up again, and the speakers worked great. A great speaker for $2!"

Hartley's guitar-playing friend Sonny Roth was impressed by the big amp with the castoff speakers, and he told Hartley that if he would make him one, too, he would give him guitar lessons—real rock 'n' roll guitar lessons. So Hartley made an amp for Sonny, and spent the next eight years trying to become a rockin' guitar player.

"Truth is, I was the world's worst guitar player," Hartley admits. But Mr. Mutt was impressed enough by his efforts to give him a real electric guitar—a Gibson that he had repossessed. "It was a very used and abused Les Paul Special. I painted it white and carved a forearm curve and rib relief in the back, which made it look somewhat odd but very comfortable to play. I ended up giving it to George Cummins, and he told me a while back that he still had it. He was a great guitar player and was primarily responsible for introducing me to jazz. He later went on to be the lead guitar player for Dr. Hook & the Medicine Show and a songwriter not only for Dr. Hook but also for other groups in the Nashville area."

> "Truth is, I was the world's worst guitar player."
> —HARTLEY PEAVEY

Hartley eventually saved enough money to buy a new instrument. "It was a Fender Jazzmaster, which was the first and only new guitar I've ever owned in my life. You know, Leo Fender was my idol—he was the only guy that I've ever met that actually gave me goosebumps, and I've had the good fortune in my career to meet a number of superstars and several presidents."

In high school, Hartley joined a fraternity that booked bands to play at dances, bringing in rock 'n' roll stars like Chuck Berry, Bo Diddley, and Larry Williams. He lost a couple of girlfriends along the way because he wouldn't dance with them when the band was playing—he was too busy watching the guitar players and studying the equipment being used onstage.

On the weekends, Hartley sometimes worked as a disc jockey at the local radio station, earning $1.25 an hour and calling himself "Dee" (for his middle initial) Peavey so his school friends wouldn't know it was him playing those country music records. And he often stuck around to help out his boss, Dan Hollingsworth, with the maintenance of the broadcast equipment, which was all tube-based in those days, further enhancing his knowledge of electronics.

There was time for fun, too. Hartley likes to tell the tale of how he slipped into a dance for a rival fraternity where he had been denied admittance. "There was this guy named Dale Hawkins who was on the Chess label," he says. "The only record he ever had of any significance was called 'Susie-Q.' I asked Dad if he had any guitar cases that he didn't need, and he gave me this old steel guitar case. I painted 'Dale Hawkins' on it, dressed up in black pants and a black shirt, and walked in with the band." That old guitar case is now on display at the Peavey Museum. Hartley was reunited with it many years later, when one of the girls who went to that dance with him, Darryl Sanders, found it in the attic of her mother's house in Meridian.

▲ *Graduation — soft focus*

Hartley graduated from high school in 1960, and he was glad to leave the regimen of school life behind. He had been a dreamer, often doodling in his notebooks instead of paying attention. "I used to sit for hours, while I should have been listening to the teacher, drawing pictures of guitars or little logos or whatever," he says. The first guitar he designed was sketched in a notebook sometime in 1958 or '59. Years later, that drawing became the basis of the Mystic model—and looking closely at that early design, you can see the scoop cutout on the headstock that was eventually incorporated into the headstock of the Van Halen Wolfgang instruments.

During his senior year, Hartley dreamed up the famous Peavey logo that would later appear on thousands of products. "I came up with an angular logo," he says. "Some people call it the 'lightning bolt' logo. What I wanted to do, since Leo Fender was my idol, was to have a very distinctive logo, as Fender did—I mean, you could be across the room and recognize that backwards 'F' and the script. So I came up with the concept where the 'P' and the 'V,' and the 'A'

▲ Hartley's first patent, filed April 10, 1963, while he was still at college

▲ *The first Peavey amplifier with the famous logo — tube amp built by Hartley Peavey in his parents' basement (early '60s, pre-company)*

▶ *The drawing in Hartley's notebook of his logo concept*

and the 'Y,' would more or less intersect." The instantly recognizable Peavey logo was the result.

As a teenager, Hartley's consuming passion was music and bands—and the electronics he read about voraciously in *Popular Electronics* magazine. He also liked to talk with Ed Sheely, the service technician at Peavey's Melody Music, who showed Hartley how he repaired gear. The store was a Magnavox and Curtis Mathis dealer, and the new stereo equipment was all the rage. Hartley's father gave him the task of converting his old stock of mono phonographs to stereo, and this became his first paid electronics employment. Stimulated by this hands-on work, Hartley supplemented his knowledge of electronics by taking an RCA electronics correspondence course.

In the summer of 1962, Hartley enrolled at Mississippi State University to pursue a degree in general business. But he also studied business on a more personal level. "All through college I was a 'horse trader,'" he says. "I always had a guitar or an amp or something under my bed to trade."

Although Hartley still dreamed of being a professional guitarist, it was becoming clear that his primary talent was in building things. His basement workshop at home was soon filled with components ordered from McGee Radio, a mail-order outfit in Kansas City, Missouri, and Hartley's friends kept him busy building amps for them. He also made one for his brother Bob.

The first branded Peavey amp (complete with "lightning bolt" logo) was built in the basement workshop in 1961; today, it's a star exhibit at the Peavey Museum. Although the company bearing

16 THE PEAVEY REVOLUTION • **PART ONE** • FORMATIVE YEARS

his name would not be founded until 1965, Hartley was already beginning to make a name for himself in the music business. He filed for his first patent (#3,151,699) on April 10, 1963, and received it on October 6, 1964; it was for a "telescoping speaker cabinet" that could be compressed for easy transportability and adjusted for optimum bass response. He offered the idea to Fender and Gibson, but both companies turned him down outright.

During his summer vacations, Hartley did manual labor, digging postholes for the REA (Rural Electrification Authority) or lugging 100-pound sacks of sand as a sandblaster's assistant. These experiences provided steady cash for his electronics projects—and also encouraged him to continue his studies, lest he spend the rest of his life doing such work.

While Hartley was in college, he played in a band called the Spades and several "no name" groups. Inevitably, each band he joined would need an amp, an instrument, or a PA system, and Hartley would make it. Soon it became apparent that once each band had the equipment it needed, they would bring in a new guitarist who was a better player, and Hartley would be squeezed out. What he thought was bad luck became a realization that the bands wanted him for his skill at building equipment, not as a musician—and reality started to set in.

"I had a fateful, pivotal experience," Hartley says. "I had to look in the mirror and be totally honest with myself. I said, 'Okay, big boy, your future as a rock star is looking very dim, so I think

◀ *Peavey's Melody Music store— Hartley opened Peavey Electronics above the store*

CHAPTER 4 • CANCEL THE INTERVIEW! **17**

▲ *Hartley enjoys some downtime with Uncle Leslie Boyd*

it's time to take a little inventory. If you're not going to be a rock star, what are you going to do?' I hated business school; principles of management, insurance, labor economics—what a boring course that was. The answer was, 'Well, if I can't play music as well as I'd like, I still love music and I like musicians, so I think I'll just do as my idol Leo Fender did—I'll build good gear at a fair and reasonable price.' I decided I wanted to go into the manufacturing business."

Hartley graduated from Mississippi State in May 1965. "In my senior year, my dad wanted me to go for job interviews," he recalls. "I had an interview with Continental Can, and I was in my room putting on my tie and then . . . I canceled it!" (The hatred of neckties has remained a Peavey characteristic ever since.) Mr. Mutt was unsympathetic, and he scolded his son. He had to work for a living, so Hartley would have to work as well. Right?

Hartley, ever the persuader, explained that he had this idea—he was going to start his own company and make amplifiers. His father thought he was out of his mind. "Do you honestly think you can compete with the big companies?" he asked. Hartley replied, confidently, "Well, honestly, yes, I think I can."

After the initial shock wore off, J.B. realized that Hartley was serious and set about helping him. In 1960, he had sold his music store to Mississippi Music (who continued to trade as Peavey's Melody Music), but he had retained ownership of the property, and the attic floor of the building was empty. It had previously been rented to an optical glass company. So, when Hartley said he needed a place to start his business, his father said he could move in upstairs. In typical style, Hartley says the place was a "hellhole" when he moved in, with aluminum oxide residue everywhere. But he set up shop there, starting up his company with $8,000 that his father got by cashing in bonds. It was late 1964.

"A lot of people told me I was crazy," Hartley says. "In retrospect, they were probably correct. I call it the bumblebee effect. Everybody knows the bumblebee can't fly—its wings can't support its body. Of course the bumblebee doesn't know this, so it flies anyway. That's kind of how I started."

THE PEAVEY REVOLUTION • **PART ONE** • FORMATIVE YEARS

PART TWO

From Dream to Reality

CHAPTER 5
Vertical Integration

"I graduated thinking that I actually knew something — not realizing my education was just beginning!" —HARTLEY PEAVEY

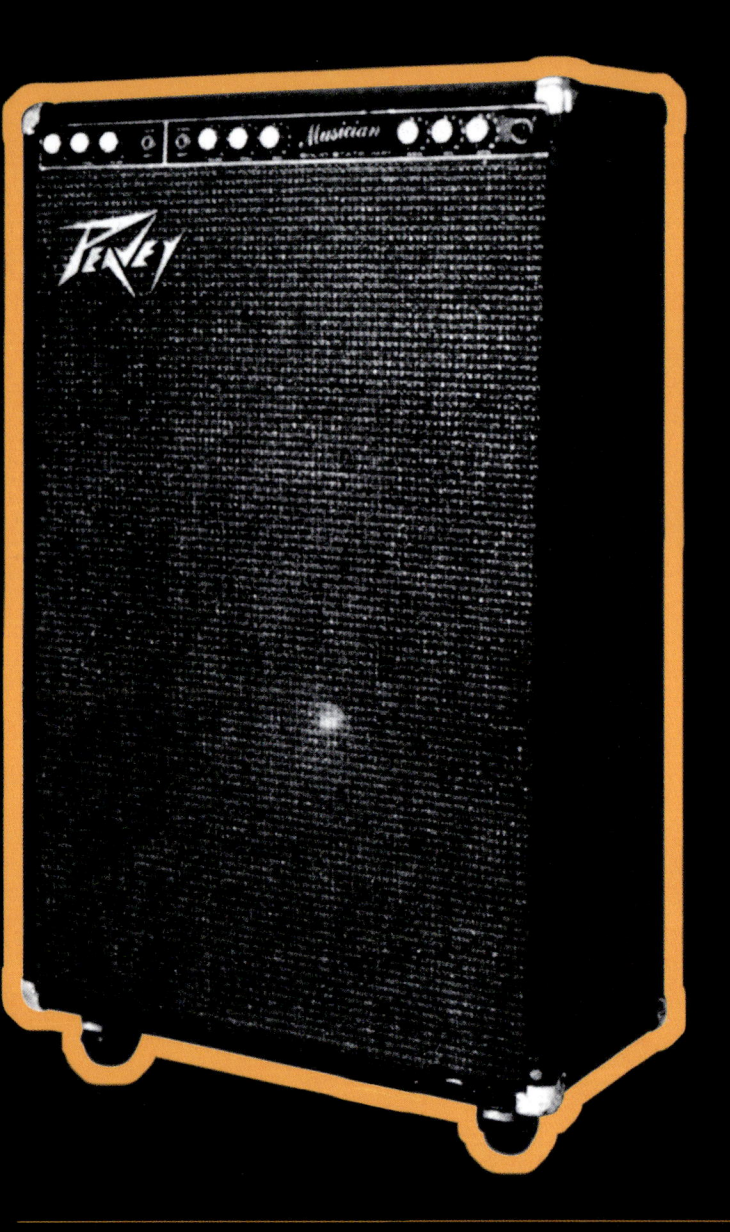

IT was time. The talents that Hartley Peavey had developed in the vocational school and the basement workshop of his home were ready to be applied. He started out as a modest one-man operation, with Mr. Mutt offering encouragement and keeping the books.

Materials were hard to find in Meridian, but that only encouraged Hartley's creativity. The manufacturing concept of Vertical Integration—building everything in-house, from the ground up—was driven by necessity in these early days, but it soon began to fuel the company's innovations. Hartley built things *his way*—and that was often quite different from the way it was done by his unsuspecting competitors. But they would find out soon enough.

Like most of the major musical-instrument amplifier manufacturers of that time, Hartley had been building tube amps. He was fascinated by the emerging solid-state technology, though, and believed it represented the future of instrument amplification. He set out to learn all he could about transistor circuits, and soon spotted an advertisement for a company called Orrtronics, based in

◄ *Hartley's first solid-state amp—the original Musician amplifier*

1967

• *The young engineer at his bench*

CHAPTER 5 • VERTICAL INTEGRATION 21

▲ *Peavey Electronics—in the beginning—assembly*

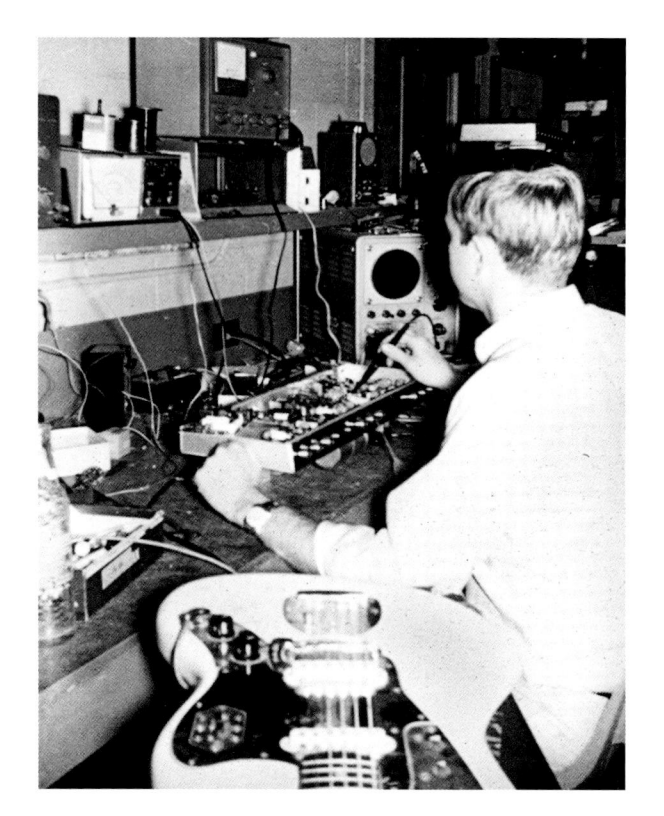

▲ *Peavey Electronics—in the beginning—at the bench*

Opelika, Alabama. The company's founder, J. Herbert Orr, had been in the intelligence service during World War II, and his unit had helped to round up German scientists at the end of the conflict. Orr was assigned to work with scientists from Telefunken, where he obtained information on making recording tape. Orr brought the formulations back to the U.S. and used them to establish a company, Orradio Industries, that made Irish brand recording tape (later acquired by Ampex). After that, Orr founded a company called Orrtronics, which developed tape and various electronics products, including an unsuccessful 8-track tape format.

Hartley's father drove him over to Alabama, where the young amp builder met Ron Matthews, a manager at Orrtronics, and got a look at some of the company's circuits. With the assistance of the Orrtronics engineers, Hartley designed Peavey's first solid-state amplifier—which became the basis for the company's first two products: the Musician amp for guitarists and the DynaBass amp for bass players.

Hartley officially founded Peavey Electronics in May 1965. The first commercial Peavey amps had identical closed-back speaker cabinets, with two 12" speakers for the guitar version and a single 15" speaker for bass. The power amp circuits, which used germanium transistors, tended to heat up inside the cabinets and distort badly. Hartley quickly redesigned them, replacing the germanium transistors with ones made of silicon. "We had the first instrument amplifier that I know of designed with silicon transistors," he says.

The initial amps produced 35 watts, and Hartley was making one unit a week. He would build the entire amp from the ground up, test it, and then go out on the road to sell it. He was the designer, circuit-board layout artist, metal worker, cabinet shop, assembly line, and sales force—all rolled into one. After a while, Mr. Mutt introduced Hartley to a traveling watch salesman, Bill Gleaton, who attempted to sell a few amps farther afield, but Hartley is quick to pay tribute to the few area dealers who accepted his amps in the early days and provided the market intelligence he needed to improve his products.

Hartley soon realized that a 35-watt solid-state amp could not compete with a tube amp of similar power because of the differing distortion characteristics of the circuits. He needed more power—but if he pushed the transistors too hard, the amp blew up. That was happening to the solid-state amps produced by the major companies, too. Everyone, it seemed, was grappling with transistor reliability problems.

1967

After about a year, Hartley hired his first employee: a woodworker named Denzel Covington. He was a fireman who worked one day on and one day off, so he could build cabinets for Hartley on his off days. This freed Hartley to concentrate on the electronics and chassis fabrication. The two-man workforce was soon augmented by Peavey's first full-time employee, Sonny Lewis, who helped Hartley with almost everything except checking out the finished products. Hartley went to Sears Roebuck and bought a 10" table saw for $179, and this became the first piece of production machinery at Peavey Electronics. It was in use for more than 25 years—and Peavey still has it!

The sales force began to grow in 1967. Hartley was still building amps upstairs over the music store, and from time to time he would be called downstairs to fix something or evaluate new gear coming into the store. One day the manager, Jimmy Ball, asked him to take a look at what a new salesman was touting as "the finest amp in the world."

Hartley picks up the story: "I went down, and there were two guys with this big ugly Kustom amplifier, the first one I'd ever seen in my life. It had two Altec speakers, at least 15 knobs on the front, and that rolled-and-pleated covering. This guy was talking about how it's got tremolo and all these features. 'Go on, plug in.' So I plugged in, and the first thing you'd hear with those Kustoms was *Boomp! . . . ssssssh*. I said, 'It's mighty noisy,' and he said, 'Well, with so much gain there's going to be a bit of noise.' I played a couple of my signature licks, and he said, 'Whatcha think?' I said, 'It sounds okay.' He said, 'What do you mean, okay? This is the best amp in the world! What do you think is better than this, big boy?' I said, 'Well, to be honest with you, I make a few amplifiers myself, and I think I can blow this thing out of the room.' 'Well, just roll it in here,' he said."

At the time, Hartley was building a 60-watt version of the original Musician, equipped with four Utah 10" speakers. The Kustom salesman had claimed that his was a 200-watt amp, but Hartley noted that it had an 8-ohm load and was probably more like 50 watts. He relished the comparison. Hartley brought in his amp and cranked it up. "I looked at him," Hartley remembers with obvious satisfaction, "and the blood drained from his face. He didn't say a word. He and this other guy just rolled the Kustom amp out the door. I said, 'Look, sir, I didn't mean to piss you off, you just asked me to try your amp. . . .' I'm feeling bad because this guy was so cocky, but I knew my amp was going to blow him away."

▲ *Peavey Electronics—in the beginning— final assembly*

▲ *Peavey Electronics—in the beginning—quality control*

CHAPTER 5 • VERTICAL INTEGRATION 23

Later, the cocky salesman's colleague came back to Hartley's shop upstairs and knocked on the door. He told Hartley how good he thought the Peavey amp sounded, and said that he knew he could sell amps like that in quantity. Hartley was gratified but openly admitted that he could not afford to pay a salesman. The salesman then suggested a deal: Hartley would give him one amp; after he sold it, he'd come back for another one.

That salesman was Don Belfield, who became the first full-time Peavey representative. Hartley gave him an amp, as he had asked, and Belfield sold it immediately to a pawnshop in Alabama, returning with cash in hand and asking for another. (Unbeknownst to Hartley, Don had been fired from his job with Southland Distributors and was as destitute as he was.) Belfield traveled all over the Southeast in the late 1960s, often sleeping in his '62 Chevette station wagon, spreading the word about this new company and helping to put Peavey on the map. Hartley later dubbed him "the Don Quixote of the amplifier business." The Kustom salesman Hartley had scared off was Don's brother Bob, who also later went to work for Peavey. The Belfield brothers became the core of the Peavey rep force, working various territories well into the 1980s.

Bill Everitt of Brook Mays Music was one of the earliest Peavey dealers, and he remembers the Belfields well. "Don and his brother did a tremendous job in getting the right dealers for Hartley," he says. "I can still remember the lecture I got from Don concerning the prompt payment of bills if we were to be a Peavey dealer. I think it had more to do with him promptly getting his commission than anything else! In some ways, Don made it difficult to get the line—which made you want to have it even more. And Don and Bob knew how to network to utilize the relationships that existed among the dealers."

While the Belfields were establishing accounts for Peavey, a friendship was forming in Meridian

▲ *This Audiotronics Inc. 60-watt stereo power amplifier was the first Peavey O.E.M. product—made in 1968. This stereo version is two mono amps (serial numbers 001 & 002) mounted on a 19" rack plate.*

▶ *This Craftsman table saw is the first piece of manufacturing machinery purchased by Peavey. It's currently in the Peavey Museum.*

that would have a significant impact on the fledgling business. Willie Hatcher was a cameraman at the local TV station, which was located in the block behind the music store. He would drop by the workshop from time to time and chat with the young entrepreneur. "George 'Skeeter' Gordon, the station photographer, and I took photos of Hartley's equipment for his early advertising brochures," says Hatcher. "His dad had a desk outside the workroom, and he would write the letters to vendors and keep up with the accounts. It was during those visits with Hartley that I decided I would do what I could to help him grow his company."

Although he could not yet afford to exhibit at trade shows, Hartley always attended so he could evaluate the competition's gear and stay in touch with trends. When he discovered that effects units were making cheap guitars and amps sound better by adding gain—Mike Matthews's LPB power booster, in particular—he immediately set out to redesign the dual channels of his guitar amps so the preamp of one channel could overdrive the other and boost gain. The search for the amp designer's Holy Grail—making a solid-state amp sound like a tube amp—had begun.

Success was not immediate, though. In the mid-'60s, riding the crest of the "British Invasion" led by the Beatles and the Rolling Stones, the market was flooded with guitar amps. It was a tough competitive environment for a new company. Although Peavey would eventually become one of the best-known amplifier brands in the world, it wasn't guitar amps that gave Hartley his commercial breakthrough—it was a PA system.

While listening to the dealers he visited, Hartley realized that groups who needed a portable PA system had only two real choices: the Shure Vocal Master or the Kustom K-200, both of which sold for around $1,000. He saw an opening in the market and quickly capitalized, introducing his first PA system. The Peavey PA Reverberation Amplifier was based on the guitar amp Hartley was building at the time, with a spring reverb built in. The system consisted of an amplifier head and two column speakers and retailed at $600. Hartley could not build enough of them.

Looking back on that period, Bill Everitt reflects on what was happening in music stores and how Hartley broke the mold: "He developed a strong dealer network because of his personal skills and direct contact with the dealers. During the '60s and early '70s, there were a lot of new dealers springing up across the country to challenge the more established ones. These new dealers were more energetic than the older, more mature dealer base, which was rooted in the loyalties and practices of the past. The Peavey products were right on top of the needs of the changing market, and the

▲ *The first PA-3 PA system*

CHAPTER 5 • VERTICAL INTEGRATION

pricing was very competitive. Hartley told his dealers, 'Do not order from me if the product is not selling or does not make you a profit.' He would say, 'If I am not making you money, throw me out the door.' This was contrary to the style of his competitors, who were telling the dealers they had to stock the entire product line and re-up every year with an order to maintain the full line."

Bill believes that Hartley's understanding of his customers' problems and needs paid him big dividends. "Hartley's background in the family music store in Meridian gave him a unique perspective on the mentality of the American dealer," he says. "He wanted and expected his dealers to make a profit, and he preached the necessity of holding the margins. His approach was to give the dealer the most profitable line in their store and prove to them that it was their responsibility to promote it within their market. He was brave enough to make difficult decisions to protect his product line from being bastardized, and he attempted to control the distribution of his products through a narrow base of aggressive, quality dealers."

▶ *Hartley Peavey in his office, 1970s*

CHAPTER 6

A Real Factory

1968-1969

> "When I put my name on a product, there's a part of me in each one. It has to be the best we can make."
>
> —HARTLEY PEAVEY

Hartley's day would start at 9:00 a.m. and end the next morning in the wee hours—and there were seven days in his working week. By late 1967 it was obvious that he would need help, and that the attic workshop would have to be left behind. With a loan of $17,500 from Citizens National Bank in Meridian, the first standalone Peavey factory was established on January 25, 1968, on a plot of land on Tenth Avenue owned by Hartley's Aunt AnnaBelle Boyd. It measured 100 feet by 32 feet but would be extended several times until it occupied the whole block. Today it covers 31,500 square feet and is the Electronics Engineering Building, known within the company as "Plant 1."

▲ *Plant 1 — the original cinderblock building*

▲ *Plant 1 in more recent years*

A phenomenal period of growth was about to begin. Frank Morris, who was hired during the attic days, tells the tale:

> When I started in '67, there was Hartley and three other employees. The head technicians were Hartley and Sonny Lewis. I worked part-time for the first 18 months or so; I was 18 and going to college. My employee badge number was 11. I started drawing schematics, and when it was needed I assembled circuit boards. I don't remember the exact order [in which the employees were hired], but starting in December 1967 and within the first year in Plant 1, there was Tommy Vance and Ray Palmer covering enclosures. A guy by the name of Otho Sessions was doing some miscellaneous work and also covering enclosures. And there was a carpenter building the enclosures whose name was Wilburn Moffett; he came along a bit after me. Fred Tingle came along around 1968, I believe, and he became one of the technicians.
>
> The only two models [being built at that time] were the Musician and the DynaBass. I loved what I was doing—so much, in fact, I used to punch out and then go back to work. It was probably around mid-1970 when I began servicing the equipment. Fred Tingle became Peavey's VP around this time, so I moved into the service slot but still performed other tasks. I tried to learn it all. I also tested finished units with bass and guitar. I can't remember exactly when Martha Boutwell came to work, but I believe it was around 1969 or '70. Hartley had the impression that women were better at repetitious tasks like building circuit boards; he thought that men were too easily distracted. He was right.

The music business in the late 1960s and early 1970s was changing rapidly as industrial conglomerates rushed in, buying up established brands like Fender and Gibson. Popular music was rocking to a new beat—and the money men wanted a part of it. They bought up the companies supplying the gear that was fueling the trend, often with disastrous results. Peavey, which was making only a few amps each week before the move to Plant 1, was under their radar. Hartley could not comprehend the millions of corporate dollars being pumped into incentives, bonuses, and spiffs. The most important thing to him was still the product. His concept of making the best product at a fair price gave him a competitive edge as the corporate overhead imposed on the older companies began to be reflected in rising prices (and poorer quality).

Hartley believed that a level playing field was essential if he were going to gain the trust and loyalty of music store owners. The stores that were supporting his fledgling company were typically smaller shops that did not have the buying power of the big operators, and they were pleased by Peavey's "one-fair-price-for-everyone" policy. It was a breath of fresh air in a confused marketplace.

Reliability and first-rate customer service were also vital ingredients in the Peavey recipe. Because Hartley had grown up in his father's music store, he realized that the way his competitors did business offered him an opportunity to build

▲ *Musician amplifier and enclosure—1969*

1968-1969

better relationships with his customers. He was ready and willing to take service calls himself, and he made sure that his employees were always courteous and helpful. He hired a local guitar player, Dennis "Preacher" Smith, as his main quality-assurance auditor. A picky fellow, the Preacher would scrutinize every amp to make sure it was built to spec and operating correctly before it shipped. Jim Webb, another early employee, handled customer service and product inquiries. He went on to be one of the most successful representatives in Peavey's field sales team.

It wasn't long before word about this new company from Mississippi began to spread among both music dealers and musicians. Peavey amps, with their clean, crisp sound and rugged construction, caught on with many of the top country players in Nashville. Exposure at the Grand Ole Opry and on regional TV shows increased awareness of the brand, and with it the interest of jazz, pop, and rock musicians. Merle Haggard became one of the earliest official Peavey endorsers, and the artist list soon included such names as Hank Williams Jr., Jerry Reed, George Hamilton IV, Mel Tillis, Dr. Hook & the Medicine Show, and the Nitty Gritty Dirt Band.

The ever-inquisitive mind of Hartley Peavey drove product innovation, and the line began to expand. In the early 1970s, the Musician and the DynaBass were augmented by the Vulcan head and the Concert, a bass combo amp with one 15" speaker. With various permutations of speaker enclosures—such as a 6x12 model and one with two 15" and two 10" speakers—plus new PA systems, a full product line was taking shape.

The first Peavey PA system was built in the traditional way, with the columns having a separate front and back, each attached by many screws. Fabricating, covering, and assembling the individual pieces was time-consuming—so Hartley set out to invent a better way of doing it. By front-loading the speakers and dadoing in the baffle board, Hartley and Ray Palmer developed a technique for building and covering the enclosures that was quicker and more efficient. The Peavey speaker enclosures worked better, were easier to build, and could be priced 30 percent cheaper than the competition—and sales escalated again.

The new PA-300 design was not without its problems, however. With the front-loaded speakers, the grille cloth had to be mounted on a frame—and when the material was stretched across the frame, the frame would bend in the middle. Hartley contacted Miami Window, a local company that made aluminum extrusions, and purchased extrusions of the proper dimensions to fit on the back of the frame, for reinforcement. One day Hartley happened to put the extrusions on the wrong side, so there were aluminum strips running down each side of the front of the frame. He liked the cosmetic effect so much that it became part of the design—and those aluminum strips would soon become a distinctive trademark, especially noticeable onstage or on TV, instantly identifying the speakers as Peavey products.

▲ *Original Vulcan amplifier head and 612H enclosure*

▲ *Concert 115 combo — 1969*

CHAPTER 6 • A REAL FACTORY   **29**

▲ *Hartley landed many major country endorsers early on, including Merle Haggard*

The young crew at Peavey put in long hours building these new products, but there was still time for some fun. Frank Morris tells this story:

> I was 18 years old, very naive, and working part-time for Hartley. Some of the other employees were constantly playing practical jokes on me—Tommy Vance, Otho Sessions, and Ray Palmer. Now, I could take a joke, but one particular prank took it a bit far. I made the mistake of telling these guys that I had taken an AWOL serviceman across the Mississippi–Alabama line. I didn't know that was illegal, but these guys proceeded to set me up to make me believe I broke the law. While I was working in the front part of the plant, one of them went across the street to a pay phone and called me using a fake voice. He said he was with the FBI, and he wanted to talk to me regarding an AWOL serviceman. He said he needed me to come to the FBI office in Meridian. Well, the FBI office was in the Post Office, so I went down there. Thank goodness they were closed, because I had fallen for this scheme hook, line, and sinker. When I went back to the plant they started saying things to me, and it finally hit me that they had set me up. They went home feeling very good about all the hell they put me through. I was hot, but I couldn't think of anything I could do to make me feel better. But there was a great mind in the room listening to me rant and rave—Hartley. Nobody ever knew it was Hartley that put the cookie idea in my head. He even went into great detail about how to do it, so they wouldn't suspect anything. He said I should wait until they least suspected it, but that wasn't going to work for me. I needed revenge. I would not sleep until they had paid dearly for what they did to me.
>
> I went home that night and told Mom that these guys had really pulled a dirty trick on me, and I needed to even things up. She was more than happy to whip up a batch of her best homemade chocolate chip cookies—replacing the chips, of course, with chocolate-flavored laxative. The next morning I was off to work with Mom's fresh cookies. Now, most employees came to work without having eaten breakfast, so by the 9:30 break everyone was usually starving. These guys were not without suspicion, and they immediately said, "You got to be crazy if you think we're going to eat any of those cookies." Well, I had a schemer who was responsible for making it possible to pull this off. Fred Tingle knew about the cookies, so he went into the back, got a cookie or two, and moved towards the front room taking bites around the chocolate. Fred even said he didn't care if the cookies worked on him a bit. In less than 30 minutes, the cookie tray was empty. I didn't say a word, but I guess my face was a complete giveaway. Within a hour or so, the three villains were lining up at the bathroom door. It was not a pretty sight. Otho, the ringleader, said, "What did you put in those cookies?" And of course I said, "What do you mean?" I held out as long as I could before I finally told them. Otho kept saying, "There's no way you came up with that. Who did you get that idea from?" Well, he was right, but until now none of them

30 THE PEAVEY REVOLUTION • **PART TWO** • FROM DREAM TO REALITY

1968-1969

knew it was Hartley that gave me the idea. Otho thought it was such a good gag that he actually gave me the 50 cents I paid for the laxative. Hartley has always said it cost him a lot of money for the time the guys spent in the john, but it was worth it for the laughs.

Not long after the cookie caper, Hartley purchased the first company vehicle. He needed a truck to transport raw materials and finished products, and its acquisition became something of a famous saga in Meridian. Mr. Mutt had banked for years with Merchants and Farmers Bank and was a friend of the manager, so Hartley went there to borrow $2,400. He had $2,600 in the company account, but the manager refused to lend Hartley the money unless his father co-signed the note. As a matter of principle Hartley did not want to do that—especially as he had more money in the bank than he wanted to borrow. And, in any event, he had been in business in his own right for several years and wanted to be treated as his own man. Disappointed, Hartley began to make his way home. As he passed Citizens National Bank, he thought he would stop in and see if they were interested in his business. He got the loan, and to this day Hartley banks with Citizens National Bank.

Hartley had met his first wife, Dawn, during his senior year at Mississippi State. She was from Philadelphia, Mississippi, and attended MSCW (Mississippi State College for Women, now known as Mississippi University for Women) in Columbus, Mississippi. "She was a freshman when I met her," Hartley says. "We dated for a couple of years and were married in 1968. She was a librarian and probably about as different from me as it's possible to get." Contemporaries recall that the couple had intellectual common ground but turned out to be very different personalities. Hartley was completely immersed in building his business, doing whatever it took to chase his dream, while Dawn was a homebody. They were married for seven years and had two sons, Joe (born January 29, 1971) and Marc (born September 8, 1974). The marriage ended in divorce in 1975.

Jim Wilson, who joined the company in the early 1970s, was Peavey's first representative west of the Mississippi. In fact, at first he covered all of the western U.S., traveling from town to town in his Winnebago. After a while, he enlisted his younger brother, Jack, to help him. Based in California, Jack Wilson was officially hired by Hartley in 1973 to handle artist relations on the West Coast. Several years later, Jack took over as the sales rep for the West when Jim left to breed and train

▼ *Inside an original Vulcan chassis — hand wired by Hartley Peavey*

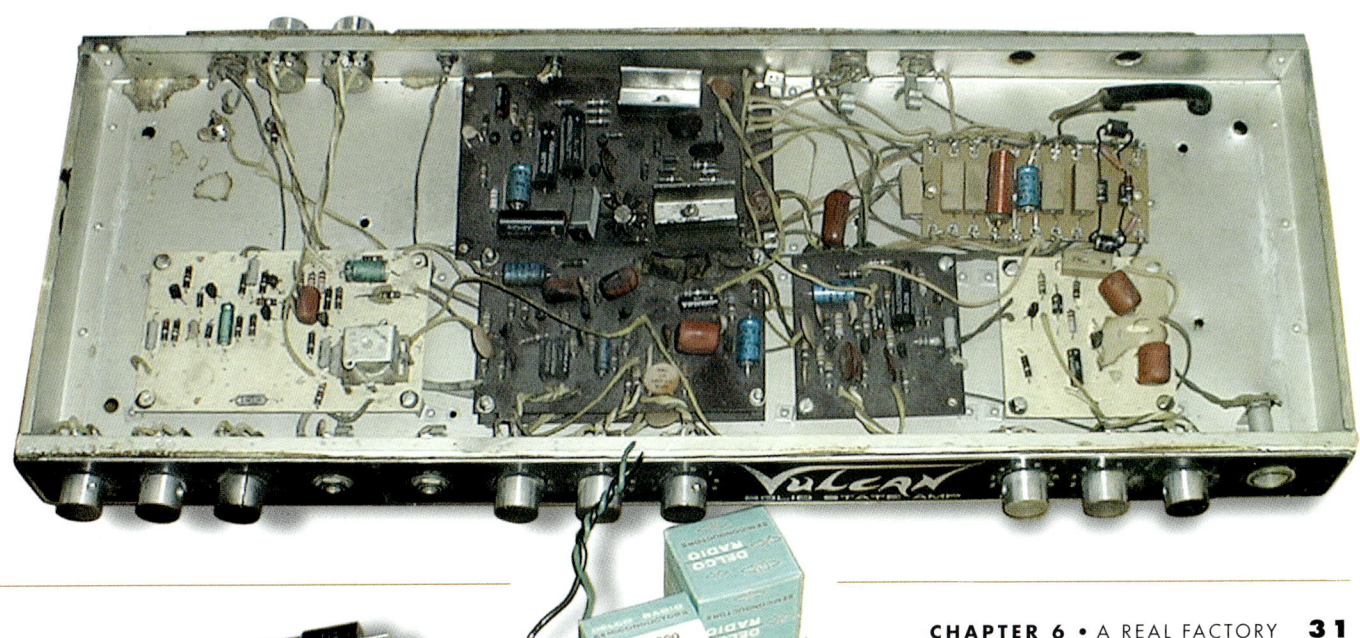

CHAPTER 6 • A REAL FACTORY 31

Peavey restored the custom "Blue Yodel" guitar of folk and country music hero Jimmie Rodgers, a fellow Meridian native

horses. Jack became a key employee, and in the 1990s he was made vice president, moving to Meridian to head up the marketing and engineering effort. Much of the company's early success in securing endorsements from top session players and rock stars in California was due to Jack's networking and marketing skills.

Reese Marin of Bellevue American Music in Washington remembers working with Jack Wilson during the "crazy, effervescent times" of the late 1960s and early '70s. During that period, Reese was at Don Weir's Music Center in San Francisco, and he helped to connect Jack with such top Bay Area–based acts as Sly & the Family Stone, the Grateful Dead, the Buddy Miles Express, and Huey Lewis & the News. Hartley would send prototype equipment to the Music Center for evaluation, and this method of obtaining feedback and refining ideas before production continues to this day. "Hartley had charisma, and he opened up lines of communication with the dealers," Reese says. "He could be quite verbose, but he meant what he said. His products were reliable, too. And if you went to Peavey Electronics in Meridian, what you found there was a bunch of open, free folks."

CHAPTER 7
Liftoff

1970-1971

> *"Fat cats don't hunt."* —HARTLEY PEAVEY

L ike the rockets Hartley had built for his junior-high science project, the fledgling Peavey Electronics of the late 1960s had been carefully assembled and was poised on the launch pad. In the early 1970s, it achieved liftoff. Hartley's energy and spirit of discovery inspired a unique corporate environment where everyone was respected as an individual and informality was the rule—employees, up to and including the founder, referred to each other by their first names. Coupled with Hartley's oft-stated objective to offer the best equipment at a fair and reasonable price, this corporate culture was to become Peavey's great strength.

Larry Linkin, who joined NAMM in 1970 and served as the organization's president and CEO from 1981 to 2001, was well placed to observe the company's rise. "By 1970, Peavey was

▲ *VTB-300 amplifier*

▲ *Vulcan amplifier head, 1970 — endorsed by Steve Lowery*

Early '70s trade show booth, L–R: Jim Webb, Don Belfield, Hartley, Frank Camp, and Hollis Calvert

already the name on the street," he says. "It didn't take Hartley long to get noticed. He singlehandedly and successfully convinced people he had the product they needed—and he did. He was the first manufacturer who outwardly showed he cared about dealers making money. Our industry in its lifetime has not experienced a phenomenon such as Peavey Electronics. It has not seen anything else like it. Hartley has affected the industry positively, worldwide."

Peavey had 30 employees in December 1970 when Willie Hatcher signed on to manage advertising and scheduling. "After 13 years with the TV station, I had taken another job selling office equipment," recalls Hatcher, who remembers selling a photocopier to Hartley after the opening of Plant 1. It wasn't long before Hartley asked him to join the team, and on his third day the plant's production manager—Sonny Lewis, who was also the lead technician—turned in his keys and said he was going home. "No amount of talking would change his mind," Willie says, so he stepped in to fill the void. "During those early days, there were no part numbers or identifiers and no drawings—only a few simple schematics. Everything was based on guides or product models. When you wanted to assemble a particular model, one of the experienced technicians would go over to a small box and retrieve the proper wire guides, and the assemblers would make copies of those wires. I found myself in the electronics shop, and in addition to trying to coordinate the production I installed the knobs on all the amplifiers. This put me in close contact with the technicians and other workers."

It didn't take Willie long to figure out why his predecessor had quit: since he was also the lead technician, he had to fix all the problems in the newly assembled amplifiers. Very few, if any, of the amps worked when they arrived at the end of the line. Assembly errors in circuit boards were

Musician and Bass amplifier heads — 1971

34 THE PEAVEY REVOLUTION • **PART TWO** • FROM DREAM TO REALITY

1970-1971

causing all sorts of problems, and he had to fix them. Ramping up production would mean more and more problems, and Willie quickly realized that this would overwhelm him.

"One of my first tasks was to go to the office supply store and purchase little ID stamps for the circuit-board assemblers," he says. "The boards were then marked, so each one could be returned to the person who made it for repair. Errors drastically diminished! I didn't realize it at first, but I had had years of experience working in sequence. When we did live television productions and when we edited film, we worked in a specific sequence to get the desired result. The task of manufacturing a product is working in sequence."

Willie's knowledge of workflow and efficiency fit well with Hartley's engineering talents, and production increased rapidly. The two shared an entrepreneurial spirit and firmly established the "can do" spirit that was to pervade the organization.

Because of the success of the early PA systems, Peavey focused its R&D efforts in this area. The product line quickly expanded in recognition of the many different venues—from small clubs to huge auditoriums—where sound reinforcement was needed. The company's first professional mixing-console system was introduced in 1974 in the form of the PA-6, and this was just the first of many innovative designs that would become standard equipment for touring bands, clubs, and churches.

Hollis Calvert was a young guitar picker who started out working part-time for Peavey, drawing up schematics, helping with customer service, and doing artist relations work. He had met Hartley in the Air National Guard. (Hartley had signed on after graduating from college and eventually rose to the rank of sergeant in the 238th Mobile Communications Flight.) In May 1971 Calvert

◀ *Plant 2, now home of the Peavey Custom Guitar & Amplifier Shop*

CHAPTER 7 • LIFTOFF 35

Hartley, c.1970

joined Peavey full-time; by that time, the employee count had risen to 54. "At first I was placed into the Quality Control area," he recalls, "making sure that the products worked correctly before they were shipped. I was also doing finished drawings of schematics for all of our amps, while continuing to talk to musicians as we tried to convince players, mostly in the Nashville area, to try our products. We were very successful, and by today's standards it seems that we had rapid acceptance of our gear." This activity caught the eye of Allan Sharp, sales manager for Great West Distribution in Canada, and he started a concerted effort to secure the Peavey line. Allan convinced Hartley of the sales potential north of the border, and Great West became Peavey's first international customer. The fact that the territory was on the same continent and shared the same 110-volt power supply made this a simple and logical expansion.

Becky Holcombe started at Peavey in the circuitboard department in 1970. Her badge number was 77, and there were 12 other female employees in the department when she joined. The boards were built by hand, she says, and they assembled about 20 a day on Mondays and Tuesdays. On Wednesday the soldering machine was switched on, and the boards were run through. The next day the boards were returned to the assemblers for touch-up and the fitting of potentiometers and wiring harnesses. Becky says that within four years, the first computer-controlled 24-station insertion machine had been installed, and she was trained as its operator.

By the fall of 1971, Peavey had outgrown Plant 1. Hartley acquired a block of land with a vacant factory building that had been used by the Harris Box Company, adding another 32,700 square feet of production capacity. This facility, located a few blocks up Tenth Avenue from Plant 1, cost $30,000—and Hartley says he didn't sleep for a week after making this big financial commitment. This new facility would become the wood shop, freeing up room in Plant 1 for electronics and assembly. The new factory would later be expanded to 54,500 square feet and eventually become the home of guitar manufacturing.

Hartley told me somewhat ruefully that his piecemeal acquisition of buildings in Meridian was not the most efficient way to grow and wished he had been able to plan Peavey's expansion more carefully. But he didn't have much time to worry about it then—his company was growing so fast it couldn't keep up with itself.

PART THREE

Acceleration

> "I think the power to succeed is in all of us—but only if you have the inner fire."
> —HARTLEY PEAVEY

Nineteen seventy-two was a landmark year in the company's history, as Jack Sondermeyer moved to Meridian. "I'd been having trouble with my amps," Hartley says. "I redesigned about four times using silicon transistors. I was getting them from RCA, but they were blowing up. I would call up RCA in Somerville, New Jersey, and get bounced around. Then finally I got this one guy who had this New Jersey accent, and he was the only one who seemed to know anything. It was Jack Sondermeyer. I called him up so much I really got to know him. He said, 'You know, I really don't have the time to do a lot of this, but I'll make a deal with you and work on your products after hours.' He actually formed a little company of his own when he was moonlighting, called Astro Associates. He went down to the electronics district in New York and

◄ *Standard PA system*

1972

▼ *Pages from the Peavey Papers from the early '70s*

▼ *Hartley and his product range — 1972*

CHAPTER 8 • ON THE GAS **39**

bought computer-grade capacitors that he sold to me to put into my amplifiers. I kept calling and talking to him, and then one day in 1970 he called and said he wanted to see me."

Hartley was so keen to impress Sondermeyer that he went out and bought a brand-new Oldsmobile Cutlass to drive to New Jersey. "We got up there and had a very pleasant stay," Hartley continues. "I talked him into coming down to Meridian, and he did in fact bring his family down to show them. He eventually moved down in 1972 and announced he was going to trash all my power amp designs. I said, 'BS, Jack—I finally got this stuff to where it's reasonably reliable, and, besides that, they're all designed in strict accordance with the RCA semiconductor manual.' He said, 'That's the problem! That manual is BS. I helped to write it.' And I said, 'But that's the bible.' He said, 'The stuff in there is not accurate. We're going to redesign everything.' And sure enough we did!"

The reliability problems stopped. Hartley didn't realize it at the time, but one of Jack's first assignments at RCA had been to draw up a power amp circuit for their TO-3 metal-case transistors. "Jack is the godfather of all modern power amp technology and engineering," says Peavey clinician Marty McCann. Sondermeyer would have many engineering triumphs at Peavey before retiring in 2002. "Jack and I were a great team," Hartley says, "because he kept telling me what couldn't be done, and I kept telling him we could do it because I was too stupid to know it couldn't be done. We used to argue like cats and dogs, but I loved him anyway."

Despite the inevitable need for discipline and structure in his young company, Hartley was determined to maintain an open, informal atmosphere. Every Friday afternoon after work was done for the week, he would bring out a few six-packs and the employees would relax, share ideas, and get to know each other better. It was a routine that eventually would have to end, due to a growing workforce and safety concerns, but it shows how different Peavey was from its corporate competitors.

▶ *The Vintage Amplifier — 1972*

1972

The 1972 lineup of instrument amps featured twin-channel 200-watt versions of the Musician and DynaBass heads. The Musician incorporated fuzz, reverb, and tremolo and was offered with 412 and 215H speaker enclosures. The DynaBass was matched with 215 and 118FH (folded horn) enclosures. A 250-watt Vulcan guitar head and DynaBass head were offered, but these were replaced by the Festival series F-800G and F-800B 400-watt models later in the year. A multi-purpose 200-watt VTA-400 tube head and 120-watt Standard-240 unit completed the line.

The VTA-400 was designed as a multi-purpose unit and had been developed to meet the persistent market demand for powerful all-tube amplifiers. The relentless quest for making a solid-state amp that sounded like a tube amp continued to consume Hartley and Jack Sondermeyer, but this did not prevent the company from introducing some of the most successful tube amps the industry has known.

The range of speaker enclosures offered for instrument amplifiers included a 610 unit with 10" drivers; 212, 412, 412S (stackable), and 612H (horn-loaded) with 12" drivers; 115, 215S, 215, and 215H with 15" drivers; and 118S and 118FH bass units with 18" drivers. CTS was the main supplier of speakers in the early days of the company, but Electro-Voice SRO and JBL options were offered on some of the higher-power units.

The 120-watt Deuce was Peavey's first "twin" combo amp, equipped with a pair of 12" CTS or Electro-Voice SRO drivers. It was the daddy of a whole family of successful combos to come, based on a solid-state preamp with a tube power amp.

All of the amp models featured the striking black-and-aluminum finish for which the company had become known and were equipped with flat-face spun-aluminum "hatbox" control knobs.

At the summer trade show, Peavey launched the Vintage series of beige-tweed "retro" guitar combos. With 110 watts of tube power, there were 212, 410, and 610 speaker configurations. Perfectly timed to satisfy the growing interest in classic-style guitar amps, these units were an early demonstration of Hartley's marketing savvy.

The six-channel 210-watt PA-400 powered-mixer system was the latest step in the evolution of the Peavey PA designs, utilizing innovative anti-feedback circuitry. It was complemented by two smaller units, the Standard PA, based on a 130-watt power amp, and the PA-120 system comprising two 210 columns and a four-channel 60-watt "power pak" (Peavey's euphemism for a separate powered mixer or top-box amplifier).

The speaker systems offered to match the Standard and PA-400 units were 212, 212H, 412, and 412H columns with 12" drivers and a 215H enclosure with two 15" drivers and a hyperbolic horn, a format that would establish a new benchmark for portable PAs.

▲ *Jack Sondermeyer at the blackboard*

▲ *F-800B bass stack — 1972*

CHAPTER 8 • ON THE GAS

▶ *The first Monitor system — 1973*

▼ *Melia McRae*

The PA-6A (210 watts) and PA-9 (410 watts) powered mixing consoles were the basis of easily affordable, great-sounding systems. They were offered with 612H enclosures or a Festival system loaded with two 12" and two 15" drivers, with a twin-driver compound-diffraction horn in each enclosure. Equipped with variable crossovers, these units pointed the way to what would become the most successful line of semi-professional PA systems in the market. The company's sales literature was already expounding the message that Peavey offered the widest selection of PA systems available—it probably was, but it was only the beginning.

Peavey had been exhibiting at the trade shows in a small way, and the news was spreading that a young man in Mississippi had come out of nowhere to become the largest manufacturer of amplifiers in North America. Despite an increasingly embarrassing back-order situation, Hartley realized that his long-term success would depend on more growth—so he needed to look beyond the U.S. and Canada. At the June 1972 NAMM show in Chicago, he signed up his first distributor outside of North America: Bjarne Christensen, the owner of Norsk Musikk, a distributor in Norway. Bjarne, like Hartley, had been born into the music business, and he was able to allay some of the nervousness that Hartley felt as he placed his products in the hands of a distributor on the other side of the globe.

Another key event in the company's history took place in December 1972, when a young woman accepted a job in the newly created post of receptionist. Demand for Peavey products was escalating, and the phone was ringing off the wall—so Melia McRae was hired to answer it. Her arrival seemed inauspicious, but it would soon affect everything. Many years later, she reminisced about her start during an interview for Mississippi educational TV: "Coming out of high school, I had a [college] scholarship, and I was going to double-major in sociology and psychology. I knew I was going to need some money to be able to live on, so I was going to work for a year and then go back to school. I was a 17-year-old who did not know an amplifier from a microphone, but I was fascinated at how things were put together. . . . My first job was to handle the switchboard, which was a black telephone with a red 'hold' button, and there were four or five lines and two incoming lines." Melia

42 THE PEAVEY REVOLUTION • **PART THREE** • ACCELERATION

1973

added that she initially thought Hartley was a "know-it-all"—but she felt "a wonderful thing was going to happen with this company."

By the time Melia started to answer the phone, Peavey was producing more than 2,000 units per month. As an amplifier manufacturer, Hartley's company was already second in size only to Fender in the U.S.—and between May 1972 and May 1973 Peavey's output increased by another 20 percent.

1973

By 1973 the product line had expanded to cover the amplification needs of most guitarists and bass players, amateur or professional, as well as a wide range of sound-reinforcement applications. For guitarists, there was the much-refined Musician head, now offering 210 watts of power, clean and distortion channels, a six-channel equalizer, fuzz, reverb, and tremolo. A working player's dream, it had twice the power of anything else at the same price.

By this time, the Musician had been on the market for seven years and was widely praised for its value and ease of use. Its modular construction was the epitome of manufacturing efficiency and had won plaudits from service technicians and musicians on the road—the separate front-end and power amp modules made servicing a snap. Peavey's emphasis on using standard power amp modules meant that several models could be made at a particular power rating, and standardization of enclosure sizes allowed further economies in cabinetry, packaging, and inventory management. It was a smart way to build gear.

The DynaBass, which featured the same 210-watt power amp as the Musician, was equipped with a specially designed six-channel equalizer and was well on its way to becoming a firm favorite with gigging bass players. Hartley was demonstrating a good understanding of the unique needs of bassists, who recognized that this company's bass amps were more than modified guitar amps.

The PA-400 once again demonstrated Peavey's leadership in this area, with its six individually mixable channels, monitor output, and anti-feedback filtering circuitry. All three of the PA heads featured state-of-the-art infinitely variable reverb send controls on all channels, plus a master control for the Hammond Accutronix spring unit.

All of the Peavey enclosures were covered in tough, one-piece 34-ounce Tolex and trimmed with the characteristic—and unmistakable—aluminum strips down each side of the grille cloth.

At the 1973 Summer NAMM show in Chicago, Peavey took the wraps off the 50-watt Classic combo, the latest addition to the Vintage series; 212 or 412 speaker configurations were offered. Available in beige tweed or regular black Tolex covering, the Classic has become just that—and it continues to be one of Peavey's most popular models.

Peavey also introduced its first Monitor package, an innovative and affordable PA system designed to meet the needs of club bands. Its 130-watt amp unit was fitted with tailored EQ and feedback filters, and the speakers—each equipped with a 12" woofer and hyperbolic horn—were mounted

▼ *CSP (Commercial Sound Projector, forerunner to the SP-1)*

CHAPTER 8 • ON THE GAS 43

▲ *711 A Street corporate offices*   ▲ *Plant 3 — the "Banana Building"*

on swivel stands for infinite angled positioning. Two new Booster (slave) amps were also introduced; these units were designed around the 410-watt (800 Booster) and 130-watt (260 Booster) modules and were built like top boxes (heads).

By the end of the year, the Commercial Sound Projector (CSP) was in development—the first of a long line of high-power, long-throw speaker systems to come. Designed to meet the need for high-output performance in large venues such as sports arenas, the CSP was a three-way system incorporating 15" and 12" horn-loaded speakers and a large 90-degree radial horn. With this system, Peavey was putting down a marker in the commercial sound market.

More products meant the company needed more space, so Peavey acquired a vacant office building on A Street on July 3, 1973, and also broke ground for Plant 3, across the street from the office building and adjacent to the railroad tracks. At the end of 1974, all production was transferred to Plant 3, making Peavey the largest manufacturer of its kind in the United States, with almost a quarter-million square feet of manufacturing capacity under one roof.

In later years, Plant 3 was expanded to reach 308,350 square feet. There were a dozen or so houses on A Street that stood in the way of this expansion, and Mr. Mutt told Hartley that he should go to the city authorities for help in acquiring this property. Knowing that some of the houses were occupied by elderly residents who had been there for many years, Hartley refused. As a result, Plant 3 became known as the "Banana Building"—not only because it was painted yellow but because of the way its additions were dog-legged around the houses. Eventually it grew to almost a quarter-mile in length, and its expansion did not halt until it reached the U.S. Highway 45 bypass (now Mississippi Highway 39). But even this wasn't enough to keep up with the company's growth, and more buildings had to be acquired in Meridian.

With the door now open for exporting to Europe, Peavey was approached by other potential customers. The author of this book—who was operating Top Gear Music in London, a guitar retailer with a young distribution company specializing in American lines—had been in touch with the company. This eventually resulted in Top Gear's appointment as U.K. distributor at the 1973 Chicago trade show. A handful of others followed, including Omikron in Greece, Rose Music in Australia, and International Music Services in the Benelux countries (Belgium, the Netherlands, and Luxembourg) and Germany.

1973

In the June 2003 issue of the U.K. industry magazine *MI Pro*, Gary Cooper interviewed this author, who told how he discovered Peavey:

> One year I was over for the Summer Trade Show in Chicago and Bill Heath, who worked for [Ernie Ball], asked me what we were looking for. We already had Guild, Rickenbacker, Ernie Ball—we had quite a few American lines—and we were looking for an amp range. At the time there were several around, such as Acoustic and Kustom, who didn't have distribution in the UK, so I knew there were companies to go and look at. Bill said, 'Before you go and talk to anybody you want to go check this young fella in Mississippi. His name's Peavey.'
>
> "I guess Hartley had been in business eight years by then, as he'd started in 1965, and Bill was insistent—he told me all the dealers were talking about it, so on the first day of the show, I found this very small booth manned by this red-haired guy with a beard. I introduced myself and said we had this small store and a fledgling distribution company in London. And on his stand, he had the coolest thing I'd seen in ages. It was the year he introduced the original Classic, so there in the corner he had this tweed amplifier. Back in London if you had anything tweed it was very saleable, so I thought, 'This guy's really got his act together. We could sell lots of these in London.'
>
> "I don't know what it was—we just liked each other and it clicked. . . . It was 1973 and I was a young man; I didn't even know where Mississippi was or how to get there, and in those days you had to get around America by 'bus-stop' airlines. I found my way by Southern Airways down to Meridian, Mississippi. We showed [the amp] at the U.K. Trade Show and the rest is history.

Peavey's export business would eventually prove to be an important source of profits, but at first it presented another steep learning curve and required the acquisition of special voltage transformers, power cords, and electrical plugs—to say nothing of compliance with multiple foreign regulations and reams of shipping documentation. Michie Hill, a friend of Hartley's, was drafted to help out with the new export business, but it quickly became obvious that an experienced manager would be needed. He appeared near the end of 1973 in the person of Pete Wood, formerly with Ampeg, who established the first Export Department in the new headquarters at 711 A Street. Lucy Lafferty, a long-suffering but charming lady who wore an all-encompassing "marketing" hat, was given the unenviable task of allocating production between domestic and export customers at a time when there was already $2 million worth of back orders.

The concept of PA system expandability was now emerging—a concept that was to become a powerful marketing tool in the years to come. The PA-6A and PA-9A not only had a monitor line output for the connection of a separate amp and speaker system for stage monitors, but a separate main line output for connecting one or more booster (slave) amplifiers and speaker systems. This meant the console could be at the heart of a potentially much larger system. The message to musicians was that your PA system would no longer become obsolete when your group got larger or you began to play larger venues—you could simply expand it.

▲ *Pete Wood — first Export Manager*

CHAPTER 8 • ON THE GAS 45

▶ *PA-9 — precursor of many successful Peavey powered mixing consoles*

▲ *The original classroom at Plant 1 with Hollis Calvert and Marty McCann*

Back then this was innovative stuff, and Hartley realized his strength in running ahead of the market would be diminished if the message was not clear. If amateur performers didn't understand the language of professional sound reinforcement or were confused when confronted with XLR connectors instead of phone jacks—well, then he'd have to educate them. Before long, Peavey's sales literature began to feature technical tips and articles with such titles as "Power," "Tubes vs. Transistors," "Gain vs. Sensitivity," "What is impedance?" and "What is feedback?" This was an early manifestation of Hartley's belief that educated consumers would be better equipped to make the best buying decisions. People, he would say, buy sound equipment with their eyes, not their ears—and he was determined to spread the word.

The opening of Plant 3 freed up space in Plant 1, and some of this space was converted into a classroom—the first product-training facility of its kind in the music industry. The Peavey Factory Seminar program commenced early in 1975, and it has continued to this day, forming a central thread in the fabric of the organization. Peavey began to bring in its retail dealers for two-day training programs, to educate the salespeople in the physics of sound and show them how this was translated into the features and performance characteristics of Peavey products. Side-by-side comparisons with competitive products reinforced the message and helped to create believers in the sales force of many retailers. More important, the seminars created a crucial bond of trust and loyalty between manufacturer and dealer.

That bond was reinforced by Hartley's policy of "one fair price," which appealed greatly to the many small dealers who felt at a disadvantage when competing against the retail behemoths who could insist on getting a better deal from the manufacturers. Many of the smaller dealers embraced the "Grow with Peavey" mantra and discovered a profitable alternative to the usual cut-and-thrust of supplier behavior—the "deal du jour" mentality, as Hartley likes to call it.

In the early 1970s, Chuck Levin's Washington Music Center became one of Peavey's first large customers. Looking back at those days, Alan Levin—who, like Hartley, grew up in his father's store—says, "For a start, you could always talk to Hartley. You might not like what he said to you, but you always knew where you stood. You could go to bed at night knowing he meant what he said—not one thing for you and something different for someone else. Hartley didn't change with the weather. He's a gentleman who will always tell you the truth, and there's not many of them."

1974

As Peavey moved into 1974, its growing prominence was reflected by an expanding roster of endorsers—recent additions included James Brown, Phil Upchurch, and Curly Chalker—and by growing manufacturing capacity. In the *Peavey Papers* at the time Phil Upchurch said about his Musician amplifier, "The Musician has solved amp problems I've had for years. The six-channel equalizer is fantastic . . . you can get any sound you want with it." New production equipment was being purchased and new workers hired at a frenetic pace. Willie Hatcher's planning and organizational talents were proving invaluable during this period of rapid growth.

Thanks to the demand for product and the resulting healthy receivables, Hartley was able to fund a good proportion of the company's growth from within. He has always been more interested in reinvesting profits to expand his business than in enhancing his personal lifestyle, and this component of his philosophy helped fuel the extraordinary growth.

At the beginning of 1974, the Deuce II replaced the original twin combo, and the Session combo was added to the line. The Session, offered in 115 JBL and 212 Electro-Voice configurations, was embraced by Curly Chalker and other top steel guitar players, and it quickly became the industry standard unit for this purpose.

The Century, an all-purpose 60-watt instrument amp top, was added at the bottom end of the price range, and the Roadmaster replaced the VTA-400. This three-channel, 200-watt unit was the first Peavey amp to feature Automix, a new channel-selection and blending circuitry that would become standard on most professional instrument amp models. The 800 Mixer, a non-powered mixer offering eight separate channels, was the latest addition to the PA line—and the first of many Peavey mixers that would dominate the market for the next two decades. The PA-600 and PA-900 replaced the original PA-6A and PA-9A powered mixers.

That spring, Peavey exhibited for the first time at the Frankfurt Musik Messe trade show in Germany. Hartley enlisted the help of Bjarne Christensen of Norsk Musikk in mounting a small display, and they drove a truck full of gear from Oslo to Frankfurt. Hartley attended the show with Pete Wood, signing up more new customers, and they stopped off in London on the way home. Hartley has one graphic memory of that visit: "I had a very close call with a London cab. When I stepped off the curb looking left, Pete Wood grabbed me very forcefully by the collar and pulled me back as a large black Austin cab rushed by from the right at about 50 miles per hour. . . . After I got the hell scared out of me, we flew back to Mississippi and continued our export program." (Which, we could note, was moving as fast as that London cabbie.)

At the Summer NAMM show in Chicago, two small 45-watt combo amps were introduced: the Pacer for guitar and the TNT for bass. At first these amps did not have the characteristic aluminum strips on the grille, although they were added later. These units were the forebears of an extensive line of small combos to come. The first Peavey microphones were also introduced at this time. The original PML (low-impedance) and PMH (high-impedance) models were outsourced from

▲ *The first Peavey microphone*

▶ *Hartley mans a computer workstation*

Turner, and later from Astatic. Later, in the spirit of vertical integration, Peavey microphones would be built in-house, but the goal of providing a "one-stop shop" for the entire audio chain made the inclusion of microphones inevitable.

Well into the mid-'70s, Hartley would often work late into the night. He loved to lay out the circuit boards himself, saying it was "his meditation." This didn't help out at home, and even with the birth of their second child in the fall of 1974 the strain on Hartley and Dawn's marriage was becoming quite apparent. Within a year they would be divorced. Quite separately, the marriage of Melia McRae Gibson was going the same way. She was now working in sales and becoming more and more immersed in the world of Peavey Electronics.

Marty McCann started work at Peavey on June 4, 1974. He had been a service tech at Zambo Music in the small town of Boston, Pennsylvania, near Pittsburgh. The store didn't carry Peavey gear, but Marty began to learn about the company when he got Peavey amps in for repair. He would call Meridian with technical questions—and often Hartley would answer the phone. This amazed Marty. Hartley would answer Marty's questions, and then pump him for market intelligence. Sometimes he'd even offer tips on how to repair the competition's products. One thing led to another, and pretty soon Marty had a job offer.

Marty arrived in Meridian just as Hartley was setting up the educational program with Hollis Calvert. Hollis would cover the musical instrument products, and Marty would assist him with the sound reinforcement training.

Marty likes to tell the story of how Hartley decided to start a product-education program: "One weekend in the early '70s, Hartley was down in Gulf Shores, Alabama—affectionately known locally as the 'Redneck Riviera'—and he stopped by a bar where a solo act was performing. The artist was a good singer, but the PA system sounded terrible. Hartley spoke to the guy, and when he

48   THE PEAVEY REVOLUTION • **PART THREE** • ACCELERATION

was shown the mixer he was shocked to see it was one of his products. Hartley made adjustments and soon had the performer sounding much better. Driving back to Meridian, the experience gnawed at him, and he found himself blaming the dealer for not explaining how it worked. By the time he got back to Meridian, he realized it wasn't the dealer's fault at all—it was his fault. He decided there and then to develop an educational program."

Bill Everitt committed his Brook Mays Music staff to the seminar program from the outset, and he believes it was a huge factor in cementing customer relations. "A lot of Hartley's early success was [due to] the Peavey School in the old cinderblock building in Meridian," he says. "He was aggressive with regard to education of the dealer base. During the sessions, the sales staff and dealer principals were tattooed with the Peavey mantra, which was often delivered by Hartley himself. As Hartley used to say, 'There is no free lunch in this business, except when you come to my school in Meridian.' The dealers had to pay all the expenses for their staff to attend the Peavey School, which meant that they were making an investment in their business and in Peavey's business. Hartley paid for the lunches!"

Peavey achieved another industry first when it introduced the MF-1X horn. John Gilliom, an engineer at Electro-Voice, had spent months designing the first patented constant-directivity horn—but E-V's owners, Gulton Industries, decided not to invest in the tooling to make it. So Gilliom called Hartley. He explained he knew how to design a superior horn without infringing on his own patent, and he made the trip down to Meridian to show how it could be done. Hartley immediately identified the product's potential and hired him. Gilliom stayed in Meridian for several years—living in a commune, which raised some local eyebrows—and he helped to establish Peavey's dominance in the transducer business.

Though outfoxing the competition was serious business, Peavey's employees still liked to have fun. One famous incident in company folklore involved an employee named Don Brown, who decided he would streak through Plant 1. Service Manager Grant Brown (no relation) tells the story: "Don was doomed to be caught, as he wore only his motorcycle helmet and he was the only one who rode a bike to work that day. He actually clocked out and asked Hartley if it was okay—would he be fired if he did it? Hartley said no, he wouldn't be fired, but he had to go through Martha Boutwell's department if he did it. Her department was circuit-board assembly and there were more than 40 women working there. Martha pegged it after she found out it was Don by saying, 'I bet that Hartley Peavey put you up to that!' Don didn't say a word." At one point during his naked sprint, Brown ran headlong into Hartley's dad. Mr. Mutt was so shocked that he wanted him to be fired, but Hartley wouldn't do it. The episode caused considerable consternation among the Southern Baptist ladies in the factory, but is still remembered fondly by many of the older employees.

▲ *Peavey gear on the Dr. Hook Medicine Show, with Shel Silverstein, left, and Dustin Hoffman, right*

Breaking Waves

"If we do the same things tomorrow that we did today, we will know what to expect in the future... status quo, or worse."
—HARTLEY PEAVEY

▲ *Inside Plant 3 — an extensive facility!*

▲ *Plant 3 — a hive of activity*

BY 1975 the first phase of the Plant 3 project was up and running, and most of the cabinetry and metalworking production had been transferred from Plant 1. Another important transition was also under way: Hartley and Melia were separating from their spouses and divorce proceedings had begun. Their initial dislike for each other had turned into mutual respect—and then it became something more. After Hartley's divorce was finalized, they began to date. As the romance blossomed, Melia's interest in all aspects of the business increased, and she set out to learn everything she could about manufacturing, scheduling, and programming from Willie Hatcher.

Product introductions in 1975 included a new Festival twin-channel head with aluminum trim strips that matched the cosmetics of the speaker enclosures. A 160-watt Mace combo (212 or 412) and a 120-watt 112 Artist model joined the Classic and Deuce in a revitalized line of combos. These units were hybrids, with solid-state front ends and

1975-1977

- *Hartley Peavey with the T-60 guitar and Deuce amplifier*

▲ *The first CS-800 power amplifier*

CHAPTER 9 • BREAKING WAVES 51

▲ Festival tube amp head introduced in 1975

▼ T-12 Tweeter Bank

6L6 tube power amps that exhibited remarkable tonal range for their time. With the added flexibility of Automix they enjoyed runaway success. The concept of Automix took root during the development of the VTA-400 in 1971. For years there had been twin-channel guitar amps, but to Peavey the provision of two separate channels seemed wasted unless both could be fully utilized. Working on ways to manipulate gain and sustain for overload distortion effects, engineers gave the VTA-400 a front-panel facility that enabled the two channels to be run in parallel or in series (one driven into the other). These early attempts to provide more flexibility and performance from the two channels faltered because they necessitated patching and were not remotely controllable. Two years later the Roadmaster design incorporated remote foot-switching to change and combine the channels, and this became known as Automix. Twin-channel amps would never be the same again, and Peavey set itself way in front of the pack with dramatically enhanced performance from this development that filtered down into the main guitar-amp range.

The PA line continued to evolve, with HF tweeters replacing horns in the column speakers; the new columns were the 1210-TS (one 12, one 10, and three tweeters) and the 1210-T (two each of the 12 and 10 units plus the tweeters). The tweeters were also offered as high-frequency components, in T-300 (three-tweeter) and T-12 (12-tweeter) configurations. The Monitor enclosure was upgraded to incorporate two tweeters in the newly designated 112-TS, a slant (wedge) design. The power rating of the PA-120 and the Century instrument amp was raised to 100 watts.

The hugely successful 1200 mixer arrived, along with Peavey's first component graphic equalizer, the EQ-10. For larger venues, Peavey offered the Vocal Projector sound-reinforcement speakers (115HT with a 15" woofer, mid-range horn, and two tweeters; 215HT with twin woofers and twin horns), based on the Festival Projectors they replaced. Peavey's expansion from packaged portable systems to flexible component systems was well under way.

New products meant new product literature—and lots

1975-1977

of it had to be printed for NAMM. "Hartley got the bill for the literature printing for the trade show and threw a fit," says Marty McCann. "He exclaimed that for the price of this printing bill alone he could probably buy a printing press. Willie Hatcher reached in his pocket and said, 'As a matter of fact, Hartley, a printing press is less than this. I shopped around and got a couple of proposals. . . .' It wasn't long before Hartley bought his first printing press and the company started producing its own literature—and that press is still in operation today."

The increased power ratings of the guitar and bass amps, the development of the CSP speaker system, and the new power amps being created by Jack Sondermeyer were pushing speakers and drivers to their limits. The premium speaker options from JBL and Electro-Voice were offered to address this—but reliability issues and the high cost of reconing, combined with the suppliers' inability (or unwillingness) to respond to Peavey's demands for improvements, drove an in-house transducer research program. Hartley had the idea of making his own premium horn driver and die-cast chassis speaker with replaceable cone/voice-coil assemblies, allowing for field replacement of the blown voice coils.

Working with John Gilliom, Peavey R&D created the Model 22 Driver, which appeared in 1976 and was incorporated initially in the Spider System (SP-1) to complement Gilliom's constant-directivity horn. This high-power compression horn driver featured a field-replaceable 2" voice-coil diaphragm and a massive 52-ounce square magnet. A rugged high-performance device, it has been constantly upgraded and retained its place as the key component in Peavey's sound systems in subsequent years. (The Model 22 Driver got its name from the throat diameter; although it is known as a 2" driver, the voice coil is actually 2.2" in diameter.)

The success of the Model 22 owed much to the company's machine shop, under the direction of master machinist Sam Moore. Forming a one-piece aluminum-dome diaphragm for the 22, at field-replaceable tolerances, required the design and construction of special jigs and tools. Sam's crew handled the task with ease.

▲ *The EQ-10, introduced in 1975, was Peavey's first signal processor*

▲ *The ubiquitous Deuce*

▼ *Vocal Projectors introduced in 1975*

CHAPTER 9 • BREAKING WAVES 53

The original Spider Model 22 high-compression horn driver

▼ *The Machine Shop*

The Model 22 Driver was spun off from the work being done on a new chassis speaker, and the announcement of the Spider series Black Widow speakers followed soon after, in 1976. The Black Widow is one component that has undeniably set Peavey apart from its competitors. It featured a number of revolutionary design concepts, including the detachable magnet-and-cone assembly Hartley had dreamed up, which allowed for replacement of a blown speaker cone in minutes by a dealer or in the field.

The Black Widow's design combined superior performance with rugged reliability, thanks to a 4" voice coil of edge-wound aluminum ribbon wire. Using ribbon wire instead of conventional round wire made manufacturing more difficult, but it meant that 24 percent more wire could be wound on the voice coil—and the extra turns yielded much greater efficiency. The speaker's finely machined narrow coil gap concentrated more energy for greater power handling, and its massive 96-ounce magnet was vented through the middle for superior heat dissipation. The whole design was a massive technical advance in transducer technology. Not surprisingly, a large portion of Plant 1 was turned over to Black Widow speaker fabrication.

Hartley showed his unflinching devotion to reliability by hiring Hal Aiken to oversee quality control. "I managed Sounds Unlimited, a retail store in Greenwood, Mississippi, before I met Hartley at a NAMM mini-show in Washington, D.C.," says Hal. "In 1975, I drove from Greenwood to Meridian to interview for the job. I met with Hartley at about 4:00 p.m. and then went to have cocktails and dinner with him and Melia—they had just started dating. He was driving a Cadillac, and she had an older black Porsche that he made fun of. He and I hit it off, and I went to work for Peavey. My first job was quality control manager. The check-out musicians at the end of each assembly line used to make minor repairs to help out the workers, but I instructed them to reject every fault that came into the booth. One day, as a joke, one of the assembly guys stuck a chicken bone under the handle of an amp. The QC guy rejected it and wrote up 'chicken bone under handle.' Well,

54 THE PEAVEY REVOLUTION • **PART THREE** • ACCELERATION

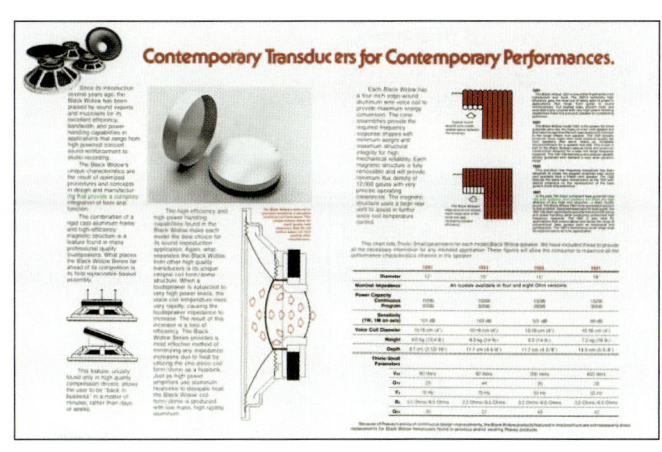

The introductory literature on the Black Widow speaker

Hartley was giving one of his factory tours that day, and he loved to show the reject pile to illustrate just how quality-conscious we were—and the first thing he found was the chicken-bone reject. Boy, did the poop hit the fan! He told me, 'Go fire the S.O.B. that put that chicken bone under the amp handle.' I told him that I couldn't fire the guy because he worked for production. It blew over quickly, but that was too funny!"

In 1975 Peavey began to get into guitar production—somewhat reluctantly. Although his high-school scribblings had included sketches of guitar designs, Hartley had not entered the music business with any intention of becoming a guitar builder. But the competition forced his hand. "Gibson and Fender started putting lots of pressure on dealers," Hartley explains, "because we were getting into their thing [with instrument amplifiers], but they couldn't get into the PA business. They started telling dealers that if they wanted to get their guitars they would have to buy their amps as well. I decided I had to return the favor, so I entered the guitar business—to fight fire with fire!"

During the 1970s, Peavey's conglomerate-controlled competitors were pushing up their production levels, looking for ways to make more guitars with less overhead, and, not surprisingly, quality often suffered. The traditional methods they used required lots of handwork done by large numbers of skilled (and expensive) craftsmen. Hartley determined that he would find a better way to do it, one that would apply his "make the best product at a fair and reasonable price" philosophy to building guitars.

Hartley found inspiration in his gun collection. As an engineer, he marveled at the way the gunsmith's art had been applied to mass production. The wood of rifle stocks was being married to the barrels with metalworking tolerances—why couldn't guitars be made that way? "I've always been amazed at how the wooden stock on a rifle fits the metal so precisely," Hartley says. "In many cases, you can't fit a sheet of paper between them. So I figured that whatever machine was used to make those gun stocks could make guitar necks that way. I could make them very fast, very precise, and at much less cost. I went to some German companies that made the machines and asked, 'Can you make this?' They said, 'We've never done it, but, yes, we think so.' So we started making guitar necks on a copy lathe—the first company in the world that ever did that. Of course, my competitors all said, 'That can't be done—everybody knows you can't make guitars with computers.' Well, we weren't making guitars with computers; we were making guitar parts, which were assembled into an instrument with human hands."

Hartley Peavey

Hartley put Chip Todd in charge of the guitar-making venture. Chip had arrived from Texas late in 1974; he was a well-respected luthier who had turned to mechanical engineering as a career. He had worked on race car engines and also designed and patented a sinusoidal braking system that is used to this day on many airport and shuttle transit systems. Chip shared Hartley's vision of making a better instrument using state-of-the-art production techniques, adapting numerical-controlled routers to carve guitar bodies and copy lathes to make necks.

> "There's something magical about taking a magnet, a piece of paper, and a coil of wire and making music."
> —HARTLEY PEAVEY

Hartley took the plunge, investing in the new machinery. Peavey would be the first to make guitars in a new way, with parts cut identically every time, ensuring consistent quality. In setting up the copy lathe, it quickly became apparent that a new method of construction was feasible whereby the truss rod could be inserted into a bi-laminated blank before carving. This meant that the insertion of the truss rod could be achieved before the wood was prepared and carved. The resulting neck would be stronger, more stable, and easier to produce. This idea formed the basis of one of several patents obtained from the research done by Hartley and Chip.

Chip wrote about his pioneering work with Hartley in the Peavey publication *Monitor*; that article is reproduced here with his kind permission.

Bolstered by a successful amplifier operation, the Peavey guitar program had the luxury of not having to go to market prematurely. Hartley and I are co-holders of the patent that made it possible to build strong necks at a price that would change guitar making throughout the world. This method of building guitar necks was so far-advanced that no one other than Leo Fender chose to copy the method, using an overlooked loophole in the patent's wording. The patented method of neck manufacture and the numerically controlled body-carving techniques allowed Peavey to get a foothold in the tightly knit guitar market by not only reducing the price but also upgrading the quality of each and every part. The neck idea came spontaneously from Hartley and me when we were scribbling ideas on paper napkins over a Meridian plate lunch in 1975.

Sometime in 1980, it was decided that two presentation T-60 guitars would be built, with the serial numbers 00000001 and 00000002. One was to be presented to Hartley and one to me, as engineer of the guitar program. The bodies were to be made of American black walnut without pick-guards (a first for Peavey), and the necks from special pieces of bird's-eye maple saved from the first wood samples received in 1976. The instruments were assembled on the regular production line by all the guitar plant employees, under the special supervision of Jerald Pugh.

Hartley wanted me to have the #1 serial number, but I declined, thinking that in later years he would regret not having the lower serial number around for history's sake. He couldn't convince me to take it, so #1 was painted with a non-gloss finish for him, and #2 with a glossy finish, my preference. The instruments were presented to Hartley and me sometime in mid-1980. At the time, nobody could foresee how closely the two guitars would be intertwined with the future.

Later in 1980, with the design work caught up and the guitar plant's supervision turned over to another, I received an offer from one of our competitors [Fender] that I just couldn't refuse. So with mixed emotions—sadness and the excitement of a new challenge—I moved to California in March of 1981. The serial #00000002 T-60 resided on a special wall hanger in my different residences until November of 1990.

Sometime in 1984, I left the music industry to return to mechanical-engineering design. In mid-1989, I moved to a small town near San Diego called Ramona. I was involved with electromechanical engineering in the computer-graphics and satellite-communications industries, but Hartley and I still corresponded and I did special work for him from time to time.

On November 20, 1990, three burglars chopped a hole in the side of my home and stole quite a large portion of the nicer things my wife Arlene and I had—things like the serial #00000002 T-60, my late father's Winchester rifle, and Arlene's personal mementos, all of which were

1975-1977

irreplaceable. One of the items missing from my firearms collection was a pistol Arlene had given me for my birthday that I hadn't even seen yet. Later it would play a vital role in this drama.

Trying to appraise the value of the rare T-60, I calculated a figure and called Charley Gressett, the third person hired for the Peavey guitar program, and Hartley to see what figure they would turn in for insurance. Indicative of the mind meld the three of us developed during the oft-argued pre-production decisions, all three arrived at the same dollar amount.

Several days after talking to Hartley, I checked the front porch for possible UPS shipments to my gun-smithing business and found a large package from Peavey. Opening it, I found T-60 serial #00000001 with a note from Hartley. After some real soul-searching, Hartley had decided that he wanted me to have this special instrument and sent it to replace the stolen one.

As much as receiving the #00000001 meant to me, nothing could compare with the note I received with the instrument. It was a message from one friend to another that showed the depth of character that Hartley is usually reluctant to expose (most people can't imagine him having a shy side). Arlene and I wanted to copy the note and put the original in our safe, as we had learned that burglars took lock boxes with things that were valuable only to the victims, and nobody would be walking off with the post-office safe we used for important papers. While copying the note, I inadvertently ran the original through the slot for the clean copy paper and re-copied the note over itself. I thought—I don't need burglars to make me miserable—I can manage that myself.

Although the sheriff's deputies told me that the stolen things were probably in Mexico, I never gave up hope that the guitar was around the little town of Ramona, the nearest town to our house. I looked in the pawnshop and hoped that it would turn up there and not be down in Mexico.

▲ *T-60 presentation model guitars, serial numbers 00000001 and 00000002.*

Around April of 1992, I received a call from the sheriff's department telling me that they had recovered one of the stolen pistols and that a deputy had been killed with it. It turned out that he had only been shot once, was very much alive, and wanted the revolver as a souvenir, as the sheriff's department was keeping his Kevlar vest for training purposes. There was still no word on any of the other items stolen along with T-60 #00000002, and the officers offered little hope of recovering anything else.

In January of 1994, I moved to Austin, Texas, to design x-ray fluorescent analyzers. I put the California house on the market and locked T-60 #00000001 in a safe-storage facility until I transported it to Austin in May. Murphy's Law prevailed again, as I discovered that the neck was back-bowed due to being stored so long in one of the original vacuum-formed cases. Needless to say, I felt responsible for "Hartley's guitar," and much to my relief, the neck was restored to playing condition without having to paint it. It now played more easily than even the Peavey factory specifications demanded.

One September evening, Arlene, who was still back in California trying to sell the house, got a call from a gun-smithing customer and friend, Rick Stangler. Rick said an ex-convict had offered him T-60 #00000002, and he wanted to get it back for me. He told Arlene he had notified the San Diego County sheriff's department and volunteered to set up a sting to buy the guitar and testify against the person involved.

Arlene had planned to surprise me by having the guitar in her trunk when I came to Ramona for Thanksgiving, but the ex-con had disappeared after allegedly being kicked out of the Corvette shop he frequented for stealing. The surprise was not to be. Rick had his work cut out for him, as the case was not an active one with the San Diego sheriff, due to the time that had passed since the robbery. Arlene told me about it, and I met with Rick to express my support and offer what I could. It would be up to Rick to orchestrate the sting, as he was the only one who knew the ex-con even slightly, and who wouldn't put him on the alert. The sheriff's detective and I warned Rick that he might be in danger, but Rick is a large and stout-hearted man who felt sure he could handle it—and that he did. The ex-con was a familiar suspect around the Ramona sheriff's department, and Detective Schaffer was quite willing to try to make an arrest.

In early February, I received a call from Detective Schaffer saying that the sting was successful and the sheriff's department had T-60 #00000002 in its possession. He said he would have to keep the guitar for a month to see if the district attorney wanted to file charges against the persons who had the instrument. He felt there would be little chance that the DA would charge the men, as they weren't the ones who stole it; the thieves were killed in a car accident shortly after they burglarized our home.

The actual holders of the guitar were a father and son who had a small recording studio at their home (they had a Peavey 24-channel mixer and other Peavey equipment), and they claimed to be

CHAPTER 9 • BREAKING WAVES 57

unaware that serial number 00000002 of a company's product line would be worth more than the $200 they claimed they paid for it. Typically, neither was charged with possessing stolen property.

The guitar was in good shape, although its original case had been lost. Not feeling that I could risk #00000001's case, I asked my daughter Catherine to send the T-60 case that Hartley had so graciously given her, so that #00000002 could be shipped back safely. Her case was one of the later blow-molded models, but it fit all T-60s equally well, and the guitar arrived in Austin without a blemish on it. As intended, the careful attention given to finish, plating, and wood treatment had prepared the instrument to stand up under extreme conditions, even being hauled down a quarter mile of dirt road when it was stolen five years ago.

I wanted to drive to Mississippi and return #00000001 to Hartley but my work schedule and commitments kept me from it. I can think of no other act of kindness and generosity that has so touched me in my entire life, and to come from someone like Hartley Peavey—well, that is hard to express in words. Only a true friend could be so generous considering I left his company to go to work for a competitor.

▲ *Marketing for the T-60 and T-40 from the Peavey Papers*

With speaker cabinet production shifted to Plant 3, Plant 2 was renovated and re-equipped for building guitars and basses. Many new fixtures and machines for fretting necks, winding pickups, shaping hardware, and other instrument-building tasks had to be designed and made in the machine shop. The first robot ever used in a guitar factory—named Onan—was installed to automate buffing and finishing.

The final design of the first Peavey solid-body instruments was completed in 1976, and the programming and installation of the factory equipment continued during 1977. By the end of the year, pre-production pilot runs were under way.

The first Peavey T-60 guitars and T-40 basses rolled down the production line in 1978, and Peavey became a truly diversified musical instrument and sound equipment company. The launch of these instruments was greeted with some skepticism in the industry, and competitors continued to scoff at the idea of "making guitars with computers." There was more to it than that, of course—the work of skilled craftsmen was still required, but they were, as Hartley pointed out, assembling precision parts made with computer assistance. The efficient production techniques being pioneered by Peavey resulted in a better instrument made for (and selling for) less money. Within a few years, Peavey would be building more guitars in the U.S. than anyone—and Peavey's competitors would be scrambling to embrace the technology they had laughed at.

Bill Everitt attended a dealer seminar shortly after guitar production began. "I can still remember the meeting where Hartley presented the T-60 electric guitar to the dealers at one of the Peavey schools in Meridian," he says. "He demoed it himself by attempting to play the song 'Wildwood Flower.' After everyone stopped laughing, he began to tell the dealers how much each part cost and how he could make a profit for the company and for the dealer while selling it for less than the price of Fender and Gibson electrics at the time. By the time Hartley finished his presentation, which included his characterization of the pricing strategy of the competition as 'padding the pockets of their corporate sugar daddies,' he had convinced the dealers that the T-60 was going to revolutionize the guitar industry."

As if plunging into the guitar business were not enough, Peavey's product launches in 1976 included the CS-800 power amp, the Black Widow speaker, and the SP speaker series. These three products would prove to be among the most successful in the company's history.

The CS-800 reflected the brilliant design collaboration between Hartley and Jack Sondermeyer.

58 THE PEAVEY REVOLUTION • **PART THREE** • ACCELERATION

1975-1977

The combination of Jack's unrivaled knowledge of solid-state technology and the well-established engineering skill of the Peavey R&D staff combined to create a super-rugged and reliable power amp that could withstand the rigors of touring and sound great night after night. Legend has it that the reliability testing involved throwing the amp down the stairs outside Jack's office—so it's not surprising that Peavey's service department still gets calls to support the oldest models. The fact that a power amp can remain serviceable for the better part of three decades is testament to the original design. The stereo CS-800 featured an octal socket on the rear panel of each 400-watt channel, and a series of plug-in electronic crossover modules was offered. This feature enabled easy bi-amping and proved to be an instant winner.

The CS-800 became an industry standard for power amps, and it often took center stage at the dealer seminars where Hartley was teaching the industry how to sell sophisticated sound equipment. "Hartley's folksy style of presentation," Bill Everitt says, "was often prefaced with 'I submit to you . . . ,' as in 'I submit to you that the competition is misrepresenting the facts when they feed you the specifications of the XYZ model. Let's look closer.' One time Hartley was comparing the CS-800 to a competitor's power amp. 'You would have to hook up two water hoses to the XYZ power amp just to keep it cool because of its bad design,' he said."

A 212-TS wedge monitor was added to the lineup of PA speakers, and an 810 bass enclosure joined the instrument enclosure line. The SP-1 replaced the CSP; it was a two-way system featuring the new 22 horn driver and configured for easy bi-amping with the CS-800. The horn section was sold as a separate unit called the MF-1X.

The PA-700, a stereo mixer amp, was added to the PA line, along with several non-powered mixers: the 600S Mixer, 900S Mixer, and 1200S stereo mixers and the 12- and 24-channel Festival mixers. To fill out the amplifier offering, a 400 mono and 260S stereo Booster were added. (These amps featured the new black-center aluminum control knobs.) Two new windscreen-equipped ball microphones built by Astatic were also added to the catalogue—and, in deference to the "one-stop shopping" approach, the first Peavey multi-core snake was produced.

Other new products included a top-box version of the Session 400 and the LTD, a 115 Black Widow–equipped version of the combo. Because the Session 400 was so popular with steel guitar players in Nashville, Hartley entered into an agreement with Maurice Anderson to distribute his M.S.A. steel guitars. The arrangement did not last long, but it hinted at a widening interest in diversification in Meridian.

Imitation may be flattery—but in the music industry it can be a financial disaster, so in the late '70s Hartley was forced to take legal action against a company called Earth, which was marketing amplifiers and speakers that blatantly ripped off the distinctive cosmetics of the Peavey line. This successful action established a corporate commitment to robust defense of patents and trademarks that has continued over the years.

The seminar program had become so successful that it was impossible to collect the folks at the airport and transport them to Meridian in two vans,

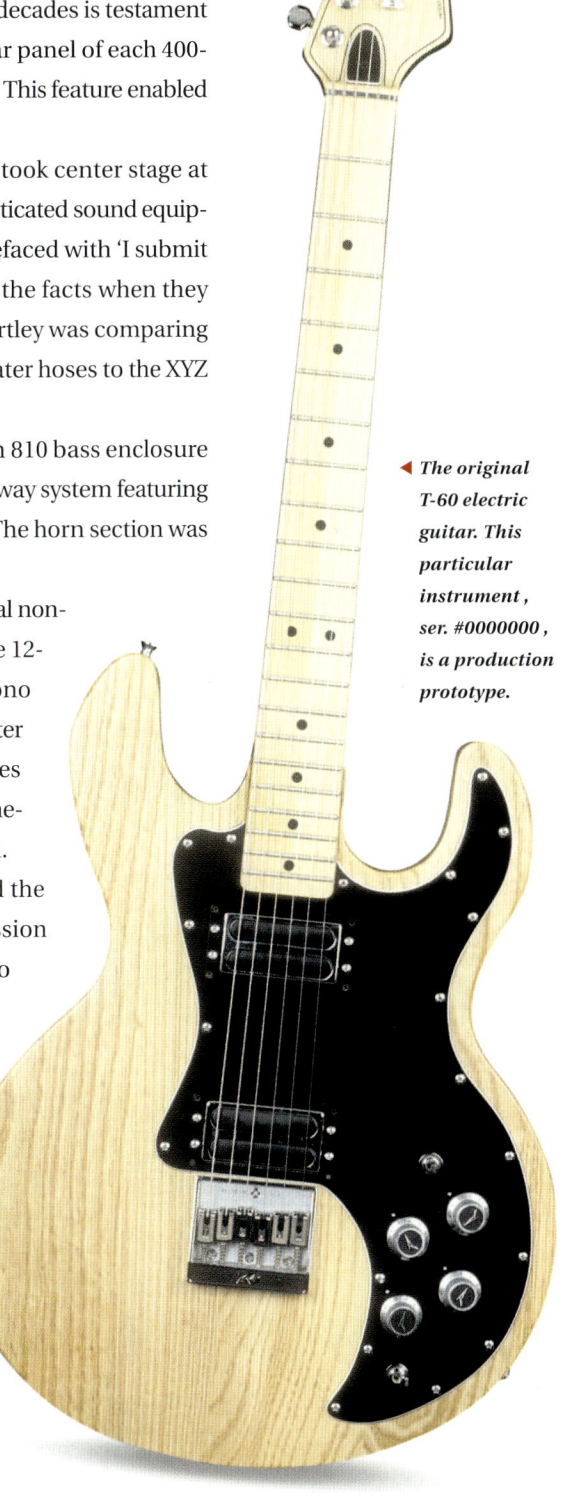

◀ *The original T-60 electric guitar. This particular instrument, ser. #0000000, is a production prototype.*

CHAPTER 9 • BREAKING WAVES

so Hartley purchased an old school bus. This utilitarian vehicle was to serve the company well for many years, until it was replaced by a full-size air-conditioned Silver Eagle coach. It is a testament to Hartley's good humor that he laughs to this day at the story of Marty McCann and the bus at the New Orleans airport. Forgetting what he was driving, McCann swung the bus into the car lane at the terminal and caught the roof on the overhang of the building, which ripped open the bus like a sardine can.

In just two years, Peavey's export effort had surged forward, with distributors established in 40 countries. In the U.K. Peavey had become so successful that the distributor split the brand away from its other activities to stand alone under the name Peavey U.K. International artists such as Elton John, Spencer Davis, Wishbone Ash, and the Cure added their names to the growing list of Peavey players during the '70s, and the influential domestic artists who endorsed Peavey gear during the decade included the Jefferson Airplane, Sly & the Family Stone, Santana, the Grateful Dead, Lynyrd Skynyrd, Lee Michaels, Boz Scaggs, and Roy Orbison. It seemed that the amps with the distinctive aluminum-strip cosmetics were showing up on stages everywhere.

On November 18, 1977, Hartley and Melia were married, creating a "double act" that would leave an indelible mark on the music industry. Hal Aiken remembers the day they informed the employees: "I had been there for a year, and one day Hartley called a company meeting in the break room of the Banana Building. He announced that he and Melia were in love and were to marry."

Years later, Melia would say that together they made "a good one person." What she meant was that they had a strong symbiotic relationship that made the most of their individual strengths. Melia was detail-oriented and kept her eye on the minutiae of management while Hartley was the visionary and driving force; together, as Hartley put it, "the whole was more than the sum of the parts." At the time of their marriage, Aiken says, "Melia had [already] positioned herself over sales and marketing—obviously with Hartley's support—and before you knew it, she was controlling production,

▶ *800S — the first stereo mixer, 1976*

1978

too. Hartley maintained his new product/engineering positions, and Willie Hatcher was always the older guy who solved problems and reported to both of them."

The perpetual expansion and seemingly insurmountable back-order situation made this a chaotic yet exciting time. With the major investment in time and money required to create both a guitar factory and a loudspeaker component plant from scratch, there was little time to spare. Everyone was working full tilt. By the end of the year, the total manufacturing space was some 300,000 square feet and the workforce had nearly doubled.

By this time, Black Widow speakers were being offered as options on more and more existing Peavey models, as well as being incorporated into such upgraded models as the revamped Session 400 and LTD-400 steel guitar amps.

The latest product introductions included a 15-watt guitar practice amp called the Backstage, the IP-1 instrument preamp, and the four-channel KM-4 keyboard mixer. The rest of the new models were all in the PA field—and none more significant than the XR-600 mixer amp, which replaced the PA-400 and went on to become an industry standard. Yet another brilliant Sondermeyer/Peavey collaboration, it was offered in a regular top-box enclosure or built into a rugged flight case.

The XR-600 was the first Peavey unit to break away from the stark black-and-silver layout to a new look, with gray highlights on the control panel and Rogan injection-molded control knobs color-coded by function. These new knobs—made in different colors for designating gain, EQ, and effects—would soon begin appearing on other upgraded products.

The XR-600 broke new ground with its nine-band graphic EQ and an extensive patch bay that further enhanced expandability. Each channel had a pre-level monitor-send control that made a complete monitor mix possible for the first time in such an affordable unit. To complement this capability, Peavey offered the 260 standalone monitor amp with onboard graphic EQ. Other PA offerings included the PA-200, which replaced the PA-120, and a new 45-watt PA-100, built into a 112PT column. The 1510T enclosure was also rolled out, loaded with two 15s, two 12s, and a trio of tweeters.

The Mark I mixers were completely redesigned, with the rackmountable MR-7 model and MC-8, -12, -16, and -24 console versions featuring the new Rogan knobs and veneered end panels. The 24-channel model retailed at $1799, breaking new ground for affordability and ensuring instant success. A 12-channel PA-100S stereo powered console was also added to the line, and, on the enclosure side, the bottom half of the SP-1 was offered as a separate bass bin that could be married with the MF-1X horn as a modular system. Last but certainly not least, Jack Sondermeyer developed 200- and 400-watt "little brothers" to the CS-800 power amp.

▲ *The author with Hartley — 1976*

▲ *A modern Peavey loudspeaker showing its easy field replacement: simply remove the magnet structure and attach a new Peavey speaker basket*

1978

During the CNN "Pinnacle" documentary about Peavey that aired in 1995, Hartley said he believed that it took 13 years for his company to become fully established. "Our business was like a motorboat," he explained. "When you put the throttle down, the [front of the] boat comes up and you really can't see ahead of you. There's a lot of water splashing around and some instability. But sooner or later, if you keep the throttle down, you come up 'on plane.' It took us 13 years to actually come up on plane. When the buffeting stopped and we could see clearly ahead of us, we really

▲ *Hartley and Melia — coming together*

started to gain speed and momentum." That happened in 1978.

Looking back on those 13 years, Marty McCann offers this take on what distinguished Peavey's way of doing business from the other musical-instrument companies: "It was the feedback, the rapport that was established with the dealer network through the early inquisitive years, and then getting up and talking to them at the seminars. The dealers realized that Hartley's company was not like a lot of the other companies. Hartley was, from three months old, behind the music store counter; his mom answered the phone and did the books, and his dad did the selling. For all his life, everything he has ever had—food, sustenance, shelter—has come directly from the music industry. He empathized with the dealers, and they empathized with him. As he was growing up, he would hear his dad talking to the various salesmen who would call. He could see his father's anger at being pressure-sold and how he resented the manufacturers who mistreated the retailers. Hartley decided that he would treat his customers better. He would talk to the dealers like they were family."

In February 1978 Mike O'Neill came to Peavey. A talented young transducer engineer, he had been working for CTS, a major supplier of chassis speakers, and recognized the opportunities opening up in Meridian. Mike would stay for 16 years and develop some of the company's most popular and profitable products during his tenure. He set to work immediately to incorporate the Black Widow components into the International Series of enclosures, creating the compact, high-power Continental model aimed at the European market. A new 18" BW derivative was developed for use in the 118 International and the direct-radiating 118-DR subwoofer.

▶ *Session 400 — the iconic pedal steel amplifier*

1978

Kevin O'Brien also joined the team during this pivotal year, taking over as controller. He had been working for Rockwell International in Tennessee and brought the financial and computer expertise that Peavey needed to advance. Mike Carter, an information-technology expert, followed him down to Meridian, and together they set about preparing a move from the IBM System 3 set up by Bob Peavey—who had joined his brother's company to run its accounting and computer departments after graduating from Mississippi State—to a new IBM mainframe system.

All of the instrument amps were given a new look, featuring the Rogan knobs on redesigned faceplates, and new features. The Mark III Musician was equipped with a phaser circuit and graphic EQ, and the Mark III Bass now featured "Paramid" (quasi-parametric) EQ, a crossover for bi-amping, and a compressor. Both amps offered extensive capabilities for preamp and power amp patching. The Mark III Standard got the facelift, and a new bass version called the Centurion debuted.

> "I don't think we have the right to complain about things if we're not going to get in there and try to make a difference."
>
> —MELIA PEAVEY

The Classic, Artist, Deuce, and Mace guitar amps were updated as the VT series, with the phaser circuit and new patching capabilities included in the redesign. At the summer trade show, two new bass combos made their debut: the TKO, a compact 40-watt unit, and the beefy 130-watt Combo, loaded with a Black Widow 15, which proved to be a serious yet highly portable (and, of course, highly affordable) gigging amp.

The 210 Stereo and EQ-27 (mono) rackmount equalizers were unveiled, along with the low-cost MR-600 rackmount mixer and the SP-2.

The SP-2 would become one of the company's top sellers over the years. Together with the CS-800 it has formed a bedrock component for many thousands of Saturday-night gigs and installed sound systems, and it survives to this day as a star performer. With its distinctive two-way configuration pairing a 15" Black Widow speaker and the 22 Driver constant-directivity high-frequency horn, the enclosure was set up for optional bi-amp operation. The rear patch panel was provided with direct inputs to the horn and woofer as well as full-range inputs. Shipped from the factory in full-range setting, a passive crossover inside the unit was activated. Resetting a jump plug on the circuit board resulted in direct access to the two components, and the unit could be crossed over at 800Hz for maximum efficiency. The plug-in modules for the CS power amps made this particularly easy to achieve, and the benefits of bi-amping sound systems became a central plank of the Peavey educational seminar programs.

The 112-TS and 212-TS monitor enclosures were now offered with a BW option. The PA-400 finally bowed out, having established Peavey's dominance in portable PA, in favor of the newly established XR-600. A revitalized Mark II series of mixers benefited from the new cosmetics being introduced throughout the line.

Perhaps most important, production of the T-60 guitar and T-40 bass was finally rolling. It had taken longer than anticipated to reach full capacity, but considering the complexity of the production methods and the many jigs, fixtures, and machines involved, it is amazing that the factory was operating within three years of the decision to get into the guitar business. Teaching the robot to accurately buff a neck was, in itself, a long and arduous process. But the result of all the hard, patient work was evident in the startling and consistent excellence of the guitars and basses. The stability of the bi-laminated neck construction combined with the precise fit of the components set a new benchmark for fretted instruments. Even Hartley's hero Leo Fender got in on the act, copying the bi-laminated neck on his G&L instruments (with changes to get around Peavey's patent). The production target of 300 units per day was soon realized, making Peavey the largest manufacturer of guitars in the country at the time.

In just five years, Peavey had established a significant international reputation, and the growth of its overseas business was recognized by Hartley and Melia's receipt of the President's "E" Award for Exports. It could have been a setback when Pete Wood left the Export Department in the fall of 1978, but Rick Grigsby quickly took over the role of manager. Rick had worked for Norlin in Chicago, and he brought with him a thorough understanding of the international marketplace.

New artists who joined the roster of endorsees during 1978 included Elvis Costello, Steve Gibbons, Journey, and Bobby Cochran. All in all, it was another banner year.

▲ *Hartley packs the first guitar for shipping, 1977*

▲ *Hartley & Melia Peavey pose with award*

PART FOUR

Clear Water

Taking Center Stage

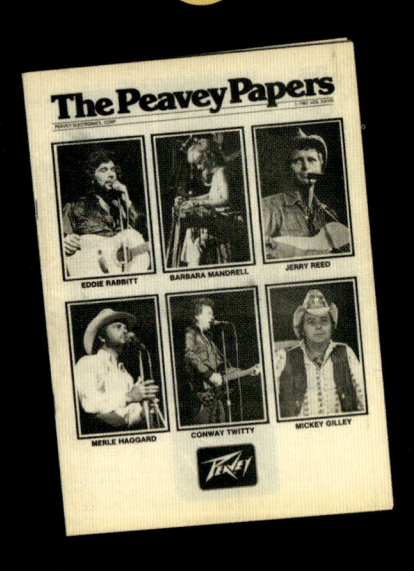

"Attitude is more important than the past, than education, than money, than circumstances, than failures, than successes, than what other people think or say or do. It is more important than appearance, giftedness, or skill. It will make or break a company... a church... a home."

— CHARLES SWINDOLL

IN the late 1970s Peavey's R&D effort was going full tilt, and Jack Sondermeyer was working on a new circuit that would become the basis of one of the company's most significant patents (#4,318,053). Distortion Detection Technique (DDT) was originally designed as an upgrade feature for the CS-800 power amp, but it would eventually find its way into most powered PA, sound reinforcement, and bass guitar products.

For applications demanding clean output at high volume levels, DDT was

▲ *Jack Sondermeyer at his bench*

▲ *CS-400 and CS-800 power amplifiers*

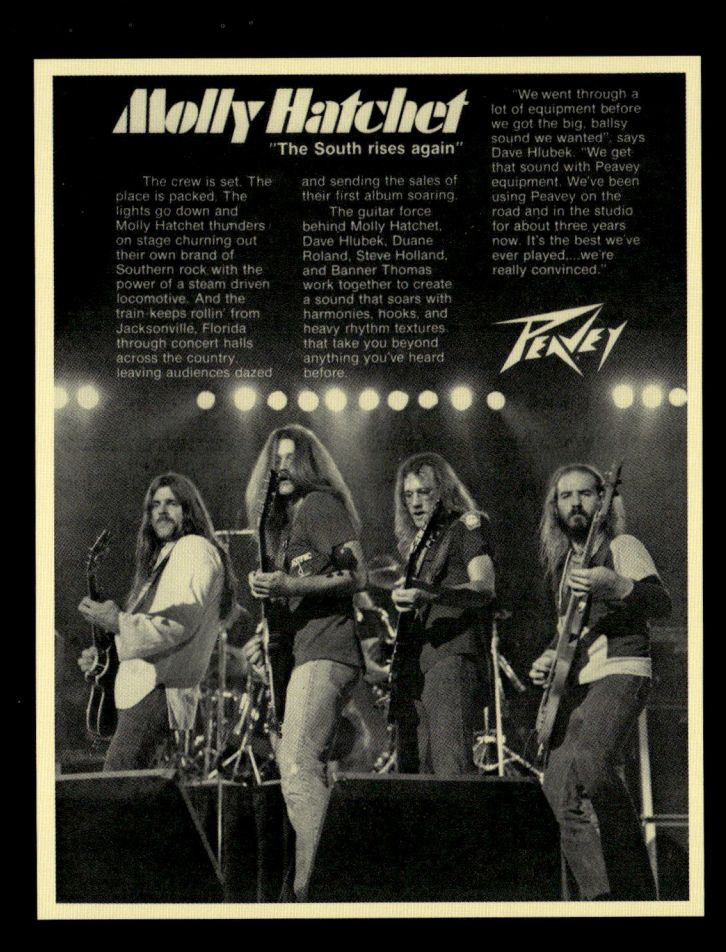

▼ *The experimental T-25 Sustanite guitar*

▲ *Molly Hatchet extols the virtues of Peavey and the "big, ballsy sound."*

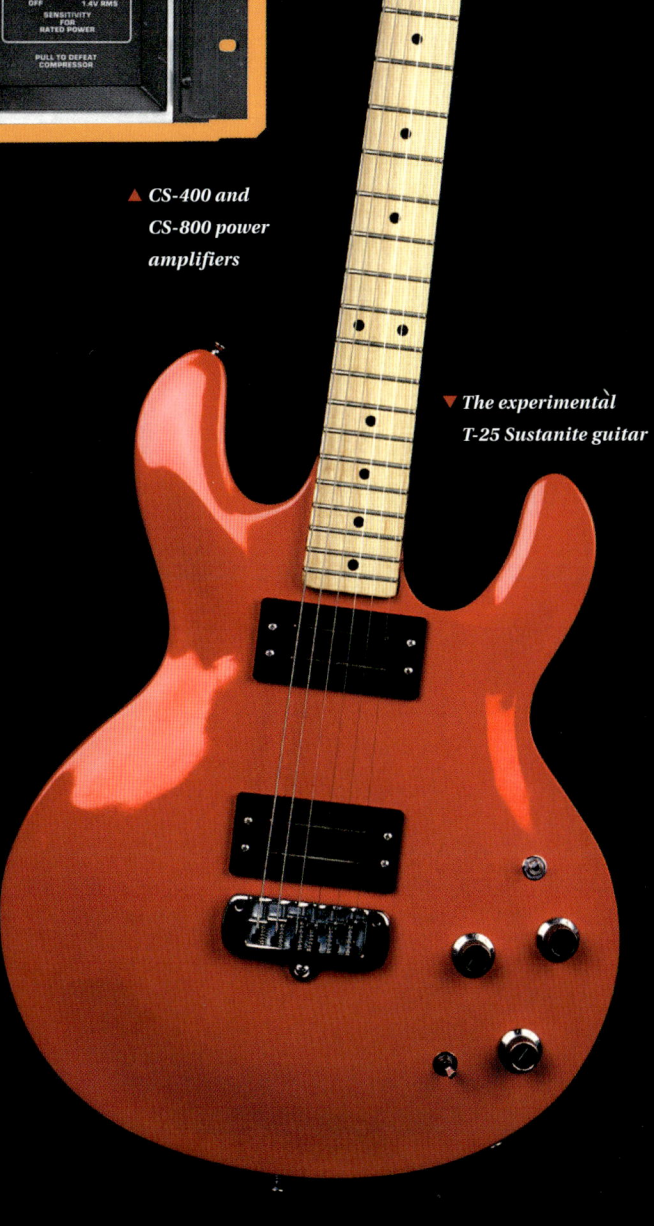

CHAPTER 10 • TAKING CENTER STAGE **67**

an important breakthrough. Jack's circuit cleverly sensed the onset of power-amp clipping, with its attendant distortion, and then used compression to prevent distorted sound while retaining the maximum headroom available. When clipping was no longer detected, the circuit automatically disengaged its compression, retaining the dynamics of the program material while wringing out the maximum wattage. Square-wave distortion is the ultimate speaker assassin, so DDT would become a cornerstone of Peavey's enviable reputation for reliability.

DDT was applied to the CS-800 and also to the newly developed CS-400, rated at 200 watts per channel. The octal-socket plug-in crossover modules were also fitted to the new smaller unit. Peavey's increasingly sophisticated engineering, coupled with its dealer education, meant that the company could make strong progress in teaching the market about the advantages of bi-amped sound systems—along with the benefits of delivering quality, reliability, and high performance at affordable prices. It was a marketing coup: Peavey was providing musicians with the performance they craved while teaching its dealers how to use and sell the tools to achieve it.

The new XC-400 was a top-box 200-watt power amp with built-in graphic EQ designed to be used in a bi-amp configuration with the Mark III Bass and its built-in crossover. For bass players looking for better performance in a small combo amp, the TNT was beefed up to 50 watts and equipped with active EQ with Paramid. To maintain its position as the steel player's amp of choice, the Session 500 was given a complete redesign, incorporating DDT and all the features requested by the many endorsers of its predecessors, such as an effects loop, volume pedal patch, string-effect phaser, and a compensated mic-level XLR output. Later the 500 would be replaced by an updated version of the original Session 400. In a *Monitor* magazine article in the early '90s, Jimmy Phillips observed, "One would be hard-pressed to find a reputable Music City steel guitarist who does not play through a Peavey Nashville 400 or Session 400 amplifier. Simply stated, these are the industry standards. From the godfathers of the instrument such as Buddy Emmons and Lloyd Green to aspiring students, the Peavey logo was a standard feature in most Nashville venues, recording studios, and TV programs. On his regular tours with the Everly Brothers, Emmons used his Session 400 exclusively. Backing Albert Lee with his Hogan's Heroes band, steel maestro Jerry Hogan also used Peavey amplification. And it has remained that way as the next generation of players emerged in the '90s, led by the busiest session man of them all, Paul Franklin."

▼ *Plug-in PL Modules for the CS series power amplifiers*

The T-60 guitar and T-40 Bass, now in full production, were offered with rosewood fingerboard and sunburst finish options.

Mike O'Neill was busy developing more products utilizing the Black Widow drivers; they included two new 45-degree wedge monitors, the 1245 and 2445, and a BW option for the FH-1. The newest member of the SP family of enclosures, the SP-3, was a lower-cost two-way system matching the SP-2 horn with a utility woofer.

The XR concept was extended to the entire packaged-PA range, with the XR-400 (four channels, 100 watts) and XR-500 (five channels, 120 watts plus DDT) top boxes and two new powered consoles: the XR-700 (seven channels and dual 120-watt amps) and the XR-1200 (12 channels and dual 200-watt amps). For smaller venues, there was a new XR-series "baby" top box, the MP-4, with a modest 50 watts into 8 ohms. Two new mixers, the 801 and 1201, also joined the lineup as Peavey's development of affordable mixer technology continued.

1980

On the last day of the 1970s, Peavey purchased a building in Morton, Mississippi, some 50 miles west of Meridian and close to Jackson, the state capital. Abandoned by Talon, a zipper manufacturer that had been driven out of business by offshore competition, the acquisition provided more production space and a ready-made workforce. There were concerns that the Meridian employment pool had been tapped to a point where the need for more workers was as much a potential restriction to growth as space. (Brenda Slayton, who joined the company at this time, says that there were already 700 employees on the payroll by the close of the 1970s.) The addition of Plant 4 in Morton secured 100 additional employees and 48,900 square feet of manufacturing space, which would be devoted to the production of the smaller single-unit guitar amps.

▲ *Plant 4 — Morton, MS*

The artists lining up to endorse products included Molly Hatchet, Deep Purple, and Bon Jovi, demonstrating that the appeal of the Peavey name had stretched well beyond Nashville. Molly Hatchet's Steve Holland, Dave Hlubeck, and Duane Roland were using four Black Widow–equipped Mace 212 VT amps and 412S extension enclosures in 1980. Bassist Banner Thomas used three Bass amps and six 215 BW enclosures, completing an awesome backline for the time. In an article for *Monitor* magazine, Dave Glover explained how he discovered Peavey: "I was always searching. I had never settled on anything. I was using Gauss speakers, some kind of nondescript cabinet, and Crown amps. Raymond De Dario, our stage manager, came in one day and said he had some Peavey amps. So I tried those out and they were very good—I liked them a lot. For the first time I could actually turn up without distortion. Out of curiosity I tried the Peavey Foundation Bass. I was amazed. The combination of the power amps, cabinets, speakers and the Foundation Bass knocked me out. For the first time, I got on stage and could actually 'feel' myself clearly. It's one thing to play a bass guitar through an amp in a shop or a studio or home and think, 'Oh it's a wonderful sound,' but you really don't know that until you go on stage, especially with a band as loud as Deep Purple is. Our soundman, Gordon Peterson with Tasco Sound, came back to me and said, 'Wow, it's great to have a great bass sound. It makes my life a lot easier.' He does a lot of heavy metal/hard rock acts, so the fact he was knocked out makes me doubly knocked out."

In the 1980s, Peavey would become firmly established in the rock scene with such bands as Bad Company, Whitesnake, Alice Cooper, R.E.M., UB40, INXS, ZZ Top, Ozzy Osbourne, and Earth, Wind & Fire using the equipment. Peavey's roster of endorsers would cut across all styles, including performers like Steve Cropper, Vinnie Moore, Steve Morse, Albert Lee, Steve Winwood, Tony MacAlpine, George Benson, Chet Atkins, Tim Landers, Jeff Berlin, and Duck Dunn—to name but

▲ *Hartley Peavey*

▼ *Scorpion square-frame speaker*

a few. The Musicians Institute of Technology in Los Angeles also allied itself with Peavey, in a demonstration of its teachers' respect for the company's gear. Above all, working musicians appreciated the performance and reliability of Peavey gear.

Tim Landers has worked with many of the greats, including Billy Cobham and the Crusaders. In a *Monitor* magazine interview he said, "Before I became involved with Peavey, I used to use the CS-800 power amps. I purchased two of them and used one as a spare and one as the main power amp. To this day I have never had to use the spare. All the problems I was having with other power amps, I wasn't having with the Peavey. I don't know why, but it never shut down on me." In the studio too, Landers was using a Peavey Combo. "Not all the time will we use an amplifier in the studio. But when I do use an amplifier, I've been using a Combo and it's been very successful, very reliable. Just recently in a recording studio, I had the Combo amp sitting on top of another Anvil case. One of the wheels of the Anvil fell into a hole and the case fell over with the Peavey Combo. It flew three or four feet on the concrete, dented the bottom left corner and dented up the heat sink, and I said to myself, 'Well, that's it.' I brought it into the studio, plugged it in, and it worked fine. I thought, 'It's working now but I wonder what's going to happen later.' I have used it many times since then. I was amazed."

By 1980 Peavey had become one of the top manufacturing companies in Mississippi, a fact that was acknowledged by the presentation of the Governor's Industrial Glove Award. And Peavey was offering good jobs to all—an unusual policy in a state where equal opportunity had not always been the rule. Fifteen years later, Melia talked about that hiring policy with an interviewer from the local educational TV channel. "It did not matter who you were," she said. "It did not matter what color you were, it did not matter if you were male or female, it did not matter if you had short hair or long hair—and Hartley took a lot of bad rap from some locals for that."

Women in particular found a level playing field at Peavey. "My first supervisory job was in circuit-board processing, where we would take the blank, copper-clad fiberglass material and make circuit boards out of it," recalls Diane Jones. "From there I went into supervising the final assembly line. We had lots of women supervisors at that time, but in 1980 I was the first woman supervisor in final assembly. I felt a lot of pride in that."

"Peavey is all about growth," says Hartley, "and I'm fond of saying that Peavey is a company that doesn't just build things—we build people. Many of our people frankly would never have been given a chance in a 'conventional' corporate environment. I'm a prime example; I would probably never make it in the corporate world. Melia is a prime example, too. Melia has never had one day of college, but she's one of the smartest people I ever met."

Despite all of the expansion, Peavey was still hopelessly back-ordered. It was a sign of the company's success—yet it gnawed at the founder. Rick Grigsby remembers a conversation he had with Hartley at the time. "The Peavey Electronics I joined was on its way up," Rick says. "Business was steadily growing, and the attitude was like that Avis slogan: we're number two, so we try harder. But one November day Hartley walked into my office, sat down, and started complaining. 'Grigsby,' he said, 'when we started the year, we had a back order of $20 million. Over this year, we've built new facilities, hired a lot more people, and managed to increase our shipments by 25 percent. But unless I want to go out and borrow a bunch of money'—something that was a real no-no to him—'I can't do more through my own cash flow. We've busted our butts all year, and when I look at the new numbers, we're up to a back order of $25 million. All that work and we're worse off than when we started the year.' Call it what you will—an embarrassment of riches or a dream scenario—but from Hartley's perspective at that moment, he had worked very hard at a task and failed. That was unusual for him."

The transducer division followed up on the success of the Black Widow speakers—now field-proven and available over the counter as replacement parts—with more innovative designs. The new Scorpion speakers combined the detachable and field-replaceable die-cast cone-basket design with a "square" four-spoke frame. This meant the Scorpion could be used in smaller enclosures, including combo amps. Based on a 2.5" voice coil, the Scorpion delivered performance superior to most stamped-frame speakers but was less costly to produce than the Black Widow.

The Project One system was unveiled at the Summer NAMM show, and it represented Peavey's most ambitious entry to date in the competition for the high-performance, long-throw sound reinforcement market. It was a three-way system designed strictly for tri-amping, with no built-in crossovers. The twin-15" folded-horn woofer was complemented by a molded mid-bass horn driven by a special encapsulated 12" Black Widow and a 30-degree high-frequency horn. The system could deliver 109 dB at 1 watt, 1 meter, surpassing the performance of anything else remotely close to the price point.

▲ *Project I sound reinforcement system*

Encouraged by Allan Sharp in Canada and other distributors to address the increasing demand for small instrument amps, Peavey responded with a flurry of activity at the new Morton facility. The new plant was to build a line of six compact single-unit guitar amps, ranging in power from 10 to 140 watts. These combo amps were designed around a new circuit design (Patent #4,405,832) that would be known as Saturation, another Peavey innovation driven by the needs of the marketplace. (The increasingly poor quality of vacuum tubes was of considerable concern to Hartley. The music industry was rapidly becoming the only significant customer for the older tube technology, and increasingly the only supplies available were coming from unreliable and under-invested factories in Russia, Eastern Europe, and China. The need to develop an alternative method for replicating the characteristics of a tube amplifier was once again coming to the forefront.)

Jack Sondermeyer and Hartley set out to determine exactly what happens when a vacuum tube is driven flat out. It was well known that rock and blues guitarists craved the warmth and singing sustain emanating from a tube amp being pushed to its limits. But what, exactly, produced

▲ An overseas advertisement for the Decade guitar amplifier

▲ Bandit guitar amplifier prototype — 1980

that sound? The Peavey engineering team carefully plotted and analyzed the way tubes responded and the way that gain compression was synthesized. Artists were consulted to determine how close the engineering effort was getting to their concept of an ideal tone. The final solid-state circuit design allowed the saturated tube tone to be replicated at all power levels and was hailed as a breakthrough.

At 10 watts, the Decade was the smallest amp Peavey had ever built, but the Saturation circuit helped it sound huge compared to other practice amps. The scramble was on to meet the rush of orders for this ballsy little unit that sold for less than $100. The Backstage, already established as a successful practice/rehearsal amp, was beefed up to 20 watts and given the Saturation circuit. The Studio Pro was introduced to appeal to players requiring a studio-quality practice amp; it had the same size and wattage as the Backstage, but was equipped with a balanced XLR line out for direct console patching, an effects loop, and reverb.

The 50-watt Bandit had enough power for most club gigs, yet was small enough to transport easily. It offered twin channels with Automix selection and active and Paramid EQ, reverb, patching capabilities, a special output transformer with optimized damping and band-pass characteristics, and a specially designed 12" speaker—a sensational package of features for such a low-cost unit. Over the next quarter-century, the continuously updated and improved Bandit would become established as one of the best-selling guitar amps of all time.

The Bandit was originally conceived as the smallest of three models in what was to be called the Renegade Series. During the prototype stage, the other two models were designated the Outlaw and the Rebel. The Outlaw was to be a 100-watt version of the Bandit loaded with two Scorpion 12" speakers; the Rebel was conceived as a 140-watt twin combo with active and parametric tone controls on one channel and passive circuitry on the other. Prior to production, the Renegade concept was dropped, and the Outlaw and Rebel became the Special and Renown, respectively. When they were released with the Bandit early in 1981, the trio was called the Solo Series. Towards the end of the year, the Saturation circuit was also applied to the preamp of a hybrid MX combo that was slotted into the Classic, Deuce, and Mace lineup as a small 120-watt unit with a single Scorpion 12.

Peavey continued to refine its portable packaged PA systems to keep them ahead of the pack as competitors fell over themselves to clone the PA-400 format. Peavey's built-in patching and system expandability, reinforced by its dealer training, had given it a commanding position in this area of the market. So they had to keep pushing the boundaries. The XR-600 became the XR-600B, the first compact powered mixer to offer balanced XLR connectors on each channel. The new version sported the DDT circuit, had a power rating of 300 watts (at 2 ohms), and was wired to return reverb to the monitor mix. The XR-800 stereo powered console arrived to replace the PA-700S, and the XR-1200 became a stereo unit replacing the PA-1000S. The PA Series had established Peavey as the benchmark for "Saturday night gigging PA equipment," and the XR series heralded a long period of consolidation. To complement the versatile patching capabilities of the XR designs, a Mini-Monitor package was developed with two small, molded wedge enclosures that clipped together for transport and storage. It made for easy monitor setup at small venues and lounge gigs. A pattern of continual development and constant upgrading was now firmly established—there was always something new going on at Peavey.

1980

New Mark III 8-, 12-, 16-, and 24-channel mixers were introduced with the option of either flight-case or conventional end-panel design enclosures; these featured transformer balanced mains, monitor and sum outputs, LED metering, PFL/cue, and a host of other professional features. These units and the Mark IV mixers that followed shortly thereafter would revolutionize the semi-pro sound reinforcement market.

To enable the CS power amp crossover modules to be used with amplifiers from other manufacturers, the ECM (electronic crossover mainframe) was introduced as a single-rack-unit power supply and patching device for the modules. A full-blown CS-X2 electronic crossover was also introduced as a specialty product, together with the IP-1, an EQ plug-in that simulated the sound of a kick drum with a pillow stuffed inside it, as was the practice of many drummers during that period. The "Electric Pillow" kick-drum EQ circuit was added to the CS amp plug-in module series.

Guitar development was moving slower than other areas of R&D effort, but three new colors—red, ivory, and black—were added during 1980. More important, the company's strings-and-accessories offerings—which would become the Axcess program—began to take off under the management of Hal Aiken and Janis Covert. A line of "Glider" strings was marketed in unique packaging, along with hardware, cables, and component accessories. "We had begun producing guitars," Aiken recalls, "so it was logical to sell strings, and Hollis Calvert was involved with that. Melia incorporated T-shirts, caps, and so on, and that was the beginning of the accessory program. I then began reporting to Melia with the task of expanding the program. Hartley did not realize the dollar potential, so Melia was the driving force. When I introduced

◀ *T-40 Bass guitar made for the author in 1980. This instrument was made with through-body controls as a one-off special. The body is made from mineral wood — ash stained by the minerals in the earth — and a figured maple neck.*

▲ *XR-800 powered mixing console*

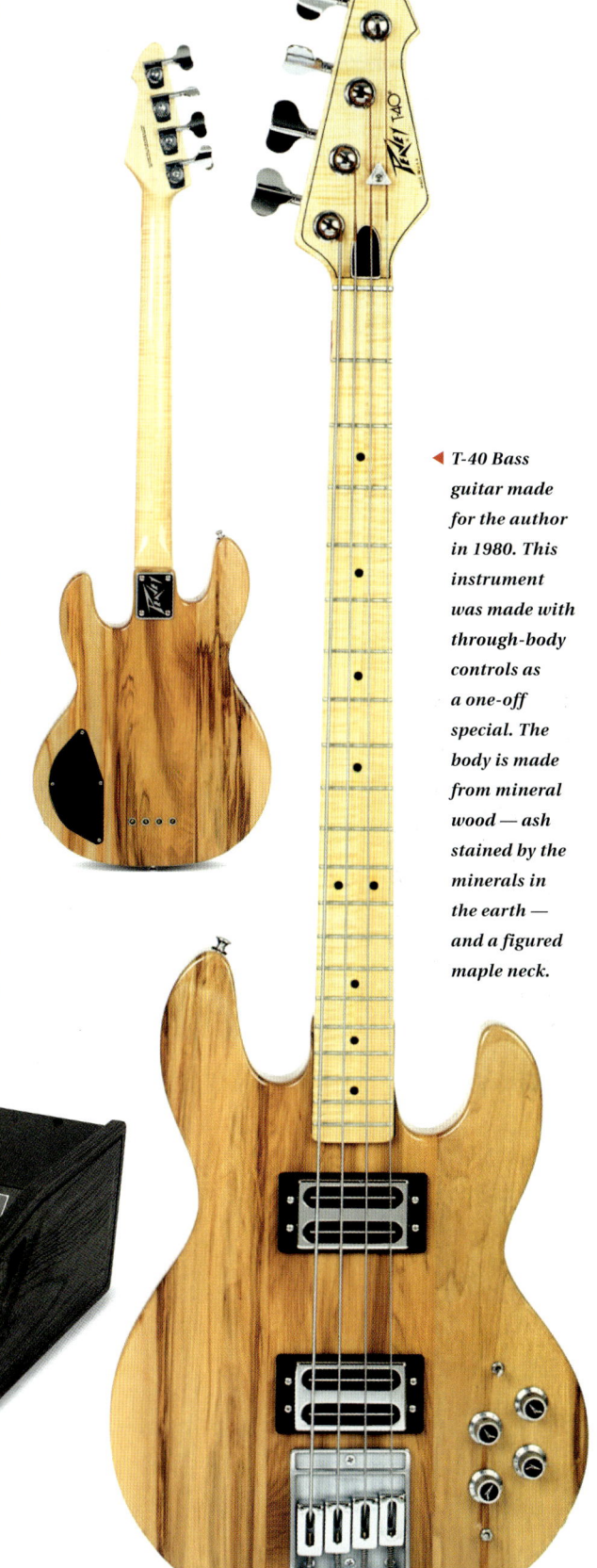

CHAPTER 10 • TAKING CENTER STAGE 73

▲ *Hartley and Melia*

▲ *Hartley and Melia introduce the T-15 short-scale electric guitar.*

▲ *Carl Perkins and his T-27 guitar*

the cable product line, Hartley got pissed off at me because I had to buy wire from Japan in order to be competitive. Three months later I was having lunch with Hartley and Melia, and we informed him that cables were doing $78,000 a month and rising. This opened his eyes, and it all skyrocketed from there."

The Axcess program grew rapidly from this small beginning, and it became a major source of revenue for supporting Peavey R&D. Hartley and Melia urged their salesmen and customers to support the accessory line if they wanted a continued stream of new, innovative products, and the fact that the sale of these small goods supported the development of big-ticket items became a central plank of the accessory marketing campaign.

The Axcess line has become one of the largest offerings of small goods, accessories, and components in the music industry, comprising thousands of items over the years—far too many to track in this book.) The promotional items and wearables side of the program became very important to Melia. Beginning in the mid-'80s, the range of shirts, caps, jackets, and other branded clothing and promotional items proliferated as a key "lifestyle" element in Peavey's overall branding strategy. Its "walking advertisement" value helped to spread the Peavey name far and wide, and the gear was sold aggressively to employees, dealers, and consumers alike. Axcess shops were opened in the factories, the classroom building, and the visitor center for sales of wearables during lunch and break times.

1981

By 1981 Hartley and Melia had become an imposing management team, driving the company to new heights. His ability to turn new ideas into successful products was matched by her skill in managing people, organizing manufacturing operations, and overseeing administrative detail. Revenue had grown substantially, reaching nearly $100 million.

Early in '81 Chip Todd moved on, and Mike Powers, a luthier from Lansing, Illinois, joined the company in July to take over the guitar program. When he arrived, a short-scale guitar known as the T-15 was ready to launch. Hartley was keen to make an instrument that would appeal to budding guitarists, and he believed a 23" scale would make it easier for them to get started. Like all the early guitar models, the T-15 came in a molded case—but this one was also offered with an optional "Electric Case" with a 10-watt practice amp built in.

Powers inherited the experimental T-25 project, which proved to be ahead of its time. Anticipating a shortage of wood for guitar pro-

1981

duction, the T-25 was to be built using plastics. R&D came up with a composite material called "Sustanite," which responded acoustically like wood. Several prototypes were made, with encouraging results—but molding a neck was difficult and the cost of the materials and fabrication exceeded wood, so the T-25 was shelved.

A three-pickup version of the short-scale T-15 was developed; it was offered in natural finish and designated the T-30. Powers, assisted by Wilburn Moffett, finished the T-26 and T-27 guitar and T-45 bass projects, which were under way when he arrived. These new instruments were launched in 1982. The first T-27 went to Carl Perkins, who used it on a TV special with George Harrison and Eric Clapton—Peavey guitars were starting to get noticed in the right places!

Neal Schon and Ross Valory of the successful band Journey became Peavey endorsers at this time, strengthening the brand's image in the contemporary rock scene.

Believing that the Black Widow speakers could be further refined, Mike O'Neill and the transducer engineering department employed new magnet technology to produce the BW "Super Structure" design. They gave the name Focused Field Geometry (FFG) to a new magnet profile that enhanced the effective use of magnetic energy in the speaker. The resulting increase in efficiency and performance helped to make the Black Widow one of the industry's most technologically advanced cone-type loudspeakers. The improved BWs were immediately incorporated into several new speaker enclosures, including the new flight-case International Series and 1545 monitor wedges. An MB-2 mid-bass horn was also built around the new speaker, providing a tri-amp option for the split SP-1 package and known as the Project Two system. The 18" version was used in a new, bi-ampable 1810 bass enclosure, along with two of the Scorpion 10s. With the built-in crossover from the bass head, this enclosure enabled an easy route to bi-amping without needing separate high- and low-frequency enclosures.

The new Scorpions were also offered in a 1210-H package, increasing power ratings and reliability.

The Mark I series of mixers was augmented with

▲ *Custom double-neck instrument made for Neal Schon*

▼ *T-30 short-scale guitar — 1982*

◄ *Black Widow Super Structure speaker*

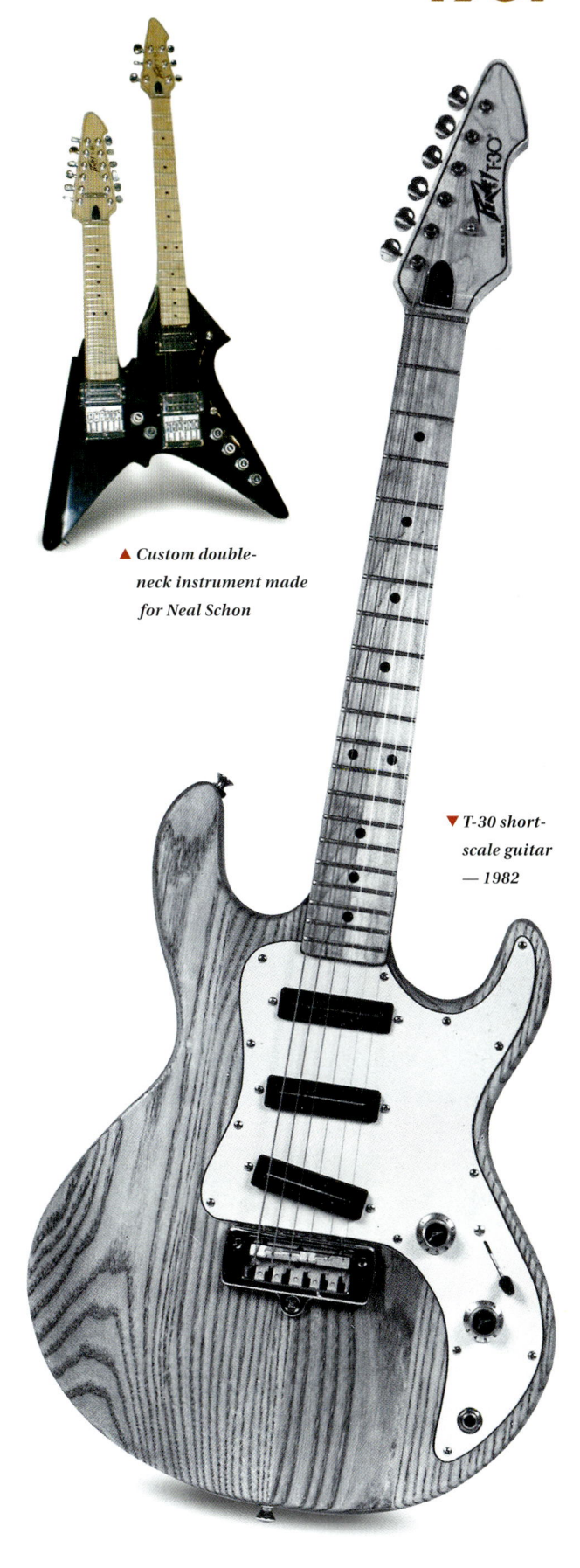

CHAPTER 10 • TAKING CENTER STAGE 75

▲ *Project II sound reinforcement system*

an MR-7 19" rackmount stereo board, and the small, six-channel 600 stereo unit was also offered. A low-cost, no-frills M-2000 stereo power amp was added to the power amp line below the CS series, which was enjoying dramatic sales growth.

In fact, the entire product line was enjoying spectacular growth at this time, both internationally and domestically, despite increasing signs of inflationary trends and rising interest rates. As many of its rivals struggled to survive, Peavey had healthy cash flow and was benefiting greatly from the dealer loyalty it had worked so hard to establish. The competition had paid little heed to the company's expansion over the previous decade as Hartley played out his "marketing by stealth" strategy. The quiet, efficient development of new manufacturing techniques and superior products incorporating such advances as Black Widow speakers, DDT, and Saturation circuitry was paying big dividends on the sales floor. Before his "friendly competitors" had fully realized what was happening, Hartley Peavey had stolen large chunks of market share from right under their noses.

Hartley was beginning to get their attention, though. He was invited to address the first general meeting of the Music Industries Manufacturers Association (MIMA), at which he exhorted the industry to lobby with one voice in Washington. He would soon be active there himself on trade issues.

1982

The growing recognition of Hartley's achievements continued in 1982, as Mississippi State University named him a Patron of Excellence, the City of Meridian designated April 2nd as Hartley Peavey Day, and the Sertoma Club presented him with its National Heritage Award as the businessman most exemplifying the free-enterprise spirit.

Allan Sharp left Great West in Canada, where he had consistently increased Peavey's sales, and floated the idea of taking Peavey direct into America's northern neighbor. For two years, he worked intermittently with Willie Hatcher to construct a distribution model for the Canadian market, and Peavey went direct with its own sales team in 1984.

Sharp had been instrumental in creating a finance plan for music retailers in Canada, and he brought this idea to Meridian, where he worked with the controller, Kevin O'Brien, to establish PVF. O'Brien had inherited a good situation when he arrived in 1978, with strong dealer loyalty and advantageous credit terms. Quite simply, if the dealers did not pay to terms, the product allocation would pass them by—so there was no bad debt. O'Brien maintained Peavey's strong receivables position, but the cash-flow implications of the company's steady growth were causing problems for even some of the most successful dealers.

1982

Peavey's growth had been mostly self-funded from carefully managed profits, but it was becoming clear that another element of growth was needed: customer credit. Financing through banks or credit companies was available for many dealers, but if Peavey were to provide competitive financing itself it could be a route to unlocking growth potential. It would also be a second profit stream for the company. Many small dealers relied almost entirely on Peavey, and PVF was designed to assist them in conducting business while boosting the company's profits—a win-win situation. Each month, approved PVF dealers were able to choose whether they wanted to finance the previous month's business, allowing them to manage their cash flow and at the same time freeing up their current-month credit line. PVF became a highly successful operation and continues to promote growth for both the company and its dealers today.

In a dramatic demonstration of the company's commitment to continuing product development, the VT hybrid combo amps were replaced with the VTX series. Although the Classic designation was retained, the Deuce, Artist, and Mace names were replaced with MX and Heritage. The series featured the new Saturation circuitry, an active presence control, "Pull Bright" treble boost on each channel (activated by pulling out the control knob), and a "Pull Thick" midrange boost. The revised Classic VTX was boosted to 65 watts and loaded with two Scorpion 12s, while the 130-watt MX got a single Black Widow 12. The Heritage, with 130 watts of power, had active and

▼ *Eighties-era guitar amplifiers*

CHAPTER 10 • TAKING CENTER STAGE

passive channels and was offered with either two Scorpion or two BW 12s. The recently introduced Renown came with a single BW 15. These were all good products made better because of new player-friendly features and improved sound.

On the bass side, the new Basic 30 practice amp joined the line of bass combos, while its partners got power boosts: the TKO went to 65 watts, the TNT to 130 watts, and the Combo to a whopping 300 watts.

The new T-20 bass, with its novel thumbrest and pickup-mounting system, provided Mike Powers with his first patent for Peavey, and a custom-order 8-string version of the T-40 also hit the market. The T-45 bass was another new model: a single-pickup variation of the T-40 with through-body controls (no scratch plate). While these models were only a modest addition to the catalogue, Mike Powers was hatching plans to considerably expand the guitar and bass lines.

In April 1982 Peavey established Plant 5 adjacent to Interstate 20/59 in Meridian with the intention of providing a sophisticated temperature- and humidity-controlled storage area for the seasoning of instrument wood. The heat and humidity of summers in the Deep South demanded an investment in this area, and this facility would later serve as an acoustic guitar storage environment as well. Part of this 29,500-square-foot building became a tool-and-die and machine shop where many production jigs and fittings were fabricated.

On the PA side, the Project IV was introduced as a standalone tri-amp system housed in a single enclosure, and the Tri-Flex was announced. The Tri-Flex was another one of those clever ideas that proved, like the composite guitar, to be ahead of its time. It was a system that combined two small satellite speakers with a larger subwoofer that could be placed almost anywhere in the room. The human ear cannot detect direction for sound waves below 250Hz, so all the sound appeared to be coming from the small speakers. This wasn't a new idea—it was based on cinema systems

▲ *Plant 5 — humidity-controlled wood storage*

▶ *MD-12 Mixer — 1982*

in use at that time (and found today in many home theater systems)—but it was a novel application then. The Tri-Flex was a portable package, too, designed so the satellite speakers could be packed into the port of the subwoofer for transport, then placed on microphone stands at the venue. While never fulfilling its sales expectations, the Tri-Flex initiated the development of separate-subwoofer systems that would make life easier for club musicians while greatly improving the sound capabilities of their PA gear.

The MD series of mixers and monitors also appeared at this time; these were "budget" units, although their features made them highly competitive within their price range.

Late in the year, Hartley and Melia decided to make another large investment in the company's future by building a state-of-the-art Research and Development facility incorporating an anechoic chamber. Hartley was convinced that having a facility normally associated with scientific research institutions would give Peavey a big advantage over its competitors. Plant 6, a 47,000-square-foot building, was commissioned in December, and the project was named Audio Media Research (AMR). In addition to providing R&D services to Peavey Electronics, the building also became the new home for the transducer engineering group—and its proximity to the highway made it the ideal location for expanded customer service facilities, repair shops, and spare parts warehousing.

Peavey expressed its corporate confidence by publishing its first "image" brochure, extolling the virtues of the company and articulating the philosophy behind its products. For the first time, Melia was featured prominently alongside Hartley in presenting this message to the world. Their beliefs are summed up in this quote from that publication: "Our company was founded back in the '60s with the goal of producing not only the best musical instrument and sound reinforcement products available but also as a means to allow creative and talented people to express their abilities and talents within a new type of commercial endeavor. Here at the factory we have gathered what we feel is a most impressive array of abilities. The structure of our company has been carefully put together in such a way so that the talents, interests, experience, and overall expertise of our people react in a combining manner as opposed to the typical 'helter-skelter' kind of corporate politics found within many companies."

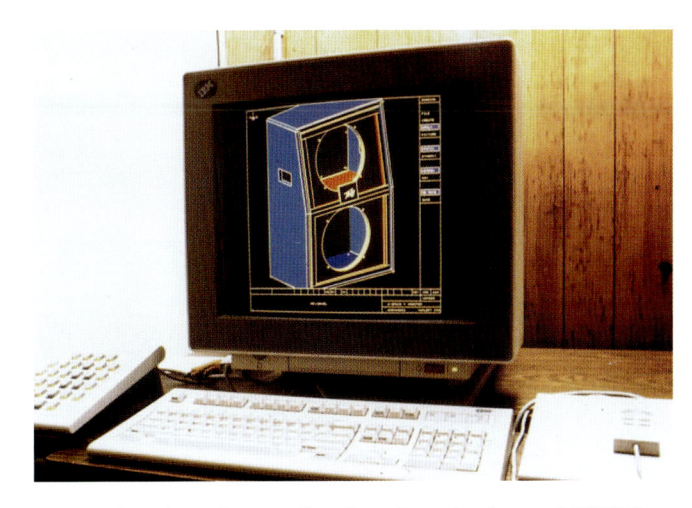

▲ *Peavey has always harnessed cutting-edge technology — CAD/CAM computer-aided design and manufacture was embraced from its infancy.*

▲ *Plant 6 — built as a research and development center*

▲ *Inside the anechoic chamber at Plant 6*

▶ *Hartley & Melia sailing near Pensacola, Fla., in the eighties*

1983

In 1983 Peavey was honored with the Mississippi Excellence Award in recognition of its increasing economic importance to the state and expanding global role. By this time, Melia was taking on more and more responsibility for managing the company and had established a loyal coterie of supporters around her. Hartley has said that Melia had more ambition as a businessperson than he did, so he was happy to immerse himself in the exciting technologies unfolding within the engineering groups and leave the administrative details to her.

Always looking ahead, Hartley had come to the conclusion that the role of digital electronics in the music industry would eventually transcend the world of keyboards and have a profound effect on signal processing and even amplifier design. It was inevitable, he thought, that digital technology would become more affordable as it was used in more applications—and, as ever, he was keen to be a leader rather than a follower. Hartley engaged the services of an English engineer, Brian Attwood, as a consultant, and together they set about researching the possibility of making a digital power amp.

As ever, Peavey relied upon feedback from top players, and the West Coast scene was becoming more influential thanks to Jack Wilson's efforts in Los Angeles. Jack's small showroom had become a hothouse for new ideas and dialogue about product development, and it helped Peavey to blossom in the '80s. Wilson was an irrepressible dynamo of a man (he held a third-degree black belt in the martial arts and shared Hartley's passion for sailing) whose strong artist relationships and marketing savvy ensured that the engineers back in Meridian were getting the best input from the field. He was at the center of the strategic-planning process and was ultimately appointed vice president of the company.

In a television documentary broadcast in 1991, Melia said that one of her goals had been to take the company's revenue to $100 million by her 30th birthday. She turned 30 in August 1984—and had achieved her goal with time to spare. Peavey was recognized as one of the largest employers in the state, and Hartley was feted by the Mississippi Broadcasters' Association as their Mississippian of the Year. Not to be outdone, the *Meridian Star* newspaper named him Man of the Year.

Hartley has never been one to rest on his laurels, and however firmly he was committed to keeping music stores as the company's main channel of distribution, he also began to cultivate an interest in exploring other markets. To that end, Larry Blakely was hired to develop AMR as a separate unit to exploit the home and studio recording market. Much of the mixer and signal-processing technology already developed could be applied to products for this new market, and a whole new dealer structure and customer base could be developed.

With Peavey Canada established as a direct operation, attention was turned to Europe. The strength of the dollar had made it difficult for American-made products to compete effectively, and rising prices were driving down sales. Direct distribution offered a good solution, because it eliminated one level of pricing markups. This concept was extended to the European markets by taking over the U.K. and Ireland operation with a deal secured in the late summer of 1984. The following year, the distributor for the Benelux countries, Austria, and Germany was incorporated into another new direct-distribution outfit called Peavey Europe Corporation.

In Canada, sales would increase tenfold in the five years after going direct, and—once the dollar turned around—the European operations began a 20-year period of dramatic expansion. Peavey was soon exporting to more than 100 countries and had become one of the leading international music companies.

Back home, another major expansion began with the acquisition of land in Decatur, a town about halfway between Meridian and Morton, to build Plant 7. Close to Interstate 20, this 67,250-square-foot facility would become the nerve center of Peavey manufacturing. Set up for circuit-board manufacturing and mixer assembly, the building would double in size within four years, making it Peavey's second-largest plant.

The town of Decatur provided a new source of skilled employees, and Plant 7 quickly became one of the most high-tech operations in the music industry. Automatic insertion equipment was transferred from Plant 3 and augmented with new machinery, including state-of-the-art production and testing equipment that greatly improved manufacturing efficiency and product reliability.

Because Peavey was producing more and more printed material each year—and Hartley now knew what printing presses really cost—sophisticated printing, collating, and binding equipment

> "Not many people realize that only 5 percent of the world's population lives in the United States. Ninety-five percent of our customers are 'over there.' The trick is you have to go 'over there' to sell them."
> —HARTLEY PEAVEY

▲ *Peavey AMR logo*

▲ *Reno 400 and Austin 400 from the City Series*

▼ *Patriot Bass*

was purchased that allowed the advertising and marketing effort to increase in the same vertically integrated fashion as manufacturing. The first full-color *Monitor* magazine was published, and new catalogues offering a wide range of wearables and other promotional items were introduced.

1984

Hartley's belief in digital technology came to fruition when the DECA-700 was rolled out in 1984. DECA (Digital Energy Conversion Amplifier) technology was designed to take the raw electrical energy from the plug and convert it to audio energy via digital circuitry. The DECA-700 was rated at 350 watts per channel, and its power-transfer efficiency was a startling 90 percent—even though the unit was just 3.5" high and weighed only 30 pounds. As John Roberts observed in an article on different classes of power amps, "Class D offers significantly higher efficiency than even Class B [analog], which at one-third power is wasting more power inside the amplifier than it delivers to the load." Basically half the energy is wasted as heat.

Hartley would later describe the process of developing the digital power amplifier as being akin to "the sunrise effect." It was like climbing a hill in the early morning, he said—you could see the sun's rays over the top as the sun was rising. But it turned out that it took this sun a long time to rise: the initial designs were finicky and unreliable on the road, causing much grief for the service department. But the breakthrough had been made, and the much-improved and more stable DECA-724 came along just three years later. The first digital effects processors, the DEP-800 and DEP-1300, were launched at the same time as the digital amplifier. Peavey was once again leading the way.

1984

Sensing another opening in the market, Peavey announced its first keyboard amps in 1984. Conscious that keyboard players had little choice in amplification and often resorted to using ill-suited PA or guitar gear, the company offered the KB-100 and KB-300 combos and KB-400 head. They were quickly accepted by working musicians.

The theme of niche products was further extended with the introduction of the City Series amps in 1985. All were based on the same 210-watt power module. The Reno 400, with its 15" Scorpion Plus speaker and CDH horn, was designed for electro-acoustic players. The LA 400 had a single BW 15 and was created with jazz players in mind; not surprisingly, it was later renamed the Jazz Classic. For players using both electric and electro-acoustic instruments at the same session, there was the twin-channel Austin 400, which was replaced a year later by the Vegas 400, an all-purpose twin-channel amp suitable for violin, harmonica, mandolin, and other electrified instruments. (Peavey designed the Vegas for endorser Wayne Newton, who wanted two channels so he could play guitar and electrified banjo through the same amp.) The already-established Nashville 400 for steel players was also part of the series.

The Backstage was replaced by the Backstage Plus, which now offered 35 watts of power and had the "Pull Bright" and "Pull Thick" preamp booster controls. The Rock Master all-tube 120-watt head, also with the new booster features, was added to the guitar amp line.

The guitar catalogue included a custom-order 6- and 12-string doubleneck called the Hydra, developed in collaboration with Jeff Cook of the band Alabama. The following year, a Jeff Cook signature model was offered, finished in a metallic heather paint job and equipped with a locking Kahler tremolo system on the 6-string neck. There was also the Milestone guitar, a controls-through-body design based on the Horizon offset-waist pattern. It was available with or without tremolo and in a left-handed version; the Horizon Custom sported a pearlescent finish with a matching headstock. To meet market demand, two lower-priced guitars were also added to the line: the Predator and the Patriot, along with a matching Patriot Bass.

▲ *Plant 7 — Decatur, MS — circuit board manufacturing*

▲ *Jeff Cook Signature Hydra doubleneck guitar — 1986*

CHAPTER 10 • TAKING CENTER STAGE **83**

New Directions

"I've always been somewhat of a rebel. I'm one of those kind of people who, if you tell me I can't do something, I've got to do it. Wet paint, I've got to put my thumb on it; I walk up to a door that says 'Pull,' you know what I'm going to do. Maybe I'm a contrarian, maybe I'm a rebel, whatever—I'm one of those people who march to a different drum."

—HARTLEY PEAVEY

▲ *Milestone 12 electric twelve-string guitar — 1986*

IN 1985 large investments were made to equip the Decatur circuit-board plant and acquire a $1 million Amada metal-punching machine for Plant 3. Becky Holcombe remembers being asked to train as one of the first operators of this giant computerized metal-fabricating machine, which boosted production to new levels of efficiency. Guitar finishing was transferred to Plant 5, where an automated drying line was built to work in conjunction with state-of-the-art painting and RF curing processes. The demand for new colors and metallic finishes was boosting demand for the latest guitar designs.

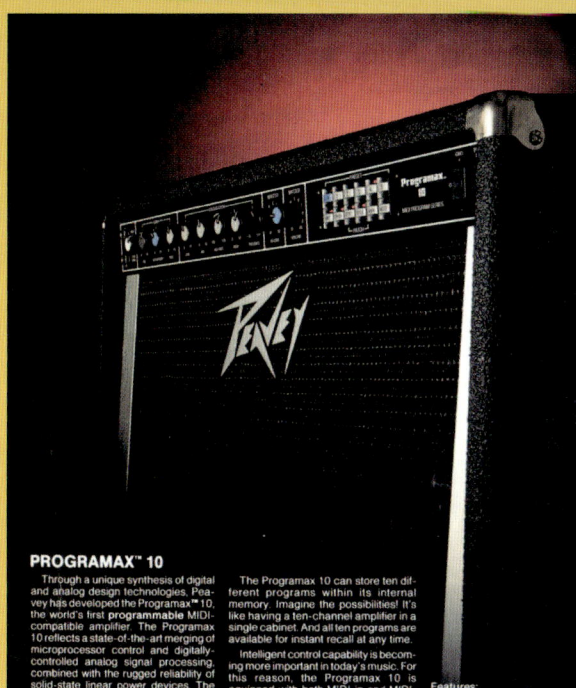

1985

PROGRAMAX™ 10

Through a unique synthesis of digital and analog design technologies, Peavey has developed the Programax™ 10, the world's first **programmable** MIDI-compatible amplifier. The Programax 10 reflects a state-of-the-art merging of microprocessor control and digitally-controlled analog signal processing, combined with the rugged reliability of solid-state linear power devices. The result is an amplifier which provides the performer with both astonishing performance and unmatched convenience.

With the Programax 10, you don't have to be a "computer wizard" to take advantage of the amp's capabilities. For example, creating and storing a program is remarkably easy. Simply adjust the amplifier's controls until you find a sound you like. Then press a button to store that sound in memory. That's all there is to it! The memory circuits in the Programax 10 will remember that sound until you next need it — next set, or next week.

The Programax 10 can store ten different programs within its internal memory. Imagine the possibilities! It's like having a ten-channel amplifier in a single cabinet. And all ten programs are available for instant recall at any time.

Intelligent control capability is becoming more important in today's music. For this reason, the Programax 10 is equipped with both MIDI-in and MIDI-thru capability. Programs stored in the Programax 10's memory may be recalled from any remote location by means of a standard MIDI interface. MIDI control signals may also be routed through the Programax 10, allowing the amplifier to act as a vital link in a complete MIDI-controlled system.

MIDI control and programmability are simply parts of what is, at heart, a great amplifier. We've also included over 200 watts of RMS power. Peavey's patented Saturation™ circuit, two 12" Scorpion® speakers, TWO effects loops . . . the list of features goes on and on.

Programax 10. Great sound, and total control. Imagine . . .

Features:
- 210 watts RMS power
- Two 12" Scorpion® speakers
- Pre Gain, Saturation™, Post G
- Bright and Thick preset EQ
- 3-Band passive EQ with MID
- Active Presence circuit
- Reverb
- Master volume control (non mable, adjusts overall ou without altering interprogram ces)
- Pre-EQ effects loop
- Post-EQ effects loop
- MIDI-in and MIDI-thru capability
- MIDI program recall

WEIGHT: 66 lbs.

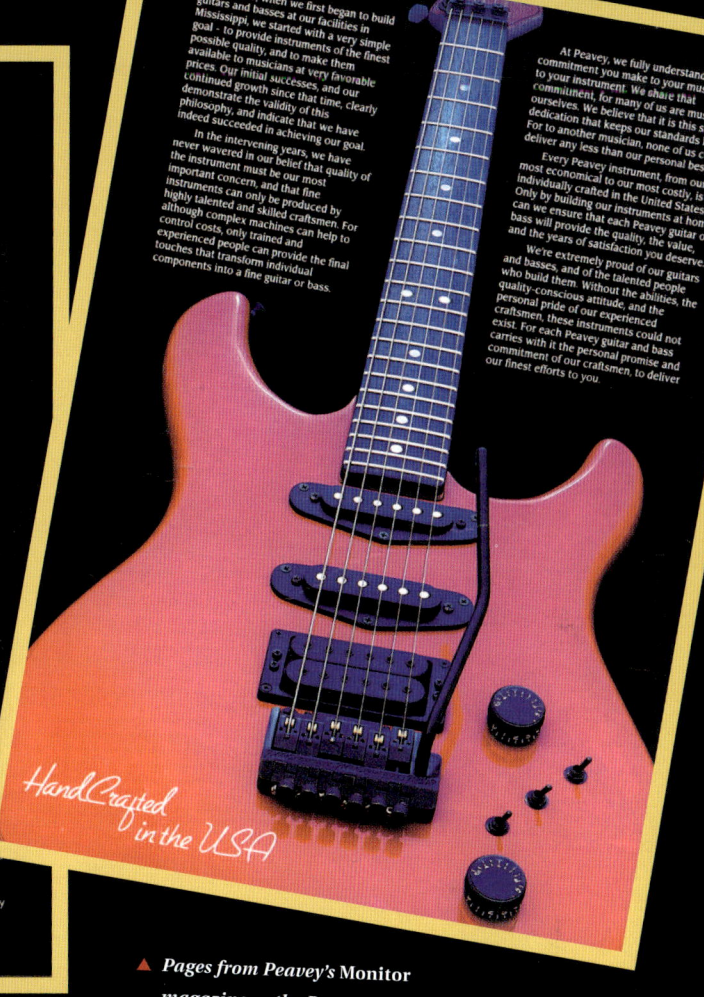

In 1975, when we first began to build guitars and basses at our facilities in Mississippi, we started with a very simple goal - to provide instruments of the finest possible quality, and to make them available to musicians at very favorable prices. Our initial successes, and our continued growth since that time, clearly demonstrate the validity of this philosophy, and indicate that we have indeed succeeded in achieving our goal.

In the intervening years, we have never wavered in our belief that quality of the instrument must be our most important concern, and that fine instruments can only be produced by highly talented and skilled craftsmen. For although complex machines can help to control costs, only trained and experienced people can provide the final touches that transform individual components into a fine guitar or bass.

At Peavey, we fully understand the commitment you make to your music, and to your instrument. We share that commitment, for many of us are musicians ourselves. We believe that it is this shared dedication that keeps our standards high. For to another musician, none of us could deliver any less than our personal best.

Every Peavey instrument, from our most economical to our most costly, is individually crafted in the United States. Only by building our instruments at home can we ensure that each Peavey guitar or bass will provide the quality, the value, and the years of satisfaction you deserve.

We're extremely proud of our guitars and basses, and of the talented people who build them. Without the abilities, the quality-conscious attitude, and the personal pride of our experienced craftsmen, these instruments could not exist. For each Peavey guitar and bass carries with it the personal promise and commitment of our craftsmen, to deliver our finest efforts to you.

HandCrafted in the USA

▲ *Pages from Peavey's* Monitor *magazine — the Programax 10 and the Kahler-equipped Nitro guitar*

▲ *CS-1200 power amplifier*

Reels of components feed the sequencing and insertion machines inserting 25,000 components an hour, 24 hours a day in 1984

The *Jackson Journal of Business*'s review of 1985 estimated that Peavey's annual sales had reached $140 million. The company now had 1,200 employees, and it had become the largest private manufacturing firm in Mississippi and the largest amplifier company in the U.S. Hartley later reflected that "Peavey Electronics' first 20 years was like raising a baby gorilla. When it's little, you can pick it up and cuddle it and love it. But when it grows up it tells you where to go and what to do."

Peavey celebrated its 20th anniversary with a gathering of dealers, distributors, and vendors in Meridian's Frank Cochran Center in Highland Park. Melia's marketing efforts were continuing to boost the company's image, and this gala event signaled a new push in an overall corporate-identity program that embraced special events and trade shows, promotional literature and wearables, stylized facilities, special products, and PR. The company was now like a snowball gathering size and momentum as it rolled forward—and Melia was increasingly becoming a workaholic. In reflection, Hartley believes her susceptibility to headaches had already started manifesting itself at this time.

As the company continued to grow, Bob Wiese was appointed CFO, and his financial management acumen drove Peavey forward. His wife, Sharon, would also play an important role as head of the advertising department.

Peavey's export business was reaching new heights. The presidential "E-Star" award for excellence in exporting is one of the most prestigious national awards any company can receive; only 18 firms are presented with the accolade each year, and in 1985 Peavey became the first in Mississippi to receive it—and the first company in the music and sound industry to be so honored. European sales continued to grow, and a new relationship with Oscar Mederos, a Miami-based distributor for South America, was about to secure significant market share in the Southern hemisphere in the form of Pexco. Started in April 1985, it went on to serve most of Latin America and the Caribbean.

While the acquisition of Peavey U.K. and its management under the careful guidance of Willie Hatcher had paid dividends, Peavey still faced challenges in the European market. For one thing, sales were vulnerable to currency fluctuations against the dollar, which could push prices too high to be competitive. And packaged PA products—always a strong point domestically—faced strong competition from such brands as HH in Britain and Dynacord in Germany. There was a need for specialized products that reflected European expectations, specifications, and aesthetics. It was decided that a manufacturing facility should be established in England, where such products could be designed, developed, and produced. This was a big step.

"Like most companies, we started out with a local view," Hartley explains. "As we grew, we learned very quickly that the world is a big place. We started our export program in 1972, and having the opportunity to travel around the world, I learned a lot. I learned that the world was quickly dividing into three trading areas: the western hemisphere [North and South America]; Europe, the Middle East, and Africa; and the Far East. We knew that to reach our potential we had to have not only distribution but manufacturing in those three areas. When we started distribution in Europe, we had distributors in the various countries. Then we took over some of that distribution ourselves and located a distribution point just outside of Rotterdam in Holland. As the company grew, we realized we not only had to distribute products made in the U.S.A. but had to manufacture on-site in Europe. At that time, we assigned a team to scour Europe for the best place, and we decided to move to Corby [England]. We leased a facility there and began a new chapter of Peavey Electronics. We selected Corby because we felt a commonality. We felt that the people in Corby, like the folks in the southern part of the U.S.A., were recovering from an adverse set of conditions. They were willing to overcome hardship and work hard, they were smart and capable, they were loyal, and—most important, I guess—they shared a value system with us folks in the South. We believe that if you try hard enough, it can be done."

In December 1985 Scott Fulton—one of the division managers in Meridian—left for Corby to set up the first Peavey plant outside the United States.

With subwoofer enclosures and bi- or tri-amped systems gaining more acceptance from working musicians, the work of the transducer group had generated a need for higher-powered amps. Jack Sondermeyer produced a new CS-1200 design rated at 600 watts (at 4 ohms) in each

▲ *Specialist component insertion at Decatur*

▲ *Every completed circuit board receives a diagnostic quality check*

▲ *Plant 7 — Decatur, MS — circuit board manufacturing*

▲ Advanced guitar-painting facilities were set up in Plant 5 during the '80s

▲ Dyna-Bass with Kahler tremolo system — 1986

of its stereo channels. The digital amplifier group, meanwhile, had applied the results of their research into overcoming the DECA-700's shortcomings to produce the DECA-1200. The new rackmount V-4X electronic crossover unit could be used as a two-, three-, or four-way device and was a successful product for many years.

Without a doubt, 1985 was "the year of bass" for Peavey. The Mark IV Bass amplifier with built-in crossover was a firm favorite on the concert stage, and its flexibility was enhanced by the 210HP powered enclosure, which allowed easy bi-amping and was engineered so the phaser could be patched separately to the high-pass circuit, allowing clear, unmuddied effects on the highs while maintaining a solid low end. A range of new small combos such as the TNT and TKO quickly gained popularity for small-venue gigs and rehearsals, and at the top of the line the recently introduced Max head was, at 300 watts, the most powerful bass amp on the market. On the instrument side, the Foundation Bass—which would prove to be one of Peavey's most enduring models—was generating admiring acceptance, and the new Dyna-Bass was offered with wide-neck and tremolo options. Jack Wilson's contacts in L.A. included such top bassists as Roger Glover of Deep Purple, ex–Vanilla Fudge bassist Tim Bogert, Mario Cipollina of Huey Lewis & the News, and session greats Tim Landers and Randy Jackson. Their input helped to bring a "pro player" slant to many instrument and amplifier features.

Guitarists were not forgotten, though. Two smaller chorus-equipped amps, the Studio Chorus and the Classic Chorus, joined the Stereo Chorus that had been introduced the previous year. At the other end of the scale—and responding to the rise of heavy metal—a stack system was introduced. The amp top, named the Butcher, was an out-and-out 120-watt all-tube rocker. Straight- and sloped-baffle 412 enclosures were made to match it, and Peavey had its first serious contender in the European-style stack market. Of course Peavey was firmly established as a manufacturer of heads and enclosures that could be configured as stacks. Gary Rossington of Lynyrd Skynyrd still uses the Mace heads he got from Hartley back in the early '70s. However, the cosmetics, style, and sound of the British-style stacks was the target for this new contender.

1986

Electronic drums were gaining in popularity, so two specialized combo amps were introduced for this application: the 65-watt ED-100 and the 130-watt ED-300. They were based on the recently developed keyboard amps, but the preamp specs and EQ had been re-engineered for drum sounds.

The transducer division continued to develop products at a feverish pace. The new Scorpion Plus speakers, including a 15" model, featured improved magnet and suspension designs and an overall performance upgrade. A super tweeter, the HT-94, was under development, and a raft of new enclosures was introduced, including the M112C and M115C church monitors, the 1545\PM powered monitor, the 1522C, and the CL-1 cluster speaker. The International Series III enclosures abandoned the flight-case cosmetic and reverted to Tolex covering. And, in keeping with the trend for touring companies like Clare Brothers to use full-range boxes, the 1510HT and 3020HT enclosures were produced.

The AMR studio-products effort was well under way, but Larry Blakely—recognizing that his strength lay in marketing, not product development—realized he needed a team of engineers for the project. He signed on a talented analog engineer named John Roberts to head the group.

▲ *Peavey's Customer Service and repairs workshop relocated in 1986 to Plant 6*

1986

When Larry Blakely left the company in 1986, John Roberts became leader of the AMR project. He quickly found out that the initial AMR product line—which had been declared ready for production when he came on board—contained what he considered to be design oversights, so he made engineering changes to almost every product, delaying their release.

The centerpiece of the AMR product launch was a four-track cassette recorder, the MCR-4, which was offered with a choice of two mixers that could be ordered separately or as a system. These were complemented by such support products as a 32-port patch bay and an interface amplifier, plus power amps, microphones, and studio monitors. The AMR signal-processing products included a compressor/limiter/de-esser, parametric equalizers, a noise-reduction

▲ *AMR multi-track recording equipment*

CHAPTER 11 • NEW DIRECTIONS

system, and—as the digital group advanced—studio versions of the digital multi-effects units. In addition to developing concert mixing consoles, Roberts was instrumental in designing Production Series recording consoles with models ranging from 24x8 to 36x24. Home recording was a fast-moving market in the late 1980s, and it left AMR behind as an under-resourced and somewhat neglected child in the Peavey family. It never reached its full potential.

Bob Wiese rolled out PVF to all Peavey dealers in March 1986, and a 4,700-square-foot property on old Highway 80 in Meridian was purchased and converted to offices for the finance company. The PVF options included flexible three-, six-, and twelve-month extended credit beyond the standard open-account terms and special product-specific stocking terms.

The relocated Peavey U.K. operation was officially opened in May 1986. Designated Plant 18, it incorporated the first manufacturing site outside the United States, where a group of PA systems was developed for production and marketing in Europe. The EuroSys model line, launched later in the year, helped to transform Peavey's profile and secure a leading position in the portable PA market in Europe.

▼ *The early European ES range of speaker enclosures — built in the Corby U.K. plant*

90   THE PEAVEY REVOLUTION • **PART FOUR** • CLEAR WATER

1986

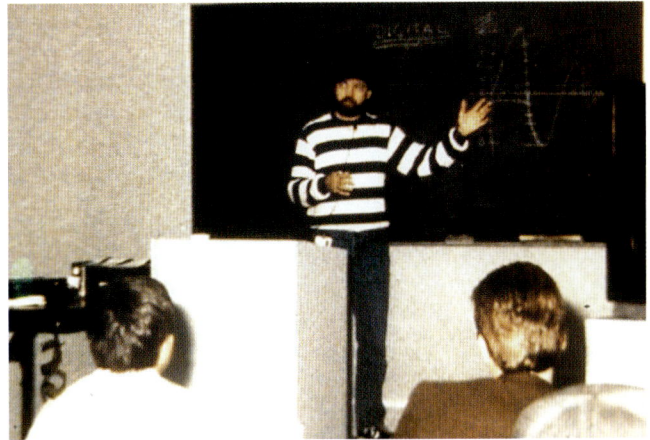

▲ *Plant 18 — the original Corby U.K. facility*

▲ *Skip Taylor teaching class*

In 1985 Dr. Skip Taylor and Larry Hand had arrived at Peavey to head up a team of digital engineers and software designers for the coming assault on the MIDI products market. Both came from the defense industry in Florida, and it was a trip back home for Taylor, a native of Decatur, Mississippi, and a keyboard player. Their efforts began to reach the market in '86 with the introduction of a MIDI-controllable instrument combo amp, the Programmax-10. Based on the 210-watt Renown twin format, it had MIDI-in and MIDI-thru connectors that allowed the unit's programmable sounds to be recalled via any standard MIDI device. Its ability to store channel gain and tone settings created, in essence, a selectable 10-channel amplifier. The MIDI-compatible PEP-4000 digital programmable effects unit and the RMC-2000 remote MIDI controller completed the digital engineering group's first MIDI offerings.

Hartley continued to believe in the growing role that digital products would play in the audio market, and he led efforts to recruit more programmers and digital engineers. Development work with Motorola was also being done on a Peavey-proprietary VLSI (Very Large Scale Integrated-circuit) chip, which would provide the digital team with the equivalent of two million transistors on a one-inch-square silicon chip. The VLSI became the basis of a whole new family of digital products over the next few years.

Peavey wasn't forgetting its past, though, and the amp line got numerous improvements in 1986. The Stereo range of guitar amps was upgraded and now consisted of the Studio Chorus 70, a 35-watts-per-channel studio model, and the Stereo Chorus 400, which became one of Peavey's most popular semi-pro units of the '80s. A busker's dream, the new Companion 15 was a battery-powered 10-watt screamer that was at home on the streets or in the practice room (where it could be plugged into an external power supply). This unit would eventually metamorphose into the Solo—more a portable PA than a pure guitar amp. The Backstage Plus got reverb and was beefed up to 35 watts, and the Basic 50 was pushed up to 50 watts. On the bass side, Peavey introduced the ProBass-1000 rackmount preamp and a new bi-amp-capable digital-powered MegaBass amp—perfect for professional and semi-pro bass players eager to get into component systems.

The guitar line featured the new Impact 1 with locking Kahler tremolo and gold or black hardware

▲ *ZZ Top's Billy Gibbons with Hartley Peavey*

and the Impact 2 with a fixed locking bridge and chrome hardware. Their contemporary design offered the fashionable two-single-coils/one-humbucker pickup configuration, with single volume and tone controls and three toggle switches for coil selection. The budget-priced Nitro Series offered contemporary styling and locking tremolos; the Nitro I sported a single humbucker while the Nitro III was equipped with three single-coil pickups. The Vortex 1, with its spiky body design, and the quasi-V-shaped Vortex 2 acknowledged the popularity of pointy, unconventional designs with the heavy-metal crowd. The Milestone 12 also joined the guitar lineup, and the Patriot bass got a new look and black hardware, becoming the Patriot Custom Bass. The popular Foundation Bass was offered in a new Custom version and also as a 5-string, acknowledging the growing popularity of extended-range instruments in the bass market.

The International Series III enclosures took on a fresh new look with the addition of the rugged carpet covering that had been previously used for the 1510HT and 3020HT enclosures. A matching 415 subwoofer was also added to the line. The keyboard-specific KB-115 and three-way multi-purpose 315S enclosures were other new additions to the catalogue. The new MS series of mixers, particularly the MS-1221 and MS-1621, reflected continuing advances in gain and EQ technology.

At the end of 1986, Peavey maintenance moved into Plant 8, the newly acquired 26,000-square-foot Barnes building in downtown Meridian. It included a carpentry shop that would provide in-house services to all Peavey facilities.

As the company continued to expand, communication became even more of a priority for Hartley and Melia, and this was reflected by the growing number of Peavey publications. *What's Happenin'*, an in-house monthly magazine, became an increasingly important tool for keeping the workforce apprised of corporate developments, news from each plant, employee awards, birthdays, special events, and more. Each week, the Wednesday a.m. newspaper was circulated to all employees to provide work schedules, administrative updates, payroll and pension information, health tips, and other news. The *Dialog* newsletter went to dealers to promote new products and publicize PVF, the seminar program, endorser signings, and events. For consumers, the *Monitor* magazine promoted the product range and carried reviews and interviews with artists and Peavey engineers. All in all, this comprehensive communications effort cemented the close relationship between Hartley and Melia Peavey and their workers, dealers, and consumers.

In '86 the Rod Stewart band chose Peavey for touring and recording, and the endorsement roster added Donald "Duck" Dunn, the legendary Booker T & the MG's and Stax session bassist. Duck used a Dyna-Bass with the new digital-powered MegaBass amp and 1820 enclosure on a tour with Eric Clapton.

1987

Ernie Lansford joined Peavey in March 1987 as an independent representative, coming over from St. Louis Music. Like Hartley, Ernie was a fan of sales guru Zig Ziglar. (At the beginning of Ziglar's book *See You at the Top*, this motivational speaker asserts, "I believe you can get everything in life you want if you help enough other people get what they want." Hartley, Melia, and Ernie certainly subscribed to this belief.) The two music-industry veterans soon found they had much in common. "During the interview," Ernie recalls, "I shared my goal of working as a national sales

1987

manager someday. I was denied the opportunity with my previous employer because I lacked an M.B.A. Hartley and Melia both told me that university degrees meant nothing to them. They promoted from within and promoted people who proved they could make a difference."

The AMR line was rolled back into Peavey, and John Roberts took over responsibility for mixer engineering. Renewed emphasis was being put on this area even though Peavey mixers already dominated many other market segments. Hartley wanted to compete for the top end of the touring and studio-console markets, so the Peavey Mark VIII and AMR large-format consoles were developed in parallel, with Jack Aubuchon as lead engineer for the Mark VIII and Roberts leading the AMR effort. The units shared common technology but had market-specific differentiation, with the Peavey console intended for touring and the AMR aimed at recording studios. In the end, Peavey was able to sell a $20,000 console that matched the performance of competitive units at twice the price—but the sound-engineer market proved to be a conservative and snobbish nut to crack.

Transducer engineering unveiled the results of their effort to improve the microphone line by introducing the first PVM models with diamond-coated diaphragms; the coating both strengthened the diaphragm and gave it smoother response—allowing for the durability of a dynamic mic with the response of a condenser mic. The PVM-38 vocal and PVM-45 instrument mics featured advanced shock mounting and were extremely rugged for on-the-road applications. The capsule was also designed for easy field replacement. For the semi-pro market, there was an economy PV model. To give the new models a publicity push, Patti LaBelle was signed on as an endorser.

Additions to the guitar catalogue included the Nitro II twin-humbucker model and the Falcon guitars. Based on the tried-and-true configuration of three single-coil Alnico pickups, the Falcon, Classic, and Custom put Peavey in head-to-head competition with the major guitar manufacturers it was now overtaking.

The digital engineering group came up with Peavey's first floor effects pedals. Although these "stomp boxes" offered attractive features like rugged die-cast packaging and sophisticated surface-mount circuitry, they were expensive and simply failed to compete with the less costly and less advanced products dominating the market. The group also introduced the new PEP-4530 digital effects unit and the DECA-424 power amp, which had been developed

▲ Monitor *magazine—Keel rocks for Peavey and the Vortex guitar*

CHAPTER 11 • NEW DIRECTIONS 93

▲ *An innovation that would make Hartley proud—a Cuban guitarist modifies his Solo amp with a solar panel (Courtesy Guanabacoa Project)*

▲ *22A high-frequency compression horn driver*

for the MegaBass amp. The PLM-8128 rackmount digital mixer was also announced, but this proved to be a brief foray into an area quickly captured by growing competition from Japan.

The analog group revived the Classic Chorus 130 stereo amp and produced a stereo practice amp called the Audition Chorus. To complement the Probass-1000, the PGP-20, a fully MIDI-controllable, programmable, and stereo-capable guitar preamp was created. Also new were the KB-15 keyboard practice amp and the 10-watt Solo, a small, battery-powered portable PA/multi-purpose amp. Seen on street corners everywhere around the globe, the Solo has become the standard of street performers around the world. The original unit delivered 10 watts into its 8" speaker and was driven by eight 1.5-volt D batteries. Peavey offered an optional AC power adapter that allowed the amp to develop 15 watts. It had two channels—one for microphone with Hi- and Lo-Z inputs, and an auxiliary channel with Hi-Z input for instrument. A two-band active EQ and a tape-out socket completed the versatile unit, which weighed in at just 12.5 lbs. A new practice amp, the Minx, was also added to the bass combo line.

In a continuing effort to serve the market for high-power tube amps, the VTM-60 and VTM-120 heads were created to replace the Butcher. The craze for hot-rodded tube amps at this time gave Peavey a marketing opportunity, and the VTM amps had a unique rear-panel dip switch for selecting among eight onboard custom amp modifications to create a personal sound. Later in the year, some of the VTM features were incorporated into the Triumph 60 and 120 combos.

Speaker enclosures rolled out this year included the 112HS, 112HS BW, and 115HS; the 1234M and 1545M monitor wedges; and a new SP-4. The latter had two 15" woofers and a CH-2/22A horn, and it was tailored to match Peavey's first speaker-system processor, the PCS, which was introduced at the same time. The 1516 bass guitar enclosure (loaded with a single 15" speaker plus two heavy-duty 8" drivers) was developed as an ultra-compact high-power cabinet to complement the MegaBass head. This was the first Peavey instrument enclosure without the characteristic aluminum strips—and a portent of changes to come.

The company's relentless expansion continued with the purchase of two of the small houses on A Street. One was converted to an "Axcess Shop" for the sale of company wearables and promotional items; the other was converted into offices for master forecasting. Bar coding was also introduced in 1987, with Peavey becoming one of the first musical-instrument companies to embrace this product-tracking technology.

1988

In 1988 Hartley was inducted into the NAMM Hall of Fame, and the *Jackson Business Journal* bestowed the "Captains of Industry" title on Hartley and Melia. Feverish product development continued, with diversification emerging as a new impetus for growth. The AMR recording products were starting to ship, and plans were well advanced for the launch of the new Architectural Acoustics

▲ *Plant 9 — distribution center*   ▲ *Plant 9 — interior*

division. Dedicated to commercial sound installations, these products would open up avenues of distribution outside of the retail music business.

Melia recalled this period in an episode of the "Mississippi Masters" series entitled *To Build a Dream*, broadcast on Mississippi Educational TV in 1997, "We were embarking on the whole digital technology theme, keyboards and things we had never built before—leading-edge for anywhere in the world," she said. "The expertise just did not exist readily in Mississippi. It didn't exist in most states."

With an increasing need for skilled workers in general, the Peaveys met with Mississippi Governor Ray Mabus, and their discussions yielded the Job Skills Education Program (JSEP). This educational effort was based on U.S. military software designed to teach skills and relate them to specific jobs. In partnership with Meridian Community College and supported by a grant from the National Alliance of Business, Peavey set out to determine if the system could be adapted to industrial employment and funded the establishment of a computer lab at the college. Beginning in June 1989, employees were authorized to take time off from work to participate in classes. There were immediate returns as workers applied their skills to the operation of computer-controlled manufacturing machinery and robotics. As an extension to the company's Vertical Integration credo and its "Peavey—People Growing Together" motto, JSEP was the key to developing high-technology production skills in a region where there had been virtually none.

In the "Mississippi Masters" TV documentary Hartley said, "People in Mississippi, given a chance, like to show what they can do. There is a tremendous amount of talent here. . . . A lot of people perceive Peavey as a company that builds things. And, yes, we do build things, but perhaps our most important product is the people that we build." He cited Melia and himself as good examples of this and said JSEP was a manifestation of this philosophy.

In the coming years, Peavey and the local community college would continue to expand their partnership to embrace pre-employment training, literacy, computer skills, management, leadership, and quality control as well as JSEP. Belief in the value of an educated workforce has remained a constant ingredient in the Peavey recipe. For those determined to improve themselves, the company pays registration and tuition fees. "Everyone is born with a talent—maybe as a mathematician,

▶ *Plant 10 — power amp assembly*

a musician, or an athlete," Hartley has said. "One of my observations is that all of us have something we can do extremely well. The trick is to find out what that is and then have the intestinal fortitude to go in that direction."

In July 1988 Peavey acquired a 90-acre tract of land east of Meridian that had been a U.S. government agricultural research facility in the early part of the 20th century. The grand plan for this site was to consolidate the company's various operations in and around Meridian into a comprehensive "Peavey City." Logistics and circumstances would conspire against the realization of this plan, but the new site was immediately developed into a centralized distribution center. By this time, Peavey had become one of the top ten manufacturers of music and sound products in the world, and a coordinated shipping point for all the plants was necessary. A 62,500-square-foot high-rise distribution center was built on the site as a staging and shipping point for all of the production locations. Architect Samuel "Sambo" Mockbee won an American Institute of Architects award for its design.

Because of the strong sales of the CS-800 and other models in the CS line, Hartley and Melia decided to open a dedicated assembly area for these revenue-generating products. The new CS-900 and M-7000 models would also be built here. A 16,000-square-foot former supermarket in downtown Meridian was acquired and designated Plant 10. The building was completely gutted and transformed into a high-tech electronics assembly facility, with automated production flow and sophisticated test equipment.

Plant 10 was the first Peavey facility to be remodeled in this new architectural style conceived by Mockbee. It became the template for stamping a new corporate image on Peavey's properties, characterized by the use of gray as base color and an "art deco" look.

The digital effort continued with the introduction of the Univerb and Addverb multi-effects processors. Raising the bar with 16-bit processing, these units were designed around the proprietary VLSI chip and, through three upgrades, became best-sellers. The Autograph was a programmable equalizer with a real-time analyzer that allowed the EQ profiles of different venues to be stored

1988

in memory. It suffered from being somewhat user-unfriendly, although the concept was good.

The DEP-3.2S was a marginal product combining delay, effects, and sampling that was outpaced by a rapidly evolving digital market. The IDL-655, however, became a successful industrial delay unit offering a maximum 655-millisecond delay time. The DECA-528 single-rackspace digital amp was announced and, in a collaboration between the analog and transducer engineers, incorporated into a new bass combo. The DataBass featured an analog preamp, a 450-watt digital power amp, and a processor-controlled Black Widow 15" speaker. Despite its promise, the complexity of what should have been a successful pro-quality unit caused its early demise after much wrangling among the engineers.

The Rage guitar amp was introduced as one of the first models with SuperSat, a progressive development of the Saturation tube-synthesis circuitry that had propelled Peavey's solid-state amps to the forefront several years earlier. Jack Sondermeyer's latest emulation of tube characteristics had been distilled from the "hot-rod" circuits in the VTM amp project and became the subject of further patents. SuperSat turned this 12-watt dual-channel practice amp into a tiny monster—one that has continued to dominate the small-amp market to this day. In the original version of the Rage, the aluminum grille strips were still part of the package, but the front panel featured the new "velvet touch" rubber-covered control knobs that would become the standard throughout the line.

The Backstage and Studio Pro were upgraded in power to 50 and 60 watts, respectively, while the Bandit went to 75 watts and got a Scorpion speaker, and the Special was boosted to 150 watts. A miniature stack, the VSS-20, made an appearance but had little impact. For steel players, the Session 400 LTD was reincarnated with updated features. In deference to session players, the Special, TNT, and Session were offered in wedge enclosures, but this format proved less popular than expected. Bass players got a new practice amp, the Microbass, and the TKO and TNT bass combos got power upgrades to 75 watts and 150 watts, respectively. Three new bass amp heads were introduced: the Mark III, VI, and VIII models.

The KB-60 was added to the line of keyboard combos. For the home keyboard market, the HKS-8, -12, and -15 combo amps were developed; their "furniture-finish" look was derived from the cabinetry developed for studio monitors and custom-install speakers that would eventually form a part of the Architectural Acoustics Division.

▲ *Peavey left no market unexplored — from electronic drum amplification to Peavey batteries*

▲ *Lynyrd Skynyrd with their Triple XXX lineup*

▲ *Rudy Sarzo and Adrian Vandenberg — 1988*

In a year marked by power and feature upgrades, the XR series was no exception—and the models were tagged with a "C" suffix to denote the changes. A John Roberts–patented circuit was incorporated into the Gatekeeper, a rackmounted noise gate, and a single-rackspace LM-8 eight-channel line mixer was added. The company made a foray into the disc jockey/dance club market with the introduction of two DJ mixers, the 502 and the 902.

Transducer developments affected products large and small. The first molded PA enclosures were introduced this year: the Impulse was a small trapezoidal molded speaker, and the Impulse II a microphone stand–mountable monitor enclosure based on the same box design. At the other end of the scale, a serious attempt was being made to impact the concert market with the HDH Series, which centered on the new Dynamic System Controller-HDH, a smart speaker-system processor. The HDH-1 was a three-way system with two 15" BW woofers, a unique HF horn manifold system with four 22A drivers, and a special 12" BW-driven mid-bass horn—all in one enclosure. Optional flying hardware made this a strong contender as a festival system enclosure. The HDH-2, -3, and -4 provided separate component options for mix-and-match systems.

An old endorsement relationship was revived in 1988 as Lynyrd Skynyrd regrouped ten years after tragedy had struck the band to embark on a new tour. They chose a full Peavey equipment lineup for their return.

A new endorsement relationship with Whitesnake produced the first Peavey signature-model instrument in the form of the Adrian Vandenberg guitar. Adrian had adopted the VTM as his amp of choice, and he then began to work with the Peavey guitar designers to conceive a radical new instrument. Its unique body styling and ultra-slim neck made it an instant winner with heavy-metal players and demonstrated Peavey's new-

1988

Plant 16 acquired to accommodate the expanding Computer and Accounting departments

found confidence in tracking guitar fashions. In a 1990 *Monitor* article, Adrian explained the process: "Peavey's artist relations manager was at one of the gigs to see Rudy [Sarzo] because Rudy had been working with Peavey for a while. He asked if I was willing to try one of Peavey's guitars. I was playing Les Pauls and other guitars that I had built myself. We talked about Peavey, and I got the feel for Peavey's approach to making instruments. He suggested I should design a guitar for Peavey, and I gave him a few parameters. I was working on designs all the time, and I just wanted to see what Peavey would come up with. A few weeks later I got a prototype, not really of a Vandenberg, but of a guitar with a neck I wanted and some other great features. The guitar felt and looked really good, which pleased me a lot. So I decided to go for it and design the guitar. When I talked to Mike Powers, things started rolling a little bit; I was impressed. You just can't build one of the best, so we sent prototypes back and forth and I tested them on the road, which is the hardest test you can get. I abuse my guitars pretty hard. I throw them around, and they go from gigs in Texas with 90 percent humidity to the Midwest where it's totally dry. So there were lots of things to be sorted out with fretting and kinds of wood and finishes. We spent months working on the detailing of everything. From the time I spent in the factory once or twice with Mike and when I started designing the guitar in my hotel room to the time the first Vandenberg guitars were in my possession was probably six months."

Rudy Sarzo, Whitesnake's bassist, had used Peavey amps when he was with Quiet Riot, and he too began working with Peavey's designers to develop the Rudy Sarzo bass.

The first neck-through-body Peavey instruments came out as the Dyna-Bass Unity and the revamped Impact I guitar, which were developed after consultation with Tim Landers, a highly regarded West Coast session bassist. Tim helped to design the TL-5, a handcrafted premium 5-string bass that was acclaimed by professional players. In other guitar developments, the pointed-headstock fashion gave birth to the Nitro III Custom and a series of Tracer guitars, and active electronics were offered as an option on the Falcon.

With Peavey's computer-system needs expanding proportionally to the rapid increase in business, more processing capacity was needed. To house the proposed IBM ES-9000—the same platform being used to run General Motors—the 11,500-square-foot Eastover Bank property was purchased in July 1988. Designated Plant 16, the building came complete with an air-conditioned computer suite into which the water-cooled processor, running 49 million instructions per second, was installed.

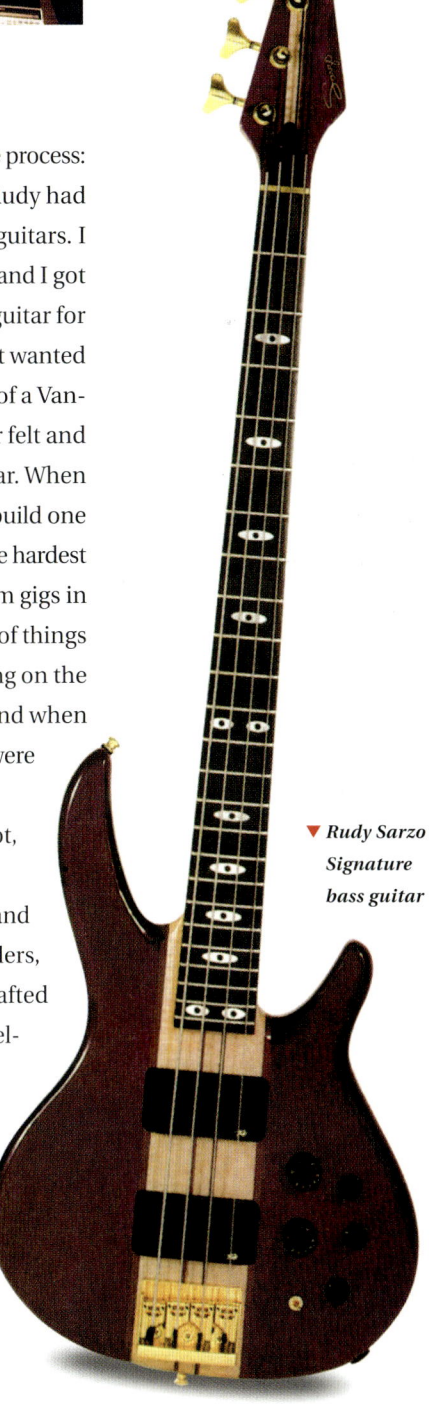

▼ *Rudy Sarzo Signature bass guitar*

CHAPTER 11 • NEW DIRECTIONS   **99**

▲ *Plant 32 — The Canadian Distribution Center*

North of the border, a building that would be designated Plant 32 was opened in Toronto in response to the company's greatly increased business in Canada. It served as a storage and staging area for distribution and as a service center for the Canadian market.

Around this time, an exclusive—and, on the surface at least, seemingly unlikely—partnership with Motorola helped facilitate Peavey's efforts to revolutionize the keyboard market. Today, Motorola is widely known as a cell-phone manufacturer, but its tentacles extend into all forms of communication, computing and networks, automotive, safety and energy products, services, and software applications that affect millions each day around the world. It is and was back then a multi-faceted giant with strong OEM business. A major supplier of electronic and electro-mechanical components, it was already one of Peavey's biggest vendors when the relationship headed on a path to develop digital signal processing. Hartley tells the story:

> For a number of years, we had been a huge customer of Motorola. Virtually all of our power transistors, most of the diodes, and most of the signal transistors and ICs were from Motorola. We had established a very successful working relationship, and Motorola was one of our top three suppliers. We were one of their largest non-automotive customers for power semiconductors and audio-type devices. They came to us and said they were developing a specific range of digital signal processors that might be useful to us in our products. They asked specifically what characteristics we would like to see, and we provided Motorola with a "shopping list" of features that we would like to see incorporated into their new DSP chip.
>
> One of the major reasons that we were interested in Motorola's specialized audio DSP is that many of our customers had complained bitterly about what had been happening to the synthesizer business. The Japanese had introduced the first digital synthesizer, and every year thereafter the various synthesizer companies introduced their new models on about a 12-to-18-month cycle. In those days, the only way to get the "new and cool" features and sounds was to trade in the old keyboard for a new one. . . . The problem was that old synthesizers, like old computers, have virtually no residual trade-in value after the new generation of products hits the market. This kept musicians as well as dealers off balance and upset in trying to follow the rapidly evolving digital synth market. Many musicians got highly insulted when their six-month-old keyboard had a trade-in value of 10 cents on the dollar. Players and dealers alike lamented the fact that this vicious cycle of obsolescence was causing severe problems and strains not only with their pocketbook but also between the vital relationship of musicians and music dealers.
>
> It occurred to us at Peavey that if we could design a digital synthesizer that was upgradeable via software instead of hardware, then we could create a digital platform that could be upgraded using optional software for at least four or five years, thus ending the vicious cycle of obsolescence of the Japanese keyboards. Working with Motorola and their newly released 56000 series DSPs, Peavey de-

veloped the first software-based synthesizer at a reasonable cost. Peavey's DPM-3 was released to the marketplace in the early '90s with great fanfare. Dealers were elated to know there was finally a platform that was software-upgradeable. Peavey engaged the services of numerous sound designers—developers to generate sounds and samples of musical instruments of all types, which we bundled with the initial DPM-3 synthesizers or sold as add-ons. The DPM-3 program was indeed a significant pioneering effort. The original premise of being able to sell the software upgrades encountered difficulties because one of our competitors at the time was giving away new sounds while Peavey was trying to sell theirs. Given the extremely high cost of developing sounds and software, we were amazed they could do this and eventually it turned out that our initial thoughts were right after all, because that company subsequently went out of business. Unfortunately, they succeeded in "poisoning the well" for software-upgradeable synthesizers where the software had to be purchased rather than given away as freebies. We eventually left the keyboard business because of the lingering expectation that new sounds and new capabilities should be gratis instead of charged for. Simply put, the marketplace expected free upgrades while our business model was essentially to build the keyboards at or about cost, and our profit would come from selling the upgrades. . . . Sadly, it was not to be.

1989

In April 1989, Peavey purchased a vacant Howard Discount store property on the northern boundary of Meridian, with the express purpose of converting it into a keyboard-assembly facility. This became Plant 17, and it was equipped to accommodate a new style of workstation production.

Community leaders continued to applaud the important role that Peavey was playing in the economic growth of the area. In 1989 the auditorium at the Ross Collins Vocational School—where young Hartley had learned many of the skills he would apply to building his first amplifiers—was renamed in Hartley's honor, and the local Chamber of Commerce established an annual entrepreneurial award in his name.

Despite the problems he had encountered with launching AMR, Hartley decided to form a separate division to address the fixed-installation and commercial PA market. Realizing that the demand for such products was considerably larger than that for musical instruments, he saw an opportunity to piggyback on the company's expertise at making amplifiers, mixers, and speaker systems—and to keep growing. "Growth is not an option," Hartley likes to say. "It's like riding a bicycle. When you stop pedaling, you fall over."

Hartley knew that sound contractors and audio-system designers played an important role in specifying the products for commercial installations. "I decided it would be a good thing to come out with a separate line of products that addressed sound contractors and their specific market requirements," he says. "I asked Jack Wilson to look into what we needed to do to break into the contractor side of the market. He did some market research and came up with the idea that we should engineer a basic line of 'bread and butter' commercial amplifiers and speakers

▲ *Hartley Peavey with Grammy-winning producer and musician Don Was*

▲ *The vacant Howard Discount lot — before becoming Plant 17*

▲ *Adrian Vandenberg with the Jigsaw Custom Signature Adrian Vandenberg electric guitar*

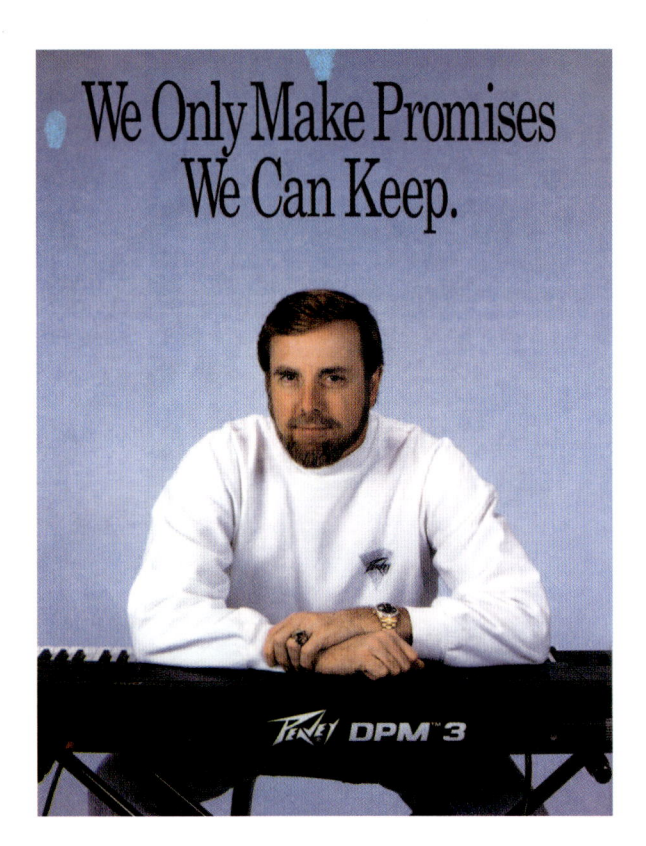

▲ *Hartley with the first DPM-3 keyboard*

and sell these through the established rep firms that were already calling on that trade. So we came up with products that were distinctly different from what we were selling to music and audio dealers, and we sold them through a different set of representatives who were familiar with that side of the market."

The initial Architectural Acoustics products released in 1989 were based on existing designs and did not make much headway in this traditionally conservative marketplace. "This first attempt was only marginally successful because we had chosen to utilize representatives who had a number of well-established but non-competitive product lines," Hartley says. "This approach was less than optimal because we needed individuals who were willing to go out and pioneer." Monte Lamb, who would later play an important role in Peavey's international business, started work as an AMR representative in March 1989; shortly afterwards, at the NSCA trade show in Nashville, he was also given the Architectural Acoustics line to sell.

Musical-instrument products introduced this year included the Envoy, a 35-watt guitar amp that filled a gap in the line between the Audition Plus and the Backstage, and a new 1x12 Bravo all-tube combo. Keyboardists were offered a wedge version of the KB-300, and bass players got the AlphaBass, an all-tube rack-mountable preamp.

Under pressure from hot competition in the mixer market, Peavey fought back with 8-, 12-, and 16-channel models in the Unity series. The MD-16 x 6 discrete monitor mixer was also added, and the CS-1000 joined the lineup of CS power amps.

In Europe, a premium line of EuroNational enclosures joined the standard ES EuroSys range. These were based on the components and configurations of the American SP series: the EN-305 emulated the SP-2, the HP-400 emulated the SP-4, and the EN-325 was a three-way unit. In the U.S., a subwoofer was added to the new HDH series along with the 112PS powered ProSys model. Two new speaker processors were offered to match systems other than HDH: the DSC-12 and DSC-23. Other new enclosures included a furniture-finish 112 Criterion, a 115-TF, and the Stadia—a weather-resistant molded big brother to the Impulse models.

Innovative new guitars continued to roll out of Plant 2. The Odyssey featured a single-cutaway body design that would also be offered in a limited-edition 25th Anniversary version the following year. The Destiny and Destiny Custom and the Generation Series followed. Mike Powers designed a special hum-canceling

1989

HCS pickup for the Generations; thanks to its use of an experimental coil-wire compound, it made this single-coil pickup almost noiseless. Peavey's first 6-string bass, the TL-6, was developed in collaboration with Tim Landers. Other examples of the fine work being produced at this factory included custom quilt-top and "jigsaw finish" Vandenberg Signature guitars.

The accessory catalogue was expanding by leaps and bounds, and cable sales were generating significant revenue. The Audiolink range of multicore cables was introduced, offering multiple send and return options and lengths from 75 to 200 feet.

Peavey's foray into the DJ market expanded with the introduction of the PV Lite System 2400, a portable light show with stands. Various controllers and configuration options would follow, but the company never invested in stage-lighting technology to the point where it could vie successfully with competitive products that were transforming club lighting during this era.

The digital group produced two new multi-effects processors—the Ultraverb and the Multifex—but its main focus was on bringing the company's first keyboard to market. The project was kept under wraps, and there was a great deal of anticipation as Peavey prepared to introduce the DPM-3 at the NAMM show the following January. The specifications of this "digital phase modulation" synthesizer included an onboard sequencer, dual effects processors and sample editing, a floppy disk drive, and a 61-note keyboard.

The DPM-3 would go into production in Plant 17, which had been set up for workstation assembly: parts kits were delivered to each workstation, where one operator would assemble a complete instrument. At first, orders far outstripped capacity and the future of the program looked bright.

The arrival of the DPM-3 was a fitting close to the 1980s. It was an enormous "can do" statement to an industry that had already witnessed a decade of impressive Peavey achievements, including the introduction of guitar and speaker manufacturing and diversification into recording equipment and installed sound systems. This step into the keyboard market was Peavey's most audacious yet.

▲ *An early Architectural Acoustics logo*

▲ *The very recognizable Architectural Acoustics logo known from products such as the Digitool*

PART FIVE

Triumph and Tragedy

Flying High

"The quality of a person's life is in direct proportion to their commitment to excellence, regardless of their chosen field of endeavor."
— VINCENT T. LOMBARDI

During the 1990s, Peavey reached new heights. The decade saw the conception of MediaMatrix and Radial Bridge drum technology, the acquisition of Crest Audio, and productive relationships with Edward Van Halen and other notable endorsers and clinicians like Jennifer Batten, Neil Zaza, Al Pitrelli, Dweezil Zappa, Bobby Rock, and Robin DiMaggio. It was also a time when the company lost its president.

n 1990 Hartley was selected for induction into Hollywood's Rock Walk of Fame alongside such greats as Chuck Berry, Jerry Lee Lewis, Little Richard, and Stevie Wonder. A popular tourist attraction, the Rock Walk is a sidewalk gallery featuring the handprints and signatures of performers and innovators who have made an outstanding contribution to rock 'n' roll as an art form.

Honors were accorded to Melia, too; she was named to the Board of Distinguished Women of Mississippi in recognition of her accomplishments as a businessperson. She was also expanding her humanitarian efforts. Appalled by harrowing stories of abused and neglected children,

▲ *Hartley's induction into the Rock Walk of Fame — 1990*

106 THE PEAVEY REVOLUTION • **PART FIVE** • TRIUMPH AND TRAGEDY

1990

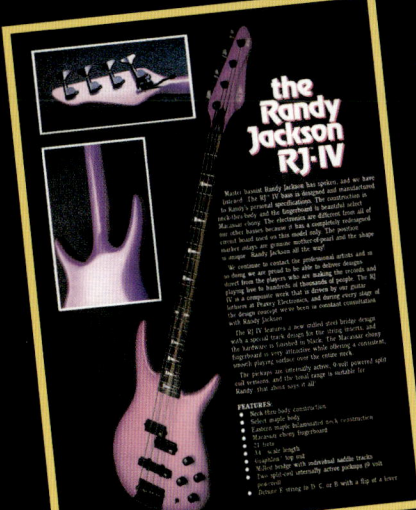

◀ *A true "American Idol": the Randy Jackson Signature model*

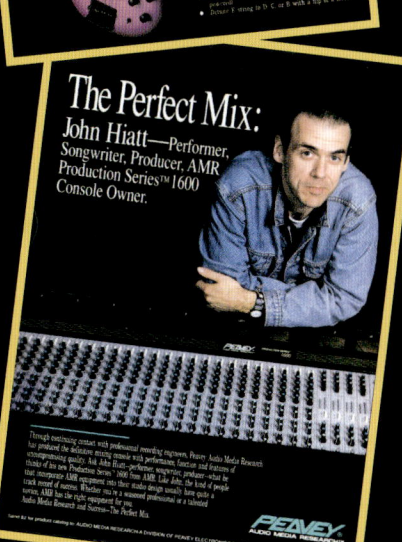

▲ *Classic 50/212 amplifier*

◀ *John Hiatt for Peavey Audio Media Research*

▲ *EVH 5150 amplifier*

CHAPTER 12 • FLYING HIGH

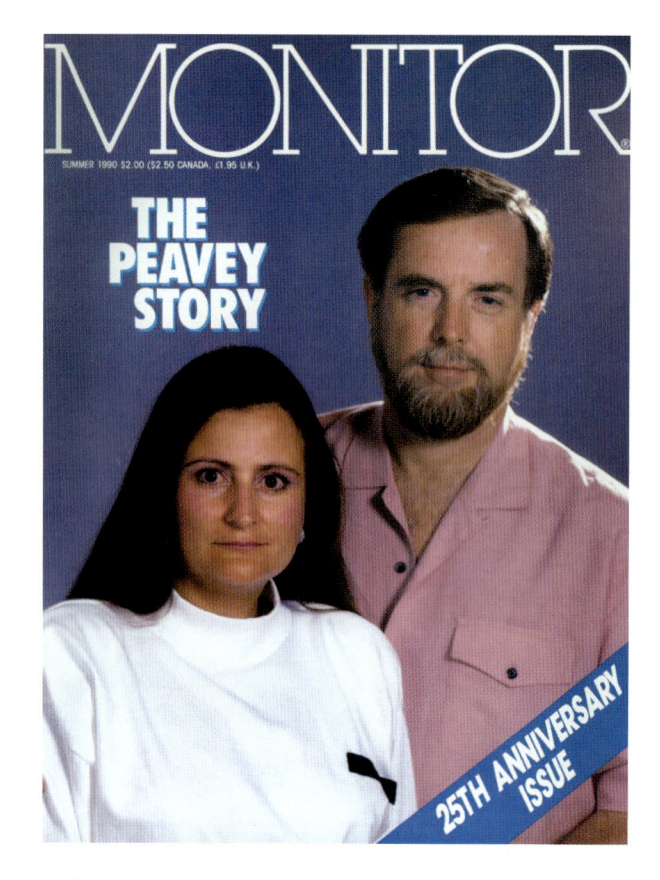

▲ *The 25th Anniversary* Monitor *magazine cover*

▲ *The Peavey Museum*

she became determined to use her celebrity status and financial resources to make a difference. "The Peavey House idea started one weekend in Fort Lauderdale," she later explained. "Hartley and I were on a business trip. I was listening to the news, and there were three episodes, one after the other, about child abuse. I was just horrified by the stories that were told. Right about the same time, I heard on the news in Meridian about someone who had left a four-year-old out at two o'clock in the morning, dropped him in a truck stop on the Interstate and left him. I just couldn't let that go on. I felt like God was saying, 'Melia, you've just got to jump into this and try to do something about it.' One thing kind of led to another."

Hartley and Melia subsequently purchased a large house in Meridian that became a shelter for abused children. They donated the house to the local Mental Health Association and began to stage a series of events to raise funds for the project, culminating the following year in ShelterFest 91, which netted $40,000 in one day. Four years later, the Peavey House became a standalone charity, and Melia continued to work tirelessly to support it.

In March 1990—three years to the day after he joined Peavey as an independent rep—Ernie Lansford was named national sales manager. Hartley and Melia hoped that sales would grow to a new level under his direction, and grow they did. In his first year as sales manager, North American sales posted a 19 percent increase. Lansford would eventually assume responsibility for global sales before leaving to become a NAMM director in 1996.

On June 14, 1990, the company celebrated its Silver Jubilee—25 years of extraordinary growth. On the land purchased for the "Peavey City" project three years earlier, there was a cluster of old buildings that Melia had decided to refurbish. They included a large greenhouse that was restored for use by the plant maintenance and landscaping department, two cottages used for catering and hospitality accommodations, and the main building, a fine old brick structure. Melia had the main building restored within historical preservation guidelines and, with the aid of Willie Hatcher's son Greg, set about turning it into the Peavey Museum and Visitor Center. It would be the backdrop for the start of the anniversary celebrations—and a surprise gift to Hartley.

Distributors, customers, vendors, employees, and local dignitaries were invited to the festivities, and they assembled outside the new Peavey Museum for the opening ceremony. A precision fly-by of Air National Guard jets signaled the start of proceedings,

1990

and then former Mississippi governor William Winter spoke of the way things were when Hartley started his business. "Some of you here," he began, "are old enough to remember what it was like in Mississippi in 1965. For some of us can recall what we were going through in this state at that time. We were not exactly the favored area of the country, and I recall conversations that I had with business leaders of this state and industrialists who were seriously considering picking up and moving out because they said they didn't see much future in the State of Mississippi; that we were always going to have difficulty competing with the rest of the country. That was not the attitude of Hartley Peavey. He started his company on the basis of having an idea, an aspiration, and along with it a motivation to make an organization succeed. Maybe the greatest contribution that Hartley and Melia Peavey have made to us in this state is to give us a sense of what we are capable of accomplishing, of raising our sights, of letting us see that we can compete with anybody anywhere."

In his address, Ray Mabus, the governor of Mississippi at the time, quipped, "I knew it was a special occasion, not because of you all being here but because Hartley has on a tie and socks!" Governor Mabus went on to thank Hartley for giving up the guitar to found his company and said: "Peavey has been an economic anchor to the whole State of Mississippi and everybody knows the story of how it started in Hartley's daddy's attic in 1965, turning out one amp a week, and today it exports to 106 countries and has a payroll of $35 million. And yet in spite of the growth, and in spite of the size, it still has the feeling of family—of no formalities, power, or rank. Everybody is on a first-name basis, and everyone can speak their mind. But I tell you this has produced a great company, this style of management. Hartley's dream didn't depend on a coat and tie, and it didn't depend on nine 'til five. It depended on persistence and determination and hope."

After the speeches, Melia presented the keys of the property to Hartley, and the crowd filed through the museum to begin three days of fun and music capped by a huge concert in the town's arena featuring Peavey endorsers.

During its Silver Jubilee year, Peavey responded to the fashion for rackmounted component instrument systems by introducing two new tube preamps, the T.B.Raxx for bass and the T.G.Raxx

▼ *Peavey Axcess clothing c. 1990: "A 'sound' fashion decision for any activity."*

CHAPTER 12 • FLYING HIGH **109**

▲ *Plant 17 remodeled as Corporate Headquarters*

for guitar. The Classic series of tube amps was updated, and the 65-watt Express 112 joined the solid-state combo line. It featured a new look, with aluminum grille strips that were narrower and profiled; the move away from the bold aluminum trim was beginning, and more new models would arrive without the characteristic strips. The Chorus line also got a makeover, with the introduction of the Backstage Chorus 208 and the other amps in the series being redesignated the Studio Chorus 210, the Classic Chorus 212, and the Stereo Chorus 212.

The 22A horn driver was upgraded to the titanium-diaphragm 22T, yielding both lighter weight and added strength. The Black Widow speakers were also improved by using Kevlar to impregnate the cone material. Kevlar, which is used to make bulletproof vests, made the cones stiffer and stronger, thus improving reliability and reducing distortion.

In December 1990 Willie Hatcher retired after directing 20 years of remarkable industrial growth.

When he started with Peavey, there had been about 30 employees in one building; when he left, there were some 2,000 employees working in 2 million square feet of manufacturing facilities.

1991

In 1991 sales growth topped 20 percent, and the need for investment in a new headquarters became obvious. The plan to develop the "Peavey City" site was abandoned in favor of a location in town, and Plant 17 was selected for remodeling. At a cost of $4 million, the building was transformed into an 80,000-square-foot corporate center befitting Peavey's dominant position in the music industry. The color scheme of purple, teal, and black that Melia and designer Judie McMullen had selected for Peavey's offices, factories, and trade show displays predominated, and the architecturally stunning result housed new offices for the chairman and president, as well as multimedia and educational facilities—including a much-enlarged classroom with superior teaching aids and an extensive MIDI lab.

The educational facilities reflected the fact that dealer seminars were as important as ever to Peavey's way of doing business. "We have the only regularly scheduled dealer personnel training system in the industry," Hartley proudly announced. "One of the big problems all retailers have is turnover of their personnel. When you have a trained person who leaves, you have an untrained person who comes in, and the whole vicious cycle starts over again. They need training. If you're a young man or a young woman and you decide you want to go into the music and sound business, where do you go to get your basic training? The fact of the matter is there is only one place to go in the whole United States, and that's Peavey Electronics Corporation in Mississippi."

The new headquarters also housed a 227-seat auditorium with an in-seat translation system, along with a sound recording studio and a video studio with non-linear editing and 3-D animation. An artist relations suite provided luxury accommodations and makeup areas for visiting endorsers. The advertising department was equipped with the latest in computer graphics, a photographic studio, and three printing presses that gave Peavey in-house four-color capability and automated collation. A catering kitchen and dining room stood ready for dealer seminars and special events—and the new facility would soon be hosting some 5,000 visitors a year.

In 1991 Washington called, and Peavey Electronics was selected as one of 20 U.S. companies named to participate in the Japan Corporate Program sponsored by the Department of Commerce. Even more recognition came on December 3, 1991, when President George H.W. Bush paid a visit. It was a big day for the town when Air Force One touched down at Meridian's airport. Twenty Secret Service agents had arrived a week earlier to make security checks, secure the airport, and plan every inch of the president's route. Sophisticated telecommunication transmitters were installed, and the president's armored limousine was flown into the airport the day before he arrived. Sentries were posted on rooftops around the factory as the motorcade arrived, and Hartley later told the *Music Trades* that "watching all this take place was like seeing a newsreel. It was certainly a day that none of us here will ever forget."

President Bush took a three-hour tour of the facilities and then addressed the 2,000 assembled employees, praising them for being part of a true American success story. On the issue of export trade he said, "Hartley once remarked that 'fat cats don't hunt.' Well, Peavey's been prowling the

▲ *Peavey has received thousands of visitors to its Seminars and Dealer Meetings over the years. This group in 1996 was from the U.K.*

▲ *Hartley with sons Marc (left), Joe (right) and Melia (taken in the early '90s)*

global marketplace with a hunger that won't quit." After the speech, Hartley and Melia presented President Bush with a one-of-a-kind, handmade Ecoustic prototype guitar painted with stars and stripes and inscribed "The Chief," as a memento of the day.

Afterwards, Hartley said of the visit: "It has confirmed some of the basic principles that have fueled the growth of our company. Unlike some of our competitors who have pursued an acquisition strategy, we have chosen to grow from within by using innovative technologies to create new products. We have also consistently operated with the long term in mind."

▶ *Letter from George H.W. Bush*

GEORGE BUSH

June 18, 2004

Dear Hartley,

For many, you epitomize the American Dream. Your entrepreneurial spirit, your ability to look to the future and see the big picture, your total integrity make you a role model for the free enterprise system.

I hope this book on your life will show a lot of young people that the American Dream is still alive, and that hard work and integrity give us all a chance to fulfill our destinies.

Congratulations on your many accomplishments and on the example you set for so many of your fellow Americans.

Sincerely,

G Bush

Mr. Hartley Peavey
Chairman and Chief Executive Officer
Peavey Electronics Corporation
Meridian, Mississippi

P. O. BOX 79798 · HOUSTON, TEXAS 77279-9798
PHONE (713) 686-1188 · FAX (713) 683-0801

1991

Hartley and Melia were in top form, flushed with the success of a quarter-century of inexorable progress and a future that seemed to grow brighter every day. They were the company's best and most tireless ambassadors, traveling some 200 days of the year, and the acquisition of a Gulfstream G-II corporate jet had extended their range considerably. But the pressure of managing what had become a multinational corporation was beginning to take its toll on the workaholic Melia, who was suffering from increasingly severe migraines. These would continue to worsen and plague her for the rest of her life.

The new Architectural Acoustics products were off to a slow start, so the project was moved to engineers working with the digital group. "We relaunched Architectural Acoustics," Hartley explains, "with greatly improved products that were much more sophisticated and in tune with what the installation industry expected from a product line. We introduced a number of important new features and new products such as our 'zone' mixers that presented multi-channel options with individually assignable channels with selective muting/paging capabilities, several automatic mixers, and power amps with our patented DDT clipping-protection system. Along with this we introduced Architectural Acoustics speaker systems and utilized an entirely different set of representatives. The relaunch of this brand was much more successful and had much greater acceptance from the installation marketplace."

One of the year's key product developments was the rebirth of the tweed-covered 50-watt Classic 212 and 410. Eighteen years after its introduction, the new Classic maintained the retro sound of its forebear but benefited from the huge strides in technology made by the company in the

▲ *Flight Operations and hangar at Meridian airport*

◀ *Hartley Peavey presents President George H.W. Bush with "The Chief" during his visit to Meridian*

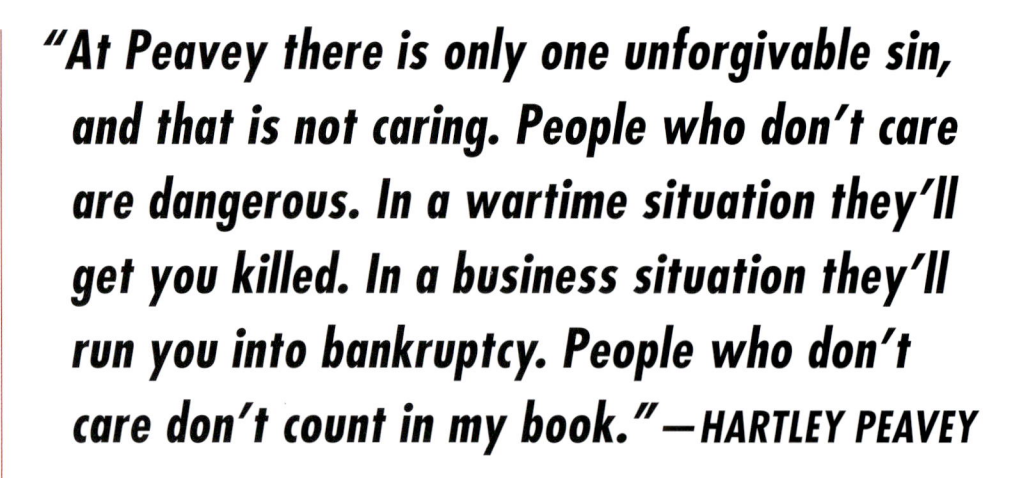

> *"At Peavey there is only one unforgivable sin, and that is not caring. People who don't care are dangerous. In a wartime situation they'll get you killed. In a business situation they'll run you into bankruptcy. People who don't care don't count in my book."* —HARTLEY PEAVEY

▶ *Palaedium bass designed in collaboration with Jeff Berlin. Inset: This was the first Peavey instrument to feature graphite neck reinforcement.*

interim. It was a big success and would spawn a host of competitive imitators in the coming years. Also new this year were two three-channel all-tube heads, the Ultra 60 and Ultra 120. These new heads not only addressed the increasing interest in three-channel amps but took the concept to enhanced flexibility. The clean channel featured 4-band passive EQ with a Presence control, while the Crunch and Ultra lead channels had a 3-band Bottom, Body, and Edge EQ set. Impedance was switchable between 4, 8, and 16 Ohms, and hum balance adjustment was incorporated. With a master-volume control completing the package, this model was covered in a new black-on-grey Tolex. The TKO-80 and TNT-160 got feature upgrades and a new look.

Development of the DPM-3 had, by design, spun off a number of projects, and several new products were launched in 1991 as a result. There were two rackmount synthesizer modules based on the DPM-3 architecture, the DPM-V3 and DPM-V2. The standalone DPM-SX sample expander and DPM-SP sample player worked in conjunction to provide full sampling and editing. And, keeping to its promise, the keyboard itself got its first software upgrade to DPM-3SE by way of a new factory-fitted or retro replacement EPROM. The PCX-4L programmable four-way electronic crossover unit, the MIDIMaster, and the Profex MIDI-controllable multi-effects preamp were all generated from the same source.

At the company's Silver Anniversary celebration the previous year, Jeff Berlin had played a startling bass solo that brought down the house. Behind the scenes, Berlin had been collaborating with Peavey on one of the company's first esoteric instruments, the Palaedium. This high-end bass guitar combined simplicity of form with tonal flexibility—its three-piece alder body was coupled to a graphite-reinforced maple neck with an ebony fingerboard and outfitted with special pickups and electronics. The RJB-4 bass—the product of another collaboration with a top bassist, Randy Jackson—was also released at this time. And the G-90 guitar and B-90 bass, both available left-handed, were added to the line.

114 THE PEAVEY REVOLUTION • PART FIVE • TRIUMPH AND TRAGEDY

1992

Hartley and Melia with President George Bush and Mrs. Barbara Bush at the White House for the National Literacy Award presentation

Over in Corby, England, a revised range of ES enclosures was produced to coincide with the plans for direct distribution on the Continent. In the States, the XR-680C was added to the XR series and the powered XR consoles got a "D" suffix to designate the addition of a 16-bit digital effects processor. The new MD-III series of mixers also arrived, along with two rackmount DJ mixers, the CD-MIX 7032 and CD-MIX 9072. These acknowledged the increasing use of CDs by DJs in this growing market segment.

1992

In 1992 President Bush summoned Hartley and Melia to the White House, where he acknowledged their support of employee education with the National Literacy Honors Award. Peavey was the first corporation in the U.S. to receive this accolade. The First Lady, Barbara Bush, read the citation:

> **Hartley and Melia Peavey**
>
> In creating a program to improve employee skills in a highly technical workplace, you have used the soundest of business practices to increase the productivity of your workers and the quality of their work. You have given them chances they might never have had for advancement and personal growth. For your continuing commitment to a model of how business can meet workers' needs and keep America competitive in the world marketplace, we are happy to recognize your exemplary accomplishments.

CHAPTER 12 • FLYING HIGH

The Peavey ID badge reminds all employees "Peavey is People Growing Together."

"Peavey is People Growing Together"—that motto was imprinted on every employee's ID badge for many years. "Peavey is not just about building products," Hartley once said. "More important, it is about building people. The company provides the structure that is necessary for growth, much like a trellis provides growth for a vine. Without the trellis, the vine could only grow at the ground level. No matter how vigorous it might grow, it still remains at ground level until it rots and dies. This company, I am glad to say, has provided the structure so that there could be tremendous growth by the people who work here. It is an essential ingredient of our success and will continue to be throughout our future."

Within the corporate structure that Hartley had created, debate and argument thrived—and one hot topic during this period was the use of the new logo that had been created for AMR. The so-called "block" logo was conceived as more modern and thus more appropriate for use on high-tech digital products, but it also began to appear on guitars, PA gear, and musical instrument amplifiers. For much of the '90s, the two Peavey logos vied for support within the company, and the sharp focus of their original differentiation became blurred. A third option appeared with the creation of the "delta" logo, which began to appear on products, literature, and wearables in the early '90s. It too had been conceived as the AMR and Architectural Acoustics products were being developed, and it was often used in conjunction with the block logo. The delta expressed the different kind of company that Peavey believed itself to be.

▼ *Manufacture of Black Widow, Scorpion, and Sheffield speakers, and horn drivers in Meridian before transferring to the Foley, AL, plant*

116 THE PEAVEY REVOLUTION • PART FIVE • TRIUMPH AND TRAGEDY

1992

"Our goal at Peavey is to be the best," Hartley explained. "This is a battle we fight almost every day—how to be the best. When I started the company, I started it for a simple reason: to build good equipment at fair and reasonable prices. I wanted to be the best company. By definition, to be the best you have to be different! We can't be the same while at the same time be different. We cannot be better while at the same time being the same. I'll say it again: you can't be better unless you are different. We're so dedicated to the difference, you will have noticed the triangle logo. The triangle is the Greek letter 'Delta.' In science and mathematics, Delta is the symbol that is assigned as the 'difference.' For that reason, we are using that Delta with the little squiggle behind it—the squiggle designates audio. We never set out to be just like this company or just like that company, or to have products just like this or that company. We set out to be the best, and by definition the best is different. We're so committed to being different we've even made that philosophy a part of our company logo, and that's what I call the Delta Difference."

◀ *The Delta Difference*

Early in 1992, another Peavey factory opened: Plant 20 in Foley, Alabama, a 64,000-square-foot facility that was equipped to build speakers. Production of Black Widow, Scorpion, and Sheffield speakers and horn drivers in this highly automated facility would increase dramatically, and two years after it opened Peavey's one-millionth speaker rolled off the line there. The new molded Impulse enclosures were also assembled at Foley.

Across the Atlantic, more changes were brewing. The distribution agreement in France was up for renewal, and the emergence of the European Union's "Single Market"—allowing free circulation

▼ *The Classic family of products spawned an industry retro revival.*

> When I first laid eyes on the Peavey Classic® Series, it reminded me of my uncle's old tube amp. Then I plugged in...
>
> They've got channel switching, effects loops, pre and post gains, reverb. And all that's great. But what really blew me away was the warm tone of the EL84 tubes in the guitar amps. And the Classic 400 bass amp head with the 810TX™ cabinet was awesome.
>
> And when you really get down to it, it's all about plugging a good guitar into a great-sounding amp.
>
> The Peavey Classic Series...
> My uncle's amp never sounded that good.

CHAPTER 12 • FLYING HIGH   117

▼ Prototype semi-acoustic short-scale Resolite bass

▲ Carving a semi-acoustic body

▲ Computer-controlled cutting, punching, and bending of raw metal

of goods, services, money, and people in one common trading area—had opened new commercial opportunities. The successful takeover of the U.K. market in 1984 and the subsequent establishment of a factory in England had positioned the company for further expansion, and a decision was made late in 1992 to plan for direct distribution to France within a year. New EuroSys-1, -2, -3, -4, and Bassflex subwoofer speaker systems went into production in Corby to provide the necessary inventory.

The tweed-covered Classic amps had been so successful that new models were added to the line: the Classic 50 guitar head and matching 410E(S) speaker enclosures, and the funky Classic 20 "baby" combo. In keeping with the retro theme, all-tube Valvex and Valverb mixer and reverb units were produced, complete with chrome faceplates and vintage knobs. Other new guitar amps included the Blazer, a reverb-equipped version of the popular Rage, and the Revolution, a three-channel version of the Bandit.

For bass players, there was the BassFex version of the ProFex (along with a foot controller for both), the new Bassist preamp, and a complete new line of speaker enclosures: 210TX, 410TX, 115 BX, and 115BW BX. These dispensed with the cosmetic strips and featured heavy-duty one-piece metal grilles and carpet covering.

The guitar line was extended with the introduction of Peavey's first electro-acoustic instrument, the Ecoustic. Its construction was another Peavey innovation. The engineers working with the numerical-controlled routers for electric guitar production had experimented with the process in

1992

reverse: instead of carving a solid body from a mahogany block, they used the machine to carve out the inside of the outline, producing a hollow body. They then glued on an X-braced cedar top. The result was an acoustic instrument with tremendous strength, since there was no back-to-sides glue joint, not to mention superior resonant qualities. Unfortunately, the process was costly and the Ecoustic failed to have much impact in that competitive sector of the guitar market.

A semi-acoustic short-scale Resolite bass was designed at the same time, but this did not get further than prototyping. Tentative steps were also being made to begin building necks for a low-cost Predator guitar in Korea—an early sign of the realization that to compete at the lower end of the market Peavey would have to look offshore, as its competitors were already doing.

The work of Australian engineer Steve Chick to perfect a bass guitar MIDI controller had come to Hartley's attention, and Chick was invited to move to Meridian and collaborate with Peavey R&D. The resulting Midibase was a technological breakthrough, using a wired-fret system and bridge-mounted pickups to achieve excellent performance without the tracking problems that had plagued earlier bass-synth controllers. For bass players who felt threatened by synthesizers, it was a dream solution. A Midibase module based on the DPM-V3 module was produced to complement it.

The DPM program moved ahead with the second software upgrade to the DPM-3SE+ and three new keyboard models: the DPM-2, a cut-down "performance" keyboard; the DPM-Si, a 78-note programmable synth with an increased 10nB wave-sample ROM; and the DPM-C8, with a full 88-note weighted-key piano keyboard. These units featured a large backlit display—which addressed

▼ *The guitar factory in the early '90s*

▲ *Kipper (left) and Jason Rebello, Sting's two keyboardists, give their DPM C8X keyboards a workout during sound-check on the 2004 tour*

▲ *Edward Van Halen with his signature EVH Wolfgang guitar*

a common criticism of the DPM-3—but the DPM-2 and DPM-Si fared poorly due to a perception that the onboard sounds were not generally useful.

The DPM-C8, however, became a flagship product for the whole program, and it found favor with many leading players for use both onstage and in the studio. It had just about everything that a demanding musician-programmer wanted in a controller, and its descendants outlasted all other Peavey keyboards. One testimonial to its utility came from Mark "Kipper" Eldridge, who discovered the C8 while writing and producing with Sting. In a 2001 *Monitor* interview, he said, "The C8 is a very powerful tool live. Layering, merging MIDI info, multi-outputs, and velocity curves on each layer are the major plus points for me."

Also new was a stereo version of the sampling module, the DPM-SX II; it was accompanied by two package modules, the DPM-Spectrum Synth and the DPM-Spectrum Bass, which had bundled collections of 200 synth and bass sounds, respectively. The latter worked well with the Midibase for producing a wide range of electric, acoustic, and synthesizer bass sounds.

Leaving no stone unturned, the digital group also designed a karaoke machine, the Protégé, which appeared as a combo or rackmount unit based around the tape deck of the AMR studio recorder. It didn't fare well against competition from less expensive units in this market. A significantly more successful product arrived in the form of the PC-1600. With its 16 programmable sliders, 16 programmable switches, programmable data wheel, and two voltage-control inputs, this MIDI controller/universal editor was an instant hit in performance rigs and the studio.

The most important new product in the year's outburst of development was the EVH 5150 amplifier. The quest for the perfect amp was an obsession for rock guitar hero Eddie Van Halen, and after he met Hartley in 1990 they agreed to work together to build a revolutionary new unit. Both men were ready to invest their reputations and the time and patience required to make it happen. Over the months that followed, the 5150 project went through a lengthy and meticulous gestation. As prototypes moved back and forth between the Meridian engineering department and Van Halen's studio, the tone and characteristics of a new 120-watt tube amp were honed to Eddie's liking. His ultimate "brown sound" was achieved only after exhausting a bewildering set of permutations for the circuitry, tubes, speakers, and materials. The 5150 head was matched to two 412 enclosures, one straight and one slant, that could be configured as a half or full stack. A key feature in the system's performance was the resonance control, a unique circuit that allowed the user to vary the amp's damping factor, ef-

1993

▲ *Expansion at the Distribution Center*    ▲ *Warehouse Warriors*    ▲ *Inside the Distribution Center*

fectively loosening or tightening the excursion of the speaker cones. Before the 5150 received its final blessing from Eddie and Hartley, the engineers toiled on perfecting the speaker design and searched for the right 11-ply birch plywood for the enclosures. The new amp drew immediate acclaim as soon as it was released, and it has become firmly established as an iconic guitar amplifier.

1993

In the January 18, 1993, issue of the *Wall Street Journal*, Peavey was recognized for its export achievements. At the time Hartley prophetically announced, "I just got back from China and it blew me away. The market there will be unbelievable."

Continuing their philanthropy for children's causes, Hartley and Melia co-founded and sponsored the Corporate Fund for Children, a statewide organization. The Peaveys also established their "Cash for Kids" cable program, donating a percentage from all audio cable sales to the operating expenses of the Peavey House.

At the distribution center, another warehouse was built alongside the first building. With 125,000 square feet of storage, it provided a consolidated site for receiving and storing incoming raw materials. This enabled further improvements in materials movement and transportation efficiency.

In Europe, direct distribution into France was established, with a new sales force recruited under the local management of Gerard Joye, who joined the team in August. In the spring of the following year, the Peavey Europe Corporation in Holland was dismantled, and distribution to Holland, Belgium, Luxembourg, Germany, Austria, and Denmark was added to the pan-European headquarters based in England. This unique operation was put together with the goal of providing multi-lingual and multi-currency resources to satisfy customers across the Continent. Subsequently, Spain and Portugal were added to the pan-European operation, giving Peavey direct control over most of the E.U. national markets.

The Bandit was upgraded with improved stamped-frame speakers, and the new version achieved the design goal of delivering a vintage "British" sound. The tweed-covered Classic line was expanded with three

▼ *Sheffield stamped-frame speaker*

CHAPTER 12 • FLYING HIGH **121**

Assembling Classic amps in Plant 3

▼ *HiSys speaker enclosure line — Europe 1998*

newcomers: the Blues Classic, a single-15 version of the Classic 50; the Delta Blues, a 30-watt vintage-style amp with a single 15; and the Classic 30, a 30-watt 1x12 model that went on to become one of the most successful amps in the line, appealing to session, blues, and jazz players alike. A new super-clean, all-tube twin combo, the Duel 212, was designed to meet the needs of country players and others searching for a classic 2x12 sound. The Combo 115 and Combo 210TX got a new look featuring steel grilles and carpet covering.

In 1993 PA enclosures took a leap forward both in Europe and the U.S. The EuroSys line built in England was expanded with a three-way EuroSys-5 system and two new EuroSys powered monitor wedges. The big news, though, was the introduction of the HiSys range. Designed with the same premium components and parameters as the acclaimed American SP series, HiSys systems delivered an affordable step-up option for semi-pro bands, and they quickly became "must have" gear. In the States, the transducer department launched their own step-up range from the SP series, utilizing the new 44T 4" high-frequency driver to boost performance. A series of trapezoidal models was also released, with grey carpet covering enhancing their stylish, modern look.

Jack Sondermeyer's group announced a complete overhaul of the CS power amp series; the improved models were identified with an "X" suffix. There was also a brand-new, lower-cost line of "no frills" models: the PV-4C, PV-8.6C, and PV-1.3K, which met the competition from rival suppliers head on. The rugged reliability of these new amps helped to secure a substantial customer base. And the DPC-1000 emerged from the digital group as the most powerful digital amplifier yet in a single-rackspace package.

THE PEAVEY REVOLUTION • PART FIVE • TRIUMPH AND TRAGEDY

Three new rack mixers appeared: the Versamix, the RSM-2462, and the DSM-752 disco unit. The Versamix, as its name implied, was designed to function as a live sound desk, home recording console, or instrument mixer. Six of the input channels had studio-quality XLR lo-Z microphone preamps, but all sixteen channels could be used as line inputs. All ins/outs were mounted on a separate module that could be oriented six different ways to facilitate in-rack, top of rack, desk, or freestanding positions. The RSM-2462 was derived from the AMR consoles as a high-quality rackmount recording desk, and the DSM-752 incorporated digital sampling for the emerging sophistication in DJ shows. Unable to upgrade the DPM-3 any further because of hardware limitations, Peavey offered the DPM-4 as a successor; it was also available with the 88-note piano-action keyboard as the DPM-488. It would be the last of the line of DPM-based keyboard workstations, as the limits of the hardware had been reached.

The fretted-instrument division rolled out the new Reactor, Predator AX, and Axcelerator guitars and basses. New Impact guitars, a new Forum bass designed to appeal to grunge players, and an RSB bass derived from the Rudy Sarzo signature model were also released.

A project commissioned by the federal government in the early 1990s helped to launch an important new phase in Peavey's development. Realizing that the sound system in the U.S. Senate had to be upgraded, the government commissioned the design of a radical replacement. To address the complex requirements of multiple-channel, multiple-zone audio plus simultaneous multiple translations and outside broadcast links, a cutting-edge solution was needed. Peak Audio, a software development group, designed a digital sound system with complex mixing and signal processing controlled by computers. Then it was time to seek out a partner with audio system expertise, plus manufacturing, distribution, and marketing skills.

"We met with the people at Peak Audio," Hartley explains, "and began talking about the possibility of a digitally controlled and implemented sound system." He quickly realized that much of the work that had been done in developing the DPM-3 was in sync with this project. Hartley continues the story:

> If you think about a synthesizer, there has to be a signal source such as a tone generator or an oscillator, various sound-shaping circuits such as gates, equalizers, compressors, and a litany of audio-processing circuits that enable the instrument to synthesize the sounds of many other instruments. With a digital synthesizer, there can be numerous presets that can be instantly called up at the touch of a button. This is accomplished through the miracle of digital electronics and involves reconnecting various sound-processing modules into different chains. These settings can either be factory programmed or customer programmed, and the ability to accomplish these tasks digitally gave the synthesizer a whole new set of capabilities.
>
> Imagine a synthesizer consisting of various functions—i.e., functional blocks—that can be instantly reconfigured to yield various sounds and effects. It should not be difficult to envision that the name and function of these blocks might be changed entirely, yielding a device that could instantly reconfigure itself in a number of interesting ways, i.e., instead of the first functional block

▲ *Hartley aboard the Westship— sailing and yachting excursions like this have afforded him the perspective to conceive new products and technologies for Peavey*

▲ *MediaMatix logo*

being a tone generator/clock/oscillator, let's assume that it is a microphone preamp. Subsequent blocks could be various types of equalizers, compressors, parametric equalizers, metering circuits, and so on, and all of these blocks, as with the synth, are instantaneously reconfigurable at the touch of a button.

In short, we learned how to create DSP-based systems that were instantaneously reconfigurable, and with the help of Peak Audio we were able to build the world's most sophisticated audio system that could have hundreds of inputs and outputs with various signal-routing and signal-processing tasks being accomplished digitally. These chains were configurable and programmable and digitally adjustable. A proprietary Ethernet audiobus was conceived by Peak and called CobraNet. The entire package came together in a program that we called MediaMatrix.

In October 1993 Peavey astounded the commercial sound industry with the premiere of MediaMatrix. At the AES show in New York, contractors and audio consultants were introduced to the power and performance of this revolutionary computer-based approach to complex audio system design and implementation. The buzz was instant and far reaching for this massive Peavey innovation. On the first day, press and industry leaders filed in for a peak; the next day, there was a line to see a presentation of this new, computer-configurable and manageable audio system.

"We utilized a computer to demonstrate the implementation of a sound system via this new MediaMatrix system," Hartley recalls. "Graphically, MediaMatrix is presented as block diagrams interconnected by lines in a digitally controlled way. The way these blocks are interconnected on a computer screen is called 'rubber banding.' We illustrated how a sound system entered a computer through what we call a break-out box (BOB), which converts the analog inputs into a digital format feeding the PC. Once the signals have gone through the analog-to-digital conversion process, the

▶ *The first Media-Matrix System*

magic of DSP can do its thing with routing, signal conditioning, metering—indeed, except for the microphone preamp and the power amp/speaker combination, MediaMatrix does it all!"

The efficiency of the system in replacing racks of hardware was matched by its flexibility. Large venues such as arenas are often used for multiple purposes such as concerts, exhibitions, and sporting events, and MediaMatrix offered the ability to instantly reconfigure the sound system for each application, store it in memory, and recall it as needed—a big bonus for operators keen to maximize facility usage. "The various configurations of the sound system are set up in the computer," Hartley explains, "initialized, adjusted, and tweaked, and then can be instantaneously recalled at the touch of a button. Just as a digital synthesizer can instantaneously change its sounds by reconnecting various internal software features, so can MediaMatrix—and just as digital synthesizers changed the keyboard business forever, so has MediaMatrix changed sound reinforcement forever."*

Much of the beta testing of MediaMatrix was undertaken at Disney World in Florida and overseen by George Douglas, Disney's technology manager. The complex zoning and automation needed for theme park attractions made this an ideal proving ground. Douglas went to work for Peavey to oversee the product's initial sales effort, and he steered its development and marketing for the first 10 years.

▲ *MediaMatrix was first installed in the U.S. Capitol building in Washington, D.C.*

1994

The debut of MediaMatrix was a tough act to follow, but 1994 proved to be one of the most exciting, challenging, and innovative years in Peavey's history. At the "Powered by Motorola" awards ceremony in Austin, Texas, Peavey received the Motorola Product of Imagination Award presented by *Electronics Engineering Times* for its DPM synthesizer products. But despite such critical acclaim, market acceptance of the company's digital gear was still disappointing.

In Corby, the European operation was expanding rapidly and had secured ISO-9000 quality certification—the manufacturing equivalent of the *Good Housekeeping* Seal of Approval. The pan-European distribution effort was in full swing, and the Rotterdam warehouse was consolidated into the Corby facility. On the other side of the world, partnerships were being established for guitar manufacturing in the Far East.

Hartley was a reluctant participant in the rush to build products offshore, and his approach—as might be expected—has been different from that of his competitors. He was never interested in off-the-shelf, possibly inferior products being branded as "Peavey." If he were to put his name on a product, it would have to be designed and quality-assured by his own engineers. This dictum has continued to underpin Peavey's offshore and third-party manufacturing, and Hartley's refusal to compromise quality has enabled Peavey to maintain its edge in the face of fierce competition

---

*Early in 1993, I was riding in Hartley's car as he drove to his office in Meridian. After swearing me to secrecy, he told me about the MediaMatrix project. He could barely contain his excitement, not so much for the commercial potential but because of the groundbreaking technology that Peavey was unlocking. I asked him why a manufacturer of mixers, equalizers, effects processors, and other hardware peripherals would want to develop a computer system that replaced the hardware. Hartley's answer was simple: "If I don't do it, someone else will." What he really meant was, he was the one who could see the future.

▲ *Leakesville, MS — guitar manufacturing*    ▲ *Guitar paint line*    ▲ *Guitar neck preparation*

from an entire industry that has turned to the Far East for manufacturing.

In October Hartley completed a five-year term as state director of the National Association of Manufacturers, and it was with great pride that he accepted the Republican Senatorial Medal of Freedom—the highest honor the Republican members of the U.S. Senate can bestow.

On October 30, 1994, a 127,000-square-foot facility was acquired in Leakesville, Mississippi, south of Meridian. This new factory was outfitted to produce guitars and drums. A state-of-the-art dust-collection system was installed, and computer-controlled machinery was moved from Plant 2 to make it a world-class musical instrument factory. The EVH Wolfgang guitar, then in development with Edward Van Halen, would be handcrafted in this building by a selected team of skilled builders.

Staff training continued to be an important component of the Peavey recipe, and Hartley and Melia initiated Peavey Adult Continuing Education (PACE), a program to recognize employees taking courses that improved their skills. "Sixteen or 17 years ago, I started a program that if an employee wanted to go to college we would pay for 100 percent of the classes as long as he or she maintained a C average," Melia later explained. "We would have to approve the course first to be sure it would be something that would benefit the company, but as diverse as we are it's really hard to find something that we won't approve."

Further expansion of the distribution facilities on the "Peavey City" site occurred when a 122,200-square-foot depot was constructed adjacent to the distribution center. It accommodated D&D Transport, which handles Peavey's intercompany transfers and freight with Southeastern destinations. It soon became a thriving standalone truck line carrying much of Peavey's freight as well as taking on third-party contracts.

With suitable fanfare, Peavey entered the drum business with the announcement of its Radial Bridge System. A couple of years earlier, Steven Volpp had met Hartley and showed him his patented idea for a radical new drum design. Volpp explained his ideas in a *Monitor* article, using an acoustic guitar analogy: "Think of the head as the strings, the shell as the soundboard, and the radial bridge as the bridge. With every other drum that's ever been made, what's supposed to be your soundboard has lugs and nuts and bolts through it, and it has to be made very thick because it has to take all that tension. The radial bridge allows everything to be maximized: it gives you a surface you can make perfectly round; it allows you to make clean, sharp bearing edges; it takes all the stress, allowing the shell to be a resonating element."

1994

Volpp's idea, like many great ideas, was simple yet elegant—and Hartley realized he could manufacture the bridges on the same machinery used for routing guitar bodies. He licensed the technology and engaged Volpp to manage the project. These radical new drums were the only ones on the market that had nothing attached to the shells, so the maple shells could be made much thinner (.080") than usual. The result was superior tone, resonance, and volume. Hailed as a radical improvement by many, the Radial Pro drumkits met with a mixed reaction from the traditionally conservative percussion market—but, like many other Peavey products, they pushed the boundaries of technology.

More boundaries were pushed when, after exhaustive development, the transducer division introduced the PVM-835 and PVM-880 Diamond microphones. After reading about amorphous diamond coating in an article about NASA, Hartley met with Mike O'Neill and his engineers to discuss the possibility of using the technique in microphones. Peavey's work on neodymium magnet structures was already advanced, and the company had received a patent (#5,033,093) for its reinforced diaphragms. The use of the superior magnetic material required a larger diaphragm, and the traditional plastic material was simply not stiff enough without reinforcement. But the

▲ *Preparing microphone capsules for assembly*

◄ *RP-1000 Radial Pro drumset*

CHAPTER 12 • FLYING HIGH **127**

▲ The Peavey G-IV aircraft in the Peavey hangar

▲ The luxurious interior of the Peavey G-IV, one of many aircraft Hartley has owned

NASA article gave Hartley a different idea: Concerned about the erosion of solar-cell surfaces by space dust, scientists had discovered a way to coat the surfaces with micro-thin diamond to protect them. Would that work for strengthening a microphone diaphragm, too?

The Peavey team realized that if they could coat their plastic microphone diaphragms with a thin diamond layer, they would have the lightest yet most rigid component imaginable. After many frustrating attempts to perfect the process, they finally succeeded—and introduced the highest-spec neodymium microphones ever brought to market.

Alongside the Diamond project, the T-9000 tube recording microphone was produced, and the speaker line was expanded with a range of DS DJ speakers. Over in Europe, a new AeroSys line of PA enclosures was developed to satisfy the demand for lightweight gigging systems. The 22T driver was upgraded to the 22XT with design enhancements and ferro-fluid added to the coil gap. This new driver was incorporated into upgraded versions of the top-selling SP enclosures bearing the "XT" designation. These developments proved to be Mike O'Neill's swan song, as he left the company in August after 16 years as head of transducer engineering. One of his leading engineers, Tim Tardo, succeeded him.

Amplifier developments included the tweed-clad 100-watt Classic 100 tube head and Classic 112E enclosure for guitar players. Bassists got three new rackmount heads: the DPB (300 watts of digital power), the T-Max (500 watts with one tube and one solid-state channel), and the Kilobass (a concert amp offering two 500-watt channels or 1000 watts bridged).

With respected industry veteran Rich Lasner now in place as product manager for guitars and basses, great strides were made in the development and marketing of several important new products. To meet the challenge of low-cost competitive instruments being made offshore, Hartley set out to partner with a suitable factory in Asia. The Korean company he chose to work with was happy to collaborate with Peavey personnel, and this gave Hartley the confidence to import a range of instruments. Known as PVI (Peavey International Series), the line comprised four models based on traditional solid-body designs: two guitars, the Raptor 1 and 2 (renamed from Falcon), and two basses, the Milestone I and II. They would form the vanguard of the new assault on the guitar market.

Meanwhile, the U.S. guitar factory began to produce a new mid-price series sporting the Impact Firenza, Impact Milano, and Impact Torino names. The Ecoustic ATS was offered with a tremolo arm—quite unusual for an electro-acoustic instrument—and the Midibase was given both improved capabilities as a MIDI controller and better sound as a standard bass guitar and renamed the CyberBass.

Peavey's engineering expertise was once again demonstrated with the introduction of the B-Quad 4 bass (and a matching 5-string, the B-Quad 5). Designed in collaboration with master bassist Brian Bromberg, this striking handcrafted instrument was equipped with both magnetic and piezo pickups and offered tremendous tonal range. To assure stability with both steel and nylon strings in a wide range of gauges and configurations, it had a special 24-fret composite neck made by Modulus Graphite. (Graphite necks are stronger than ones made of wood and not prone to warping from changes in humidity or string tension.) The B-Quad's electronics were highly advanced, with a four-in/two-out stereo mixer built into the preamp to allow control and panning of individual piezo pickups for each string. The high-energy VFL magnetic pickups could be operated independently or blended with the piezos. VFL—Vertical Flux Loading—was a Mike Powers innovation based on placing the magnets between the coils, producing a field that is very efficient. Smaller polepieces mean less iron for less inductance and better high-frequency performance.

Powers worked more pickup magic with a special computer-controlled winding machine based on the same principle as a spinning reel that feeds nylon fishing line at constant tension. "That winder was called a 'Rotowinder,' " Powers explains. "The wire basically spun around the bobbin, and as far as we know we are the only people to ever use it for pickups. It was very, very accurate, and we could wind a coil in less than 30 seconds. Pickups were within a 2 percent tolerance range because the wire wasn't stretched out like on regular winders. Vintage pickups sound unique because of the crude winding techniques used 50 years ago, and we actually designed a winding machine that could vary the wrap so we could do 'old sounding' pickups."

Peavey displayed its first line of acoustic guitars at the 1994 NAMM show. The high heat and humidity of Mississippi summers had long been an obstacle to building acoustic guitars in Meridian. A solution presented itself in the form of the Landola Company of Finland, a small family concern that manufactured acoustic guitars alongside their music distribution activities, which included Peavey products. Keen to expand their business, Landola suggested that they could produce acoustic guitars to be sold under the Peavey brand. With Landola's reputation for building quality instruments and an indigenous supply of top-grade spruce at hand, the collaboration seemed like a good idea. A line of eight models was created, and the dealers went nuts for them. By the end of the show, the orders had far exceeded the anticipated annual demand. Landola attempted to ramp up production, but quality suffered; Peavey was soon rejecting more and more instruments. Landola couldn't supply the 25,000 units on order, and before long the plug was pulled on the entire venture.

Rick Bos, an engineer respected for his innovations and marketing savvy, joined the team from DOD to develop the company's signal-processing products. Rick brought a bevy of ideas to the development group in the mid-'90s, resulting in many innovative new equalizers coming to the market.

Amplifier developments in 1994 included a new Class BG two-rackspace power amp, the VX-1.5K, which offered 1500 watts bridged, and the Class BBG VX-3.0K, which delivered 2800 watts bridged.

At the end of the year, *EQ* magazine named Hartley as one of the recipients of their "People of the Year" award, and Mississippi Educational TV was busy filming their documentary *To Build a Dream* for the Mississippi Masters series. On December 28, Hartley and Melia took delivery of a new Gulfstream G-IV jet airplane. Peavey's flight operations facility at Meridian airport doubled in size to accommodate the aircraft, which took its place alongside the King Air 200 turboprop and Hartley's classic car collection. The Peaveys were also building a new house in Florida, and on the surface the couple appeared to be enjoying the fruits of their considerable labor. But Melia's health was beginning to be a source of great concern. Her migraines were becoming more frequent, and they caused unexpected disruptions to her daily routine. She was unable or unwilling to let go of the details of managing what was now a giant corporation, and her condition was causing considerable stress for the key managers who worked with her—and who closed ranks to protect her.

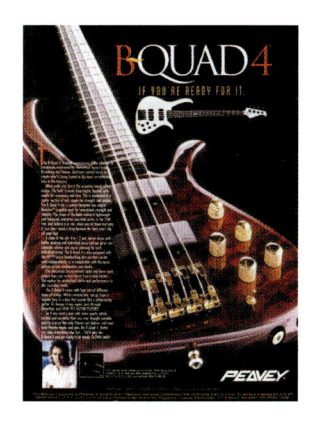

▲ *B-Quad 4 bass guitar*

CHAPTER 13

Letting Go

"We are making good biscuits, and we are not going to change the recipe." —HARTLEY PEAVEY

Peavey celebrated its 30th anniversary in 1995. "Peavey has been here for 30 years," said Hartley, "and the Good Lord willing and with the support of our dealers, we hope to be here for another 30 years. We're making the commitments in technology, facilities—in every way, we're trying to lay the foundation to build on in the future. Frankly, it would be easy to go public, it would be easy to change the recipe that we've developed over

▲ *The EVH Wolfgang*

130   THE PEAVEY REVOLUTION • **PART FIVE** • TRIUMPH AND TRAGEDY

1995

▼ *5150 Twin Combo*

▶ *Hartley featured in an international advertising campaign for Chubb Insurance*

CHAPTER 13 • LETTING GO **131**

the years, but we have a good direction and I believe that it is important that we continue this approach of building the best product we know how to build, to price it fairly, and keeping a relatively stable market structure."

CNN devoted an episode of its "Pinnacle" documentary series to the Peavey story. In the broadcast, the network estimated the company's annual sales at $370 million. Peavey Electronics Corporation has always been a private company, and Hartley would not confirm this number. Whether it was accurate or not, there was no doubt that Peavey had become an industry giant.

Under the direction of Jack Wilson, engineering and marketing were running at full speed and Meridian was bursting with creative developments. Hartley and Melia, the corporate ambassadors, were on the road much of the year, often traveling in the new Gulfstream, and the company participated in no fewer than 50 trade shows during the course of 1995.

At the January NAMM show, center stage was given to the company's bread-and-butter guitar amp line, which had been completely redesigned and given the "TransTube" name. Making the best better has always been a goal at Peavey, and the previous breakthroughs of Saturation and SuperSat had already made the company the industry leader in solid-state emulation of tube performance. But that was not enough to satisfy Jack Sondermeyer and his team of engineers in Meridian.

Although the Bandit was now the world's best-selling guitar amp, the quest continued to ensure it was also the best sounding. The breakthrough came with emulation of the "feel" of

▲ *1995 introduction of TransTube technology*

▲ *TransTube Bandit 112S*

132   THE PEAVEY REVOLUTION • **PART FIVE** • TRIUMPH AND TRAGEDY a tube amp as well as its sound. The combination of redesigned preamp and power amp circuitry plus the new T.Dynamics circuit formed the basis of the TransTube concept. The new power amp design replicated the effect of pushing a tube amp hard so it compresses and "pushes back" at the player—a feeling rather than a sound. And T-Dynamics allowed the user to alter the output of the amplifier from its full 100 watts down to 10 watts without altering the tone. The transformation was completed with an aesthetic overhaul—the aluminum strips were gone, and the amp was given a contemporary new look that complemented its performance.

Virtuoso guitarist Neil Zaza offered a strong testimonial to TransTube performance, describing his "road to Damascus experience" this way: "I had a chance to do a record in Los Angeles with fellow Peavey endorsee Robin DiMaggio, and I thought, This is going to be the best opportunity to get some of the best tones I've ever gotten, because I'm in L.A. at one of the top studios. Because of this I had all my vintage tube gear, boutique amps that cost $3,000 and everything. I had everything shipped out to Los Angeles, and I thought with all this gear and the studio and the players, I'm really going to tread the line with the greatest tone I've ever gotten. In about two hours I realized that even with all the very high-end expensive gear, it wasn't happening at all that day. So I went back into the lounge area where we were watching TV, sat down kind of dejected, kind of thinking what my next game plan is. I started playing and said, 'Why can't it sound like this?' And instantly the light bulb went on and I called the engineer and said, 'Hey, come on, check this out.' He said, 'Yeah, sounds really good.' I had my guitar plugged into a Peavey Envoy 110! He said, 'Let's put a mic on it and see what happens.' It was the greatest guitar tone I had ever had—absolutely amazing! I used it on all the record, and from that point on I was a converted TransTube fanatic."

While Sondermeyer's team was developing the TransTube circuitry, John Roberts was designing the new Feedback Locating System. FLS was granted a patent three years later (#5,737,428), but it was incorporated into Rick Bos's Q-series equalizers immediately. An LED indicator was placed above each slider, and when feedback occurred the indicator over the offending frequency band would illuminate, showing where an adjustment was needed. If two or more feedback nodes were involved, each band would illuminate. The idea, although simple in concept, was a tremendous boon for working musicians, making it quick and easy for them to eliminate feedback in a performance environment.

One of the year's most heralded developments was the introduction of a new signature guitar, the Cropper Classic, developed in collaboration with the legendary Stax guitarist Steve Cropper. Steve tells how it came about:

▲ *Hartley with his brother, Bob Peavey*

▼ *Cropper Classic guitar*

Peavey had a line of guitars called the Generation series. One of Peavey's salesmen [Paul Robinson] had been calling me, trying to get me interested in playing a Peavey. Being a devoted Telecaster fan, I just had not strayed too far. People had talked to me about making another guitar, and I really did not take them seriously. But they brought this guitar by a session one day. We took a break and I said, "Well, I'm going to see what this thing sounds like." I plugged it in and hit it a couple of times. I said, "Wait a minute there." A friend was in the session, and I said, "Play this thing. Does this thing sound as good as I think it does, or is it just fooling me?" He picked it up and said, "Man, this thing feels great. What is this?" I said, "Peavey."

I fell in love with the guitar. It was the best thing I had heard all night long. I said, "That's got to be it. It literally eats every guitar I own." I took it on tour, and I also took my regular guitar that I'd been playing, and before long I switched over. The guitar I'd been playing for years ended up being my backup guitar and the Peavey became my number-one instrument. I've been playing that particular guitar for around 11 years now. And this led us into thinking of making a guitar—one that was even a little more customized than what I was used to playing, especially in the studio and stuff like that. We came up with some ideas of maybe coming out with something a little different than had been done before, and that's how we came up with the way the neck joins the body. We came up with a patent there, which I think is fantastic. It allows you to get a little higher up the neck, and that was one of the questions they brought to me: "Is there anything about guitars that you would change?" I told them, "Yeah, I wish I could play higher up the neck without having to go to a big deep cutaway." And they came up with this idea. You know, for the most part a guitar is nothing more than a piece of wood and six strings, and it's only as good as the guy that's playing it. But to the dedication and quality that Leo Fender started many years ago, Hartley Peavey continues to carry those values to the next level.

▲ *Skid Row's Snake Sabo endorsed the 5150*

As Steve noted, he had been playing his Generation for 11 years. It had been back to the factory several times for refretting and servicing, but he had literally worn it out. Because the Generation was no longer in production, a new instrument was in order—one that would have everything Steve liked about the Generation plus anything from his wish list that could be incorporated. The neck joint he refers to was a heel-less design with a clever joining via an aluminum billet-and-bolt arrangement. The pickups, which were voiced specially for Steve, were a double-blade humbucker at the neck and a quad-blade double humbucker with a coil-tap switch in the bridge position. The top was made from bookmatched flame maple, and the elegant yet functional finished product seemed to sum up the deep mutual respect of musician and maker. The Cropper Classic was another good example of the kind of symbiotic relationship that Peavey sought to have with its endorsers.

Skid Row's Snake Sabo and Jennifer Batten, well known for her work with Michael Jackson, both became Peavey endorsers around this time. Their high-profile usage of 5150 amps onstage offered proof of the top players who were turning to the EVH amp as an accepted professional choice.

1995

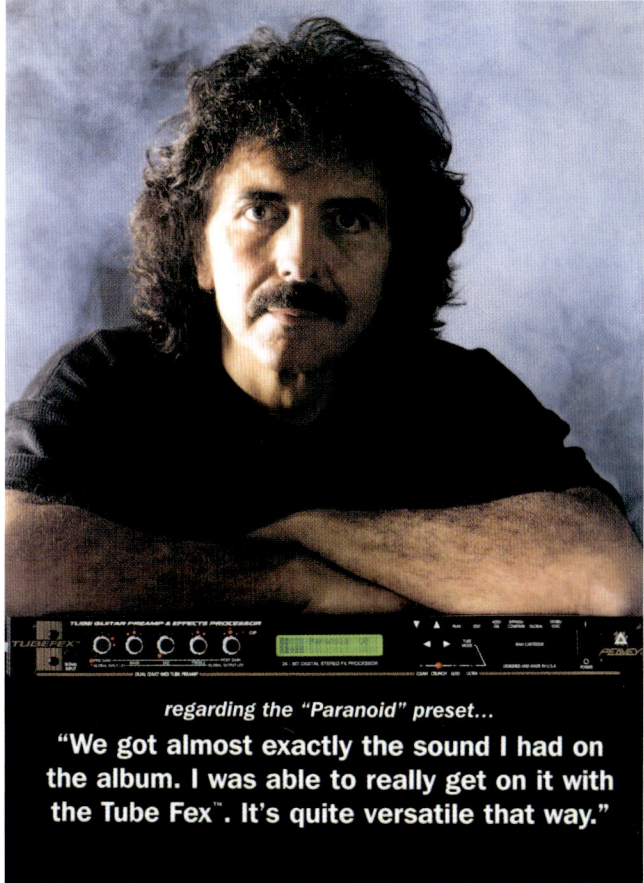

▲ Launch of the EVH 5150 — 212 Combo

▲ Tony Iommi and the TubeFex

Other significant products among the many released this year included the 5150 twin combo and the Ultra Plus tube amps. The three-channel Ultra Plus featured a transparent Peavey logo that changed color—green, orange, or red—to indicate the channel selected. Snake Sabo became an Ultra user, and he said, "I've tried everything, and there's a lot of great stuff out there—but pretty much between the Delta Blues amp, the Classic 50 combo, the 5150s, and the Ultras, I'm set. I really don't need much of anything else."

Rick Bos came up with another great idea in the Tube Fex, a MIDI-programmable tube preamp with 24-bit digital stereo effects processing built in. It found favor with a new set of endorsers who were invited to develop presets to enhance the factory-supplied set. One of these was Black Sabbath's Tony Iommi, who had this to say about the "Paranoid" preset: "We got almost exactly the sound I had on the album. I was able to really get on it with the Tube Fex." The unit was equipped with a RAM-cartridge slot so patches could be stored and retrieved as required, and it could be operated with the PFC-10 foot controller for flexibility in live performance.

Following up on the success of the Spectrum Synth and Spectrum Bass, two new modules were added: the Spectrum Organ, with a large collection of traditional and electronic organ voices, and the Spectrum Analog Synth, which capitalized on the rage for "vintage" Moog and ARP sounds. The DPM-C8P, a more portable and roadworthy version of the 88-note MIDI-controller keyboard, was released, along with the DPM-SP+, a more powerful sample player with competitor compatibility.

The speaker division introduced a molded Impulse 652S model and an upgraded Impulse 6. The powered SP-118P subwoofer was added to the SP line, and all the SP models were now equipped with a high-frequency driver circuit named SoundGuard. Three new Sheffield-loaded cabinets, the 112-SE, 212-SE, and 312-SE were also produced. For the DJ market, the MDG 1150 and 2150 two-way single-unit systems were launched, together with two three-way systems with separate subs, the DJS-1500 and DJS-1800. The DSM-752, also for the mobile DJ market, was a rackmount disco mixer with digital sampling.

There was a clutch of new AMR recording equipment, including a unique 24-channel meter bridge (the subject of yet another patent), the PS-2482 and RSM-2462 consoles, the SDR-20/20+ effects processor, the RPA-500 studio power amp, and video-shielded studio monitors, all of which were aimed at boosting the reputation of the line.

In the midst of all this product-development activity, there was an important change in the executive suite. Bob Wiese, the CFO who had guided the company's finances during an extraordinary decade of growth, left Peavey on May 31, 1995, to become a CFO in the fastener industry.

With the establishment of the pan-European distribution operation, Peavey had outgrown its original building in Corby. So, in October, Plant 18 was relocated to a 68,000-square-foot building

▲ *The European headquarters relocated to this site in 1995*

▼ *MediaMatrix literature from 1996*

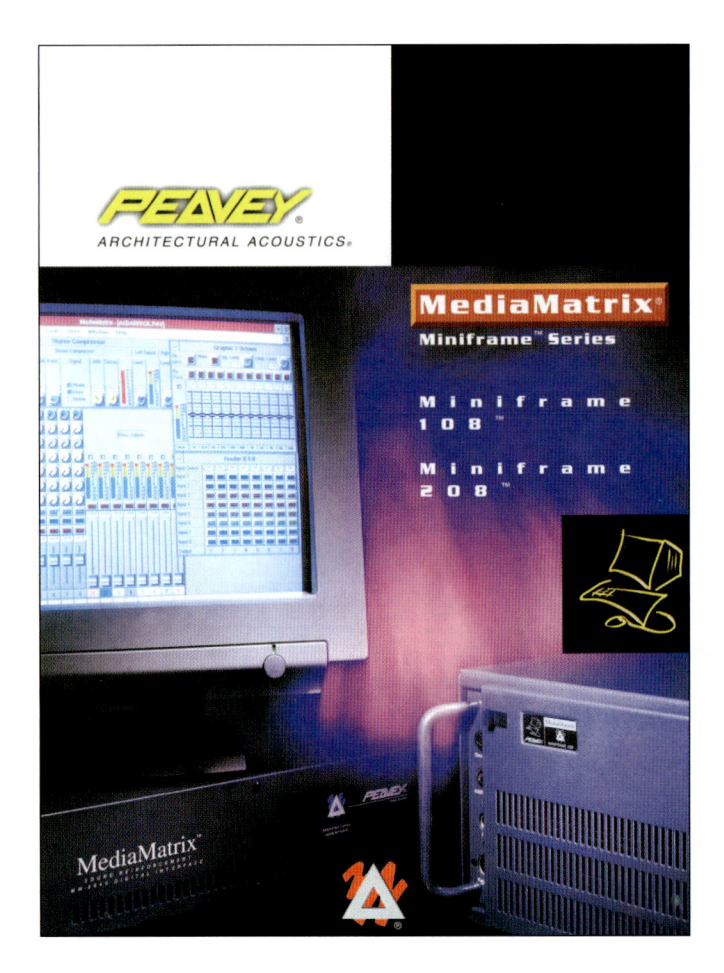

1996

that provided more warehouse space and expanded production facilities. The building was remodeled to match the corporate style of the Meridian headquarters, with the work being directed by Melia when her health allowed her to travel. In a message to the troops in Europe, Hartley reminded them of his philosophy for building the company. "Peavey is one of the most stable companies in the music and sound industry," he stated. "We're not a conglomerate; we're not a part of any big holding company. I own all the stock in the company. The stockholder has never, ever, not one single time, received a dividend. The profits of the company have been plowed back into expansion, back into technology, back into doing all those things to promote the longevity and the stability of the company. Quite honestly, I'm just as selfish as anybody else. I would have liked to have taken that cash and spent it on something else. The important point here is I didn't. I've made a commitment."

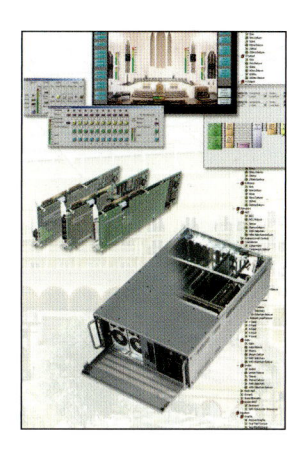

▲ *A sampling of the extensive MediaMatrix product offering*

By the mid-'90s MediaMatrix and Architectural Acoustics had become closely linked divisions, and many new products reflected this relationship. These included a series of IA "intelligent" power amps and the AC-8 interface for their control via MediaMatrix. Two new versions of MediaMatrix were developed to offer a more affordable solution for systems that could be configured on one or two DSP cards; the Miniframe 100 and 200 offered four and eight Motorola 56002 processors, respectively. The MM-A8P eight-channel microphone preamp was designed for easy interface of mics to MediaMatrix, and additional software developments expanded compatibility with other control systems, such as those offered by AMX and Crestron.

The company had attained new heights, but Melia's health was taking a turn for the worse. "Melia began suffering chronic migraine headaches in the late 1980s," Hartley explains, "and they got progressively worse. By the mid-'90s she had become somewhat inactive on a day-to-day basis, but still insisted on being involved in most aspects of management. Her health continued to deteriorate, and—unknown to me at the time—she had become heavily addicted to painkillers. By 1995 or '96, she was spending as much time in hospitals as out, all the while on constant medication."

1996

By 1996 Peavey had reached a new peak in its international activities, shipping almost everywhere in the world—and the statistics were formidable. The outgoing shipments for that year would have filled a football field to a height of almost eight stories. And incoming shipments of parts

◀ *International Sales Team — 1996*

CHAPTER 13 • LETTING GO 137

and materials were running at a level that would have filled 5,500 48-foot containers, the equivalent of 54 miles of trailers laid end to end. It was a long way from the days of the attic amp shop—and Hartley could now be seen gazing out at the business world from the pages of such major magazines as *Business Week*, *Forbes*, and *The Economist*. He was also selected to front an international advertising campaign for Chubb Insurance.

Another national education initiative took Hartley and Melia back to Washington for the launch of "Learn to Work." Peavey, partnering with Mississippi State University, was to prototype an initiative to train teachers to better understand the application of science to the workplace and teach students industrial career skills. Funded by a $1.27 million National Science Foundation grant, a dozen physics teachers completed the first course, spending three weeks inside Peavey facilities and two weeks at the university.

As gratifying as all of this was, Hartley found himself more and more troubled by his wife's condition. "I realized about 1996 that she was in trouble," he says, "so I sent her to the Betty Ford Center to get help. She was so smart that she talked herself out of that institution and convinced me that the folks at Betty Ford agreed that she did not have a problem with painkillers—but she did! She had managed to go to different doctors, who knew nothing about each other, to get prescription painkillers, which she continued to take."

Peavey's momentum was such that activity continued to gather pace despite the increasing incapacity of its president. The strain continued to take its toll on the management team, however. In January, after the NAMM show was over, Jack Wilson resigned as vice president, packed his belongings, and returned to California. It was the end of a two-decade relationship during which the company's marketing edge had been forged.

Peavey had stolen the show at NAMM that year with the launch of the EVH Wolfgang guitar. Appearing in person to introduce the instrument, Edward Van Halen had been a sensation. In the buildup to this event, Hartley and guitar engineer Jim DeCola had been working with Eddie on the next stage in the evolution of his instrument. Impressed by what Peavey had accomplished in creating the 5150 amplifier and recognizing the company's capabilities in guitar manufacturing, Eddie had signed on to work with the Meridian team on a new guitar. Although superficially the instrument was somewhat similar to his previous guitar, there were three major differences: the top was arched, the neck was set at a more comfortable angle, and a unique drop-D tuner had been incorporated into the design. Peavey was also able to demonstrate its experience in pickup design and production, creating custom humbuckers that satisfied Eddie's discriminating ear.

Named "Wolfgang" after Eddie's son, the flagship guitar was offered with a basswood body in solid colors or basswood with a quilted-maple top. Its one-piece neck was bird's-eye maple

▲ *Edward Van Halen and the Wolfgang guitar* — Monitor magazine cover

with a fingerboard carved from the same piece of wood; two graphite inserts were placed on either side of the truss rod for extra strength. The first model was offered with either a Floyd Rose–licensed locking tremolo or a stop tailpiece.

Guitar production was phased out at Plant 2 and shifted to the new facility in Leakesville. The EVH Wolfgang guitar was built in this location along with the rest of the guitar line and the Radial Pro drums. The drum line was extended to three series: the top-of-the-line RP-1000 series featured the original Radial Bridge concept with solid-maple shells, while the RP-750 kits had composite bridges with solid-maple shells and the RP-500 sets had composite bridges and wrapped shells.

The KB/A 100 and KB/A 300 keyboard combo amps were given a fundamental redesign that picked up on the TransTube look, and they were marketed for use in amplifying acoustic instruments as well as keyboards. The sales literature described these units as "basically self-contained, compact sound systems, perfect for voice, keyboards, acoustic and electric guitar, drum machine, and backing machines," and many have been sold over the years to "one-man party entertainers."

On the guitar side, the chorus amps were phased out in favor of completely new FX models: the flagship Stereo TransFex 212 featured a solid-state derivative of the TubeFex MIDI-programmable preamp; the Backstage FX 208S and the StudioFex 210S stereo amps with digital effects completed the line. The Ecoustic 112 launched Peavey's new breed of amplifiers specifically designed for use with acoustic and electro-acoustic guitars (following in the footsteps of the Reno amp of the 1970s). Finally, to fill out the low end of the bass line, Peavey introduced the 200-watt Sessionbass rackmount amp.

More XR-series products appeared this year in the form of the XRD680+ and the XRD680S+ with 600 watts of power in a twin 300+300 and stereo version, respectively. A rackmount version of the Unity 1002-8 mixer addressed the needs of the lower-price mixer market, while the Unity 4034-FC and the SRC-6024/SRC-6032 professional sound-reinforcement consoles were designed to head off some stiff competition in what was traditionally Peavey's fiefdom. The PC-4-XLA four-way digital and MIDI-controllable crossover unit set a new standard of value for professional sound

▶ *Hartley Peavey and Eddie Van Halen create the first working model of the EVH Wolfgang guitar in the summer of 1995.*

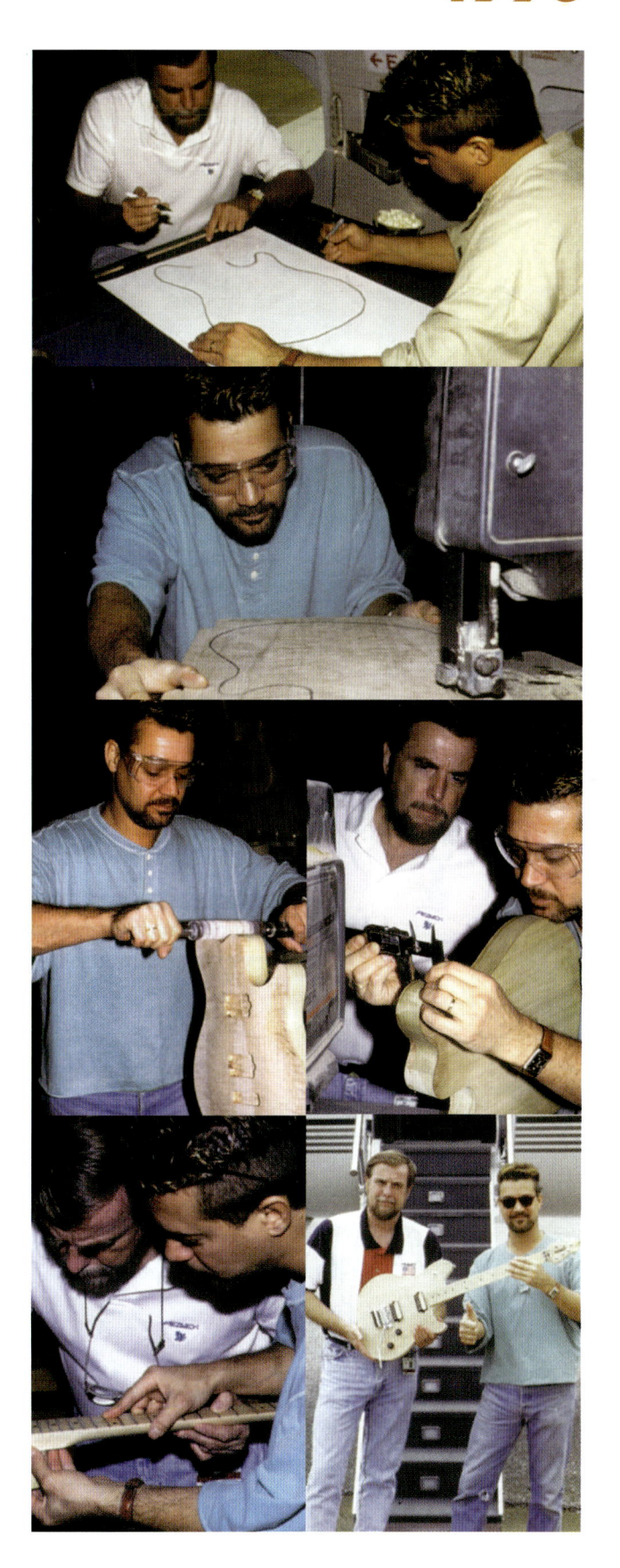

▶ Mixer assembly

gear, and an expanded series of Q equalizers with FLS did the same at the low end. FLS was also offered in two new stereo equalizer monitor power amps, the MAQ-300 and MAQ-600.

Another Sondermeyer-inspired circuit was awarded a patent, this time for the CS-3000G, a Class G power amplifier that was Peavey's biggest yet at 2x1500 watts into 2 ohms.

The Impulse 200 high-performance molded speaker enclosures (also available as the powered Impulse 200P) were launched at the NAMM show. Retailing for about half the price of the competition, these new enclosures were equipped with Black Widow and 22XT drivers and capable of handling 600 watts (program). They were an instant hit—and it quickly became apparent that the customer base for molded enclosures was quite different from that for traditional wood cabinets, the sales of which were unaffected by the newcomers. The Impulse 200 addressed a healthy market for competing products that had been established on a promotion of light weight, good looks, and performance. The new units outperformed and undercut the market leader and immediately started to return the project's substantial tooling costs and investment.

A new line of natural-wood and painted enclosures for churches and other "architecturally sensitive" commercial venues was also introduced. The Impulse 2652 for auditorium side-fills and speech systems was complemented by the HV-1280 and HV-1580 permanent-installation cabinets with flying hardware. The revised "S" series of DTH enclosures offered several permutations of the concert system components and was expanded with the DTH-118 folded-horn subwoofer and an anti-axial 218 subwoofer. In Corby, the new trapezoidal HiSys enclosures were upgraded with the 22XT horn driver and SoundGuard to make their components compatible with the SP series.

By the mid-1990s, the new and upgraded Architectural Acoustics products being introduced reflected Peavey's increasing understanding of this market segment. These included a series of IA power amps with AC-8 interface for amp control via MediaMatrix. These "intelligent" amplifiers were equipped with a module bay designed for upgrading with smart accessories or application-specific modules. For example, the ACI amp-control interface module facilitated amplifier control and monitoring by collecting data and communicating it to MediaMatrix via the AC-8 eight-channel amplifier controller. With this setup, a sound engineer at a remote location could monitor voltage, power, speaker protection activation, impedance, fault status, power status, and audio as well as switching amps on and off via the software. The new MediaMatrix mainframes featured upgraded industrial PC hardware in the 740 and two models in the top-of-the-line 900 series: the 940 and 950 supported up to 256 analog inputs and outputs and up to 32 DSPs for impressive system-configuration possibilities. Two Miniframes, the 108 and 208, offered less powerful but equally flexible solutions, and the following year the X-Frame was offered as a stripped-down two-in/four-out audio tool.

In collaboration with consultants from the movie-sound market, Peavey launched its CinemAcoustics Division. The company's 30 years of experience in power amplifier and speaker innovation translated easily to products designed for cinema use. The THX-approved line included two power amps, a digital cinema processor and monitor, a screen crossover monitor, and a series of specially designed horns, surround speakers, and subwoofers.

▼ *CinemAcoustics Division was created to market products for the cinema industry.*

CHAPTER 13 • LETTING GO **141**

1997

In 1997 Peavey's customers were once again presented with a blitz of new products. One notable innovation was a rackmountable TransFex solid-state preamp processor, derived from the circuit that had been incorporated into the Stereo FX 212 the previous year. It retailed at a significantly lower price point than the Tube Fex that had inspired it. The TransFex Pro amp top also featured this versatile circuit.

The MAX-100 floor processor was another new idea from the seemingly tireless Peavey engineers. Much more than an effects pedal, the MAX-100 was a twin-channel Transtube preamp with 24-bit effects processing that offered factory presets and user-definable patches. Permitting the use of up to six effects simultaneously, this powerful package also had a rotary-speaker effect with speed morphing, a built-in chromatic tuner, CD input, and a headphone jack for practicing.

The 60-watt Ultra 1x12 combo was added to the guitar amp line, and the keyboard combo line was extended with the KB/A-15 and the KB/A-60.

The new top-of-the-line Wolfgang guitar featured a quilted-maple top with a transparent amber or sunburst finish. Relatively few of these were made, as the high-quality quilted maple demanded by Eddie proved difficult to obtain. (They will undoubtedly appreciate in value over time due to their rarity.) Because of the supply problem, the specification was changed in the following year to a bookmatched flame-maple top. The three-a-side peghead design of the Wolfgang was adopted by three new electric guitars, the Firenza, Firenza JX, and Firenza AX, which replaced Peavey's Impact models.

▼ *The Cirrus line of handcrafted professional basses*

It was a good year for bass players, too, as a 6-string version of the Axcelerator Bass was added to the line and the Cirrus basses were introduced. Reflecting the artistry of Mike Powers, these handcrafted basses, along with the Wolfgang guitars, served to propel Peavey's fretted instruments to a new level of respect among professional players. Three years later, in an interview with Steven Volpp in the *Monitor* magazine, session bassist Mike Porcaro had this to say about the Cirrus: "I just love what Mike Powers did. I love neck-through-body basses myself. I have plenty of bolt-ons, but I've always been partial to the [neck-through] sound. Mike just put together a really nice bass. It plays well, it feels well, and it's lighter than a lot of basses out there, which is critical to me. When you're wearing it two hours a night—and I'm not Arnold Schwarzenegger—basses are so much heavier in general than guitars. Guitarists don't know how lucky they've got it. This bass is light. Its sustain, its tone—and I dig the fact that it has some qualities of a custom handmade bass. It's a really nice custom instrument that's in the [price] ballpark for a lot more people." The graphite-reinforced neck-through construction of the 4-, 5-, and 6-string Cirrus basses combined exotic hardwoods with state-of-the-art electronics and featured a 35" scale length. The longer scale, which is believed to improve the sound of the low *B* string, was also featured on the new G-Bass, introduced later in 1997. Its graphite neck was made for Peavey by Modulus (where Rich Lasner had become president after he left Peavey in 1995).

The XR 560 with digital reverb replaced the XR 500C, and the XR 886 was introduced to satisfy the demand for a powered console-style mixer. Two new Unity mixers with stereo line inputs, the Unity 300RQ and Unity 3014RQ, joined the line. Four upper-end mixers were introduced as the SRC (sound reinforcement console) series: the four-bus SRC 4026FC and SRC 4034FC flightcase units, and the six-bus SRC 6024 and SRC 06032 console models. New signal processors included the DeltaFex Twin (two independent stereo effects processors in a single-rack unit) and the Mentor (two 31-band FLS systems in a single-rack unit).

The PV 2000 stereo 2x1000-watt power amp with switchable subwoofer crossover was introduced to replace the PV 1.3K; subsequently, the other two amps in the PV line were replaced by the new PV 500 and PV 1200. Two more new stereo power amps were introduced, the DPC 1200X digital unit and the CS 800S. The latter was a completely new design with a Sondermeyer-inspired patented damping-factor circuit that compensated for amplifier output. With its smart high-frequency power supply and resulting reduced size and weight, the CS 800S had a radically different look from its CS partners. In an unusual move (and one that caused uncharacteristic confusion in the marketplace), the popular CS 800X was retained in the line and allowed to compete with the CS 800S, its heir apparent.

The transducer department rolled out the new TL line of lightweight packaged-PA enclosures and extended the SP series with the SP 1G (with 44T driver), SP 3G, and SP 6G. The importance of the church market was acknowledged by the addition of three new models with ivory paint finish and matching grille cloth: the 115TF (a two-way system with flying points) and the matching 112CM and 115CM (wedge monitor enclosures).

The diamond-coated microphone diaphragm technology was made accessible at a lower price point with the introduction of the PVM 22 microphone. The neodymium magnetics combined with the superior integrity of the diaphragm and a new suspension system gave the PVM 22 electret-level performance in a low-noise, handheld dynamic mic package that was greeted with strong market acceptance.

The PC 1600X upgrade was released in 1997 and became even more popular as the MIDI command station and editor of choice for many musicians and sound engineers. The new model was supported by Pro Tools, which made it an instant favorite in the studio.

Four years after its introduction, MediaMatrix was starting to show the full power of its capabilities and, as a result, was gaining more acceptance in the world of sound reinforcement. Such famous venues as the Sydney Opera House, the Hawaii Convention Center, Seattle's St. James Cathedral,

▲ *PVM-22 microphone*

▲ *Hartley with fellow Mississippi native Jimmy Buffet*

▼ *PC 1600X MIDI controller*

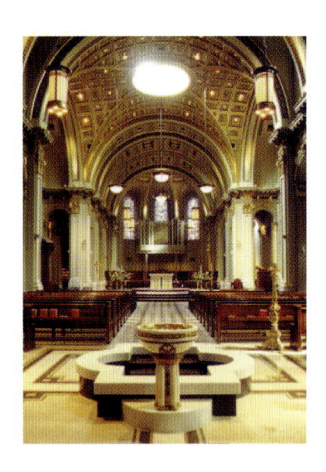

MediaMatrix is hard at work behind the stunning architecture of St. James Cathedral

Disney World, and the Edinburgh International Airport had embraced its innovative technology. As the cost of memory fell and the power of PCs increased, the Miniframes were updated to 108 and 208 designations, doubling their channel capacities. The 940 and 950 Mainframes were also upgraded in power and performance, with load-sharing redundant power supplies. The 950 also incorporated the RAID hard-disk monitoring system. When the X-Frame was announced as a rack-mount-box version of MediaMatrix for use with an external PC running Windows 95, the flexibility offered by the mainframe units and an extensive devices library became available in an easy-to-use package for smaller system applications.

Even as the company flourished, there was increasing concern about Melia Peavey's condition. Communication with her had become increasingly difficult as her illness worsened, and her hospitalizations were becoming more frequent. More and more, Hartley was carrying the burden. Things reached a critical point in November. "I came home from work late one night and found her incoherent," he recalls. "I told her that I had had enough, and that she was going to get help."

Despite the gathering clouds, Melia was still a highly visible and much-revered figure. In December, a surprise celebration was held at the Silver Star casino in Philadelphia, Mississippi, to mark her 25th anniversary with the company. A spectacular gala, it was a formidable display of the organizational skills of the company's special events team and master-of-ceremonies Jere Hess (director of public relations at the time), who had ensured the element of surprise. As Melia walked into a ballroom filled with hundreds of dignitaries, friends, colleagues, employees, customers, distributors, and vendors, her pleasure was evident—but so was her physical deterioration. It would prove to be the last significant company event she would attend.

1998

Determined to help Melia overcome her dependence on medication, Hartley made a decision. "I arranged for her to go to Hazeldon clinic in Jacksonville in January 1998," he says. "Over the Christmas/New Year holiday, she developed pleurisy [a severe irritation of the lining of the chest]. I took her to the hospital and asked her physicians not to prescribe any painkillers for her, since I didn't know whether this situation was real or just another ploy to get more medication. She was in the hospital for nearly three weeks during which time she was given no painkillers of any kind—she went 'cold turkey.' When she got out of the hospital in the third week of January, she had already gone though the trauma of withdrawal and acted almost like her old self. I was extremely thankful that, after many years, I finally had my wife back. For the next five weeks Melia was back to her old self—she was cheerful, came to work every day, and enjoyed every minute of it."

On March 6, 1998, the European team was building the display for the Frankfurt Musik Messe in Germany when the news broke that Melia had been taken to Meridian's Rush Foundation Hospital and was in a coma. Hartley recounts the events of March 6 and 7:

> Late in the afternoon Melia had gone to the dentist, and she called me at six o'clock to see when I was coming home. I was writing a letter to Ed Van Halen regarding the 5150. Somebody had told him that an amp with only one input jack sounded better than an amp with two input jacks. I was trying to explain

to him that this was BS, and I finished the letter about 6:30 p.m. I got home about 10 minutes later and found the house completely dark. This was not unusual because Melia slept most of the time during the day and into the evening. She usually stayed up all night—I would go to bed about 12 o'clock and she would come to bed at 6 or 7 a.m. and then sleep all day. We had become like two ships passing each other, going in opposite directions in the evening and in the morning.

I called out Melia's name repeatedly, with no response. I thought she was asleep in the bed, but she wasn't there. I noticed that there was light from the crack under the bathroom door, and I thought she might be in there. I knocked on the door and asked her to open it—no response. There was something about this that really pissed me off, and I remember being overcome with the feeling that I simply wanted to kick down the door if she didn't answer me. I even said that if she didn't open the door I was going to do just that—again, no response. Just then I remembered that the door to the bathroom had a small hole in the center of the doorknob that would disengage the lock if you put a small rod in the hole and pushed. I took apart a ballpoint pen and used the refill to open the door.

When I walked into the bathroom, Melia was lying there face down. My first thought was, Oh hell, she's passed out. When I rolled her over I was absolutely shaken to the core because her eyes were open and her face was blue. My thought was, My God, she's dead—what can I do? I immediately started CPR, and I got a small flush back to her face. I called 911 from the phone in the bathroom. It seemed like almost instantaneously that the paramedics were there with their equipment, and of course they made me leave the bathroom while they worked on her. I heard one of them say that they had a heartbeat, and I thought, Thank God, we have saved her. Sadly, that was only temporary.

She was taken to the emergency room at Rush medical center, and she was in there for quite a while. It seemed like hours to me. Finally they took her to intensive care, where she was being respirated artificially. At about 10:30 p.m. they did a CT scan of her brain, which showed massive damage. Then it hit me—Melia and I had agreed that if either of us got into the condition that we

> *"I want to do something to try and help make the world a better place."* —MELIA PEAVEY

▲ *Melia Peavey, August 18, 1954 – March 7, 1998*

would have to be kept alive by machine, the survivor would authorize "pulling the plug." As I contemplated the thought of having to make that decision after the trauma of the last few hours, I became physically ill. By 3:00 a.m. I was a total basket case, and I went back home to try to get some sleep. Both of my parents were getting up into their mid-eighties, so I did not tell them about Melia until early Saturday morning. While I was at my parents' house, I got a call from the hospital telling me that Melia had died. I felt awful because the second time she died I was not there, just as the first. This probably was the single most traumatic event in my life."

Melia Peavey died of cardiac arrest at 8:04 a.m. on March 7, 1998. She was just 43 years old. At her funeral, Hartley offered this tribute: "Melia began her career at Peavey in 1972 at the very young age of 17. Her knowledge of the world of business and especially the music industry grew by leaps and bounds. She had a profound impact on the company and deserves a huge amount of credit for its success. Beyond credit for her mastery of functions of the business, she is responsible for the major support that Peavey gives to the whole field of education and was the heart of the movement to protect and care for abused and neglected children. But more important than all of that, she was the light of my life and will always be the wind beneath my wings."

Melia lived by the Golden Rule: Do unto others as you would have them do unto you. Despite her success as a prominent businesswoman and her many awards and tributes, her thoughts were always for others. Although she was a shrewd negotiator, her steely resolve was accompanied by compassion and a belief in fairness. By the time she died, the company she had helped Hartley to build employed about 2,200 workers and was operating 33 separate facilities around the world.

"Melia and I were a very good team for a while," Hartley reflects. "In the early part of our relationship, she and I were like two peas in a pod. What happened to Melia was living proof of that old adage that if you don't have your health, you don't have anything. Melia burned out—and the company can do that to you! I fight it every day. No matter what you do, it isn't good enough."

Four days after Melia's death, Hartley said this in a memo to his employees: "The only way I know how to cope with all of this is to roll up my sleeves and get back to work. So starting Tuesday morning I did just that. Now I am asking all of you to focus on making 1998 the best year in the history of this company. Personally I feel it will be a tribute to Melia and her memory to do exactly that!"

At the time, Jere Hess said, "If I was the competition I'd be scared to death right now. He's going to work twice as hard, and he's going to make us twice as competitive as we are today."

PART SIX

After Melia

CHAPTER 14
Turbulence

> "To know what is to come, you have to know what's been."
>
> —HARTLEY PEAVEY

▲ The DTH S/SF pro touring flying enclosures

◂ Peavey's "Radial Bridge system" for drums and TransTube technology are touted in these 1998 Monitor magazine ads

Realizing that it would be impossible to replace Melia with one person, Hartley set about creating a new management team. At the beginning of May 1998, he announced the appointment of Walter Lutz as chief operating officer and named Chuck Tillet director of manufacturing and Paul Jernigan director of marketing. The company was about to go through some radical changes. Hartley explains:

48 THE PEAVEY REVOLUTION • PART SIX • AFTER MELIA

1998

▶ *RQ Series mixers*

▶ *The EVH Wolfgang was offered with a variety of options.*

▲ *A black-tweed-covered Classic 50/212*

CHAPTER 14 • TURBULENCE **149**

▲ *Christmas at the Peavey's: Back Row, L to R: Hartley Peavey, his nephew Daniel (Bob's son) and brother Bob; Center Row, L to R: Marc Peavey, J.B. and Sarah Peavey, Hartley's Aunt Anna Belle Boyd; Front Row, L to R: Joe Peavey with wife Jennifer and Deanna (Bob's daughter)*

Melia and I had been together for 21 years, and I was deeply depressed, to say the least. I had to adjust to a whole new set of realities. The company was also in shock. Melia had been so much a part of what was going on in the company, but everybody knew that she was not well. The company had suffered because even though Melia was not able to perform her duties, she insisted that she continue to be involved. Before her death, I had to make many decisions simply because she was not available to make them. This caused considerable strife between us, but I could not let the company go down simply because she was essentially an invalid. After Melia's death I kind of zoned out for about six months or so. I spent quite a bit of time at my house in Palm Beach. I felt that I was somehow "floating." Peavey was my baby, but in some ways I wanted to leave it—yet I knew that I couldn't walk off from what had been the center of my life for so long. So I decided to take another long look at things, to kind of back off and maybe try to restart my life all over.

Peavey began to operate on "autopilot" as Hartley deliberated on the company's future. Even in these difficult days, though, notable new products continued to appear, including a lower-cost Wolfgang Special guitar, with a flat rather than arched top, and a lot of new amps. These included the all-tube Ultra 212 and 410 and Ranger 212 guitar amps, the 700-watt Firebass head, and the KB/A-30 keyboard amp, with a unique four-channel bi-amped 40/10-watt power amp configuration driving a coaxial 10" speaker and a 1" ferro-fluid dome tweeter. For steel players, there were two new digital-powered combos, the Session 2000 and the Nashville 1000, with programmable digital effects.

New additions to the PA line included the XR 684, which updated the XR 600 concept and proved to be a highly successful mixer amp, plus the XR 2012 and MP-5+. The front end of the XR 886 was released as the unpowered RQ 880 mixer. The Unity 1002 and 2002 were upgraded and re-tagged with the "RQ" prefix. The SRC-4018 console and SRM-2410 monitor board were also added to the line. Recognizing the shift from vinyl to CD in mobile DJ applications, Peavey responded with two new DJ mixers, the CD-Mix 7 and the CD-Mix 9. FLS was added to the EQ 31 and EQ 215, which became the EQ 31FX and EQ 215FX. The DPC 1400X digital power amp was upgraded to 1400 watts and full export certification.

The Impulse molded speaker line was extended with the introduction of the Impulse 500 and the Impulse 200 matching subwoofer. A new commercial paint finish was applied to the revised DTH 4000 series of concert enclosures. In Europe, the EuroSys line got trapezoidal enclosures and the EuroSys-500 Scorpion-equipped two-way system was launched.

As Hartley pondered his future, the new management team settled in—and the hitherto "family" culture of the company began to change, sometimes to the consternation of the employees. One major change was the implementation of a strict budgeting regimen. To Melia, a budget had been a "license to spend money," a concept that did not fit well with her management style. Through three decades of phenomenal growth, financial control had rested entirely with the Peaveys and their CFO. That was changing, and now there was rigorous scrutiny of all expenditures and appraisal of all processes and procedures. In effect, the company was entering a two-year phase of changing much of what had made Peavey a unique and imposing corporate alternative.

1999

The new management began to look for growth in other directions, including acquisitions. Within six months, negotiations had commenced to buy one of the professional sound industry's most respected manufacturers, Crest Audio. A producer of power amplifiers and mixing consoles for the concert and touring sector, this New Jersey–based operation became part of Peavey on October 21, 1998. (This book will not attempt to catalogue the Crest products or document the relationship between the brands other than to note that Crest has remained a standalone operation.)

Peavey's engineering progress included ongoing development of the MediaMatrix software, which was moved to the Windows NT operating system and enhanced with the introduction of PageMatrix. Working with MediaMatrix, PageMatrix was designed to meet the paging needs of multi-zone installations such as airport terminals, theme parks, and convention centers. Various microphone paging stations were offered, together with a paging controller that established RS-485 communications and line-level audio via software for MediaMatrix control.

▲ *Crest Audio became part of Peavey in October, 1998*

1999

The new year brought more heartache for Hartley. On January 21, 1999, his mother—who had comforted him after the loss of his wife only a few months before—died at the age of 83. And then, just over six weeks later, his 86-year-old father died, too. J.B. "Mutt" Peavey had been with Hartley every step of the way, from the attic days when he helped him to find vendors and kept the books through the years of phenomenal growth and international success. In the beginning, he had been as skeptical as anyone about his son's "crazy venture," but as soon as he saw the determination with which Hartley was proceeding, he became his solid rock. It is probable that Hartley was driven in his business life at least partially by a need to prove to his father that he had learned from him the value of a dollar and the virtue of a job well done.

While Hartley was dealing with his grief and trying to put his life back together, the management team he had put in place was busy changing and reorganizing the company. Melia's loosening grip during the last few years of her life had caused problems in manufacturing, but she had refused to delegate responsibility. Things were drifting—and there was much to do to stop the drift.

The shock waves generated by the new management style were being felt throughout the company, and many long-serving stalwarts found it impossible to deal with new levels of responsibility. There was significant staff turnover, and some members of the management team were viewed with suspicion as they attempted to implement new ideas on a conservative workforce. It was, Hartley ruefully admits, "a dark period."

One bright spot was a celebration in May that marked Peavey's 25th anniversary of European distribution. Bjarne Christensen (Norway) and the author (U.K.) were honored as original and continuous managers of the brand in their countries, along with many long-serving employees and long-standing customers. The event celebrated the family spirit within a company that had successfully transcended countries and continents to become a truly global brand.

The continuing growth of the company combined with Y2K fears had set planning in motion for a new computer system. The IBM mainframe that had been so proudly installed and expanded in the 1980s and early '90s had outlived its usefulness, and a $27 million investment was made

▲ *J.B. and Sarah Peavey*

in implementing its BAAN software replacement. Before long, the entire company—still reeling from tragedy and the management changeover—was either in training or engaged in bringing the project to a conclusion. In the summer of 1999, the old system was shut down and the new one turned on—and computer chaos resulted. A painful period of lost shipments and disrupted procedures followed, and it is a testament to the inherent strength of the company that it survived.

Understandably, the new product launches for the year were somewhat muted. One of the most important developments was the expansion of offshore production. In an effort to get back into the acoustic guitar market, instruments were brought in from the Far East and launched as the Delta Series. In recognition of the musical heritage of Mississippi, the first three models were named after the towns of Clarksdale, Indianola, and Tupelo, all of which were home to musicians who were integral to America's music history. Further offshore production was heralded by the Predator Plus guitar, while an upgraded Fury II and G-Bass 5-string were produced in the American factory.

New guitar amps included the Prowler, a 45-watt all-tube combo, the three-channel Revolution 112 combo, and the TransChorus 210. A black tweed covering material was offered as an option to beige tweed on the Classic 30 and Classic 50/212, as well as on a new 210 version of the Delta Blues.

The main preoccupation throughout the year was bringing the 5150 II amp to market. When the 5150 combo was in development, Peavey's engineers had designed it to have a "tightness" to the attack on the lead channel. As an experiment, they modified a 5150 head with this tweak, but Eddie did not like it and it was abandoned. Then, during the recording of the *Van Halen III* album, he experimented with all his guitars and amps in an effort to perfect the sound he wanted. One amp stood out in the studio, he reported—and it turned out to be the modified head that he had previously rejected. With that as the starting point, Eddie and the engineers set to work on what would become the 5150 II. A second set of resonance and presence controls was added, and the channel levels were also modified.

Another example of Peavey's expansion was the RQ-200, the first product from what would be a significant partnership with a factory in China. A low-cost yet high-spec compact mixer, this board offered six channels, battery operation, and studio quality. It hit the ground running, signaling a significant return to success in the mass mixer market. The 3D Mix Pro DJ mixer also appeared, and in PA there were the new XR 600F and XR 1204.

Top musicians were still playing an important part in Peavey's promotion, including Nate Mendel of the Foo Fighters. "We were in rehearsals for the new record," he told *Monitor*, "and the rehearsal facilities in Virginia had a Peavey bass rig. It was amazing. It was super loud and crisp, and it was everything I wanted. So I got it into my head to call Peavey and see if we could work out a way to get a rig. Now I use it and people comment on it all the time." More kudos came from David Ellefson, who appeared with Neil Zaza and Steve Cropper in a promotional video and said, "I use the Peavey Kilobass and two to four 8x10 cabinets. I started using it in the fall of 1996, and I've been using it ever since. . . . I've had Peavey with me now for going on four years, and it's been bounced around every possible truck and train, airplane and shipyard, every possible concert venue around the world—and the stuff is just holding up great. Aside from it being loud and powerful, which is important for a musician like myself being in a band like Megadeth, it has great tone. I can get all of the highs, I can get all of the lows, and one of the best things about it is—and this

▲ *Hartley Peavey and golf legend Jack Nicklaus share a laugh during a press conference*

◀ *EVH 5150 II amplifier*

is probably true for any bass player out there that plays in a loud hard-rock band—the stuff is powerful and it pisses off the guitar player!"

The first of several collaborative products was introduced at that year's NAMM show. StudioMix combined a hardware mixing interface manufactured by Peavey with recording software from Cakewalk. It was an example of Hartley's belief in symbiotic relationships between non-competing entities, where joint product development and shared technologies could come together and benefit both parties. This idea came to the attention of Daniele Galanti at Generalmusic (GEM) in Italy, leading to another collaborative venture. As a keyboard manufacturer, GEM had signal-processing technology that was of interest to Peavey, and Peavey had production technology of interest to GEM. Furthermore, both companies needed distribution in each other's market. Galanti discussed the situation with Hartley, and as a result Peavey commenced distribution of GEM performance keyboards in the U.S. and U.K., and Generalmusic became Peavey's distributor in Italy.

MediaMatrix developments centered on Peak Audio's CobraNet digital audio-transport system, and the latest software reflected support for new devices associated with it. The CobraNet Audio Bridges—designated CAB-8o and CAB-8i—were CobraNet-compatible equivalents to the original break-out boxes, and a DSP-CN card was developed to harness the new technology.

For Hartley, a new beginning dawned after a chance encounter with a young lady in Texas named Mary Gray. "Fate plays a part in all of our lives," says Hartley. "I experienced what had to be fate when I met the woman who is today Mary Peavey."

Mary remembers their first meeting, where a mutual friend in the music business introduced them. "Hartley was departing for a business trip. He was charming, but he seemed preoccupied and was literally dashing out the door. I didn't expect much of a follow-up, but he did say he had an engineering office in Dallas and he would 'give me a shout' the next time he went over there. Well, he must have been more observant than I realized, since the next week he hunted me down where I was visiting my mother in Mississippi, saying that he would be coming to Dallas that week on business, and 'how about dinner?'"

Whether it was love at first sight, one cannot say, but they clicked—and for obvious reasons. They grew up in relative proximity to each other in Mississippi, and they graduated from the same university although their paths never crossed; Mary went on to study at the Harvard Business

Mary Peavey

School and moved to Dallas where she had a very successful real estate business. They share a similar drive and energy, and both have always been actively engaged in business, community, politics, and the arts. Both are high achievers.

Mary reflects, "When I think of what we have in common and what gives us such strength in business, I realize that many of our decisions are made from a similar set of experiences. We think alike on politics, religion, and values; our sense of self-worth and purpose are uncannily similar. Hartley says 'love is based on respect.' We do have a genuine respect for each other. I can honestly say that there's never a dull moment. Hartley keeps me laughing, keeps me on my toes, and gives me that marvelous, precious opportunity to 'make a difference' every day!"

Today, Mary Peavey is President of Peavey Holding Company, the umbrella of Peavey Electronics Corporation and other family business entities, where she interfaces daily with a group of outstanding leaders within the company who have their eye steadily on the future. Mary's past experiences and general business acumen equip her to handle many of the financial and legal issues relating to the company's diverse endeavors, and she meets regularly with Hartley's trusted general counsel, Sandy Sandusky—who serves on the company's executive board along with Hartley, Mary, and her son, Peavey's Executive Vice President, Courtland Gray.

2000

As the new century commenced, yet another patent was on the way for a Peavey engineering innovation. Work by Jack Sondermeyer, John Roberts, and Ronnie Goss had led to a breakthrough in power amp design with the invention of a new cooling structure called V-Cooling. The heat sinks were laid out at angles to increase heat transfer toward the outlet end of the heat tunnel, significantly improving performance. V-Cooling was incorporated into both Crest and Peavey power amps, including the new GPS series.

By the summer of 2000, Hartley was returning to form, with the new love in his life giving him astute business support. They concluded that the restructuring of the company after Melia's death had done little to restore its production efficiencies, but much to unsettle its workforce. Re-energized,

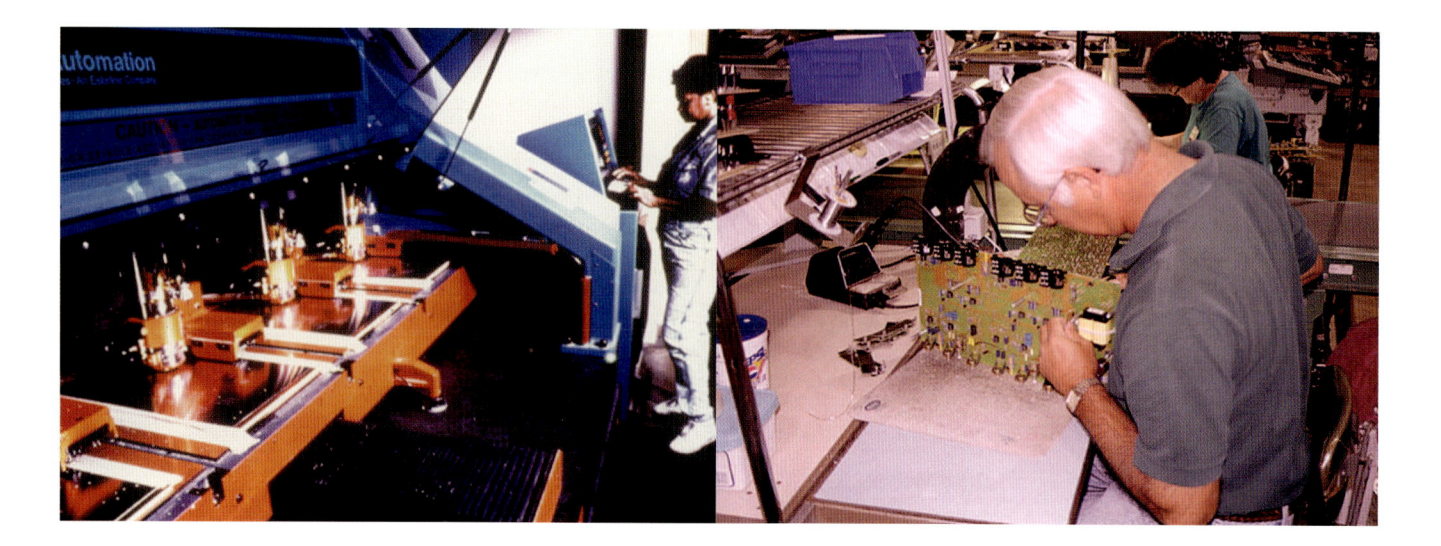

Circuit-board processing

2000

▼ *Two examples of the EVH Wolfgang line*

Hartley cleared the deck and returned to full-time hands-on management of his company. He hired a new CFO, Mark Kuchenrither, and authorized an immediate investment of $3.6 million in new insertion machinery to restore Decatur to maximum efficiency and clear up a bottleneck in circuit-board production. Product management was revitalized, and new production and scheduling managers were hired.

Under the aegis of Bill Xavier, product manager for guitar and amplifier products, the output of guitars, basses, and instrument amps blossomed. The new Millennium basses were introduced to mark the arrival of the 21st century. Built to exacting standards, these professional-quality instruments were offered in 4- and 5-string models with 35"-scale, bolt-on necks featuring graphite reinforcement and rosewood or maple fingerboards. Their twin VFL pickups were married to active electronics with three-band EQ including variable midrange. The Peavey-exclusive Quadrajust bridge made by Hipshot allowed for lateral, vertical, and horizontal string adjustment and either tailpiece or string-through-body anchorage. The Millennium Plus was dressed up with a bookmatched AAA-quality flame-maple top on the alder body and a Hipshot D-tuner. And there were no fewer than 17 color options.

▲ *The Sydney Opera House in Australia utilizes a Media-Matrix system*

The Foundation Bass was revamped as the 2000 Series, with a new body design and metallic colors. A new Fury series, with flame-maple-topped agathis bodies and active electronics, appeared in more affordable 4-, 5-, and 6-string models. A flame-top version of the Wolfgang Special was unveiled at the NAMM show, along with a new premium guitar to be known as the Limited. The offshore factories were producing more fine-quality middle- and lower-priced instruments such as the expanded Predator Plus series, which included a 7-string model and the twin-humbucking HB. And the Raptor Plus and TK offered new styles for the entry-level market.

Peavey entered the modeling amp market with the Transformer. Available as a 50-watt 1x12 or a stereo 50+50 twin, the Transformer was much more than a "me too" unit content to simulate the characteristics of a few well-known amplifiers. Its circuitry allowed the user to transform the preamp and power amp stages to match the characteristics of just about any guitar amp, and its front-panel design featured an innovative WYSIWYG (What You See Is What You Get) control indicator: the knob settings were indicated by a ring of LEDs, so any program called up included the position of every knob when it was stored.

As noted, Hartley had been reluctant to have products made offshore, but the success of the

Rage and Blazer since their transfer to the China factory and the overall quality of the guitars being produced in the Far East convinced him to agree to the expansion of this enterprise. His caveats were—and remain—that the products would be designed by Peavey engineers and production quality supervised by his own people. It wasn't long before the products were coming thick and fast from overseas. TransTube amps, mixers, and packaged-PA powered mixers led the charge, with new guitar, bass, and drum models reasserting Peavey's position in entry-level markets. The RQ mixers from China featured such market-driven expectations as sweepable mids, mute, and PFL—features that would normally be found only on more expensive units.

The rapid acceptance of MediaMatrix and PageMatrix continued. International airports such as London's Heathrow, Sydney, and Madrid followed the lead of many U.S. airports in specifying the paging system, and concert halls from China's Nan-Jing Cultural Arts Center to Manchester's Bridgewater Hall in the U.K. and New York's Carnegie Hall adopted MediaMatrix. It could also be found at such major sporting venues as London's Wembley Stadium, the Olympic Stadium in Athens, the Las Vegas Motor Speedway, and the New Orleans Superdome.

On December 1, 2000, Hartley and Mary were married, and she was subsequently appointed president of the company. "Mary has become not only my wife and business partner but also my closest friend and confidant," says Hartley. "Thank God for her."

▲ *Predator Plus-7 7-string electric guitar*

▲ *Hartley and Mary celebrating their first Christmas together*

156 THE PEAVEY REVOLUTION • **PART SIX** • AFTER MELIA

CHAPTER 15

Renaissance

2001

> *"Finish each day and be done with it. You have done what you could; some blunders and absurdities have crept in; forget them as soon as you can. Tomorrow is a new day; you shall begin it serenely and with too high a spirit to be encumbered with your old nonsense."*
>
> —RALPH WALDO EMERSON

▼ *Triple XXX amplifier*

▲ *HP Signature USA Custom guitar in tiger-eye*

With Hartley now firmly back in control, the spirit of "can do" and the emphasis on product development that had driven the company forward for so many years were fully restored. This could be seen in many ways, including the launching of a new signal processor called KOSMOS, which generated three patents. A low-frequency and stereo-image enhancement device, KOSMOS worked well in live, repro-

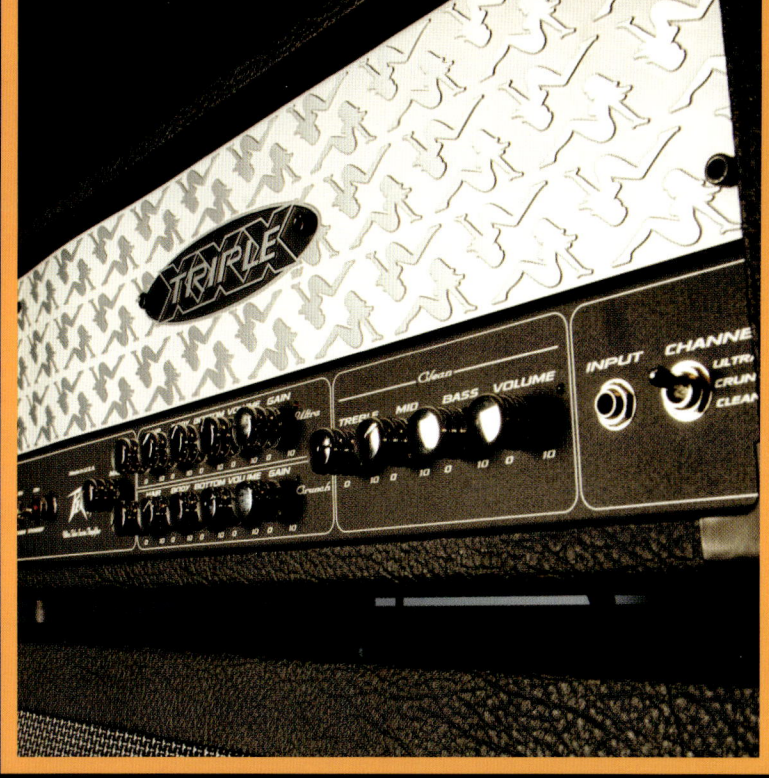

▲ *Making a point*

duced-sound, and recording-studio environments. The Feedback Ferret was another innovation, touted as a once-and-for-all solution to feedback problems. With FLS incorporated into many Peavey products, locating feedback was by now taken for granted. The simple but highly effective Feedback Ferret went a step further, not only locating feedback but eliminating it by cleverly applying narrow notch filters at the offending frequencies. Its 16 digital filters constantly swept for feedback nodes, filtering them when feedback was about to occur and disengaging the filters when it subsided.

The new instruments introduced at the 2001 NAMM show reflected the consistency of quality at both the U.S. and Far East factories. Several models, including the Limited ST and HB, were now offered as both premium American-made instruments and lower-cost EXP versions built offshore. Production of the the Fury flame-top basses was moved overseas, and a passive version of these instruments, reviving the DynaBass name, was produced for the European market.

Peavey's productive endorsement relationship with Dweezil Zappa had led to numerous successful seminars and promotions, and it now yielded the development of a unique amplifier. The Wiggy debuted with the coolest retro looks and the most unusual sounds imaginable, all rolled up into a 100-watt solid-state package. Its '50s Chevrolet dashboard–inspired control panel and automotive control designations belied its ultra-modern sonic capabilities, developed to make the most of Dweezil's inventive playing style.

The Triple XXX head brought the three-channel Ultra line up to date with a contemporary look and continued electronic enhancement. It had four 12AX7 tubes in its preamp stage and offered the switchable option of utilizing either EL-34 or 6L6GC power tubes. This concept would be expanded in the following two years with a lineup of matching enclosures and combo derivatives. Ironically, perhaps, even after years of developing and patenting highly successful tube-emulation circuitry, Peavey retained a market-leading position as a manufacturer of tube amplifiers.

Continuing the innovative approach Peavey had taken with the Transformer, in 2001 the company announced the BAM, the world's first bass-specific modeling amp. Initially offered as a 2x12 combo and subsequently as a 500-watt head, the BAM incorporated Peavey's engineering leadership in both bass amps and modeling technology.

Spearheading the resurgence of Peavey's fortunes in the portable PA market, the Escort 2000 offered a truly portable foldaway system with everything needed for great plug-and-play performance. The molded stand-mounted speakers clipped to the powered mixer amplifier to make an easily transported package that quickly became one of Peavey's most popular products ever. A completely redesigned PV Series of economy power amps, Impulse 1000 series molded speakers, and QW concert speaker systems rounded out the effort.

In April 2001, Hartley was inducted into the Mississippi Musicians Hall of Fame in Jackson, joining such great native sons as Muddy Waters, John Lee Hooker, Mose Allison, Charley Pride, Conway Twitty, and Jerry Lee Lewis. Four months later, he presented a check for $86,353 to the Peavey House. Every year since he and Melia had established the "Cash for Kids" program, the company had donated a portion of its proceeds from cable sales to help neglected and abused children—and this year's sum was a record amount.

CobraNet continued to transform MediaMatrix, as the new flexibility of system distribution using CAT 5 wiring was recognized and new products were developed to utilize it. The Mainframes were upgraded with more powerful industrial PC platforms to the 980nt and 960nt, both supporting

▲ *The Peavey display in the Mississippi Musicians Hall of Fame*

2002

◄ *Wiggy amplifier*

up to eight of the new CobraNet DPU cards, and the 760nt, supporting four. Completely new two-rackspace Miniframes, bundled with Windows 2000 software, replaced the originals. The MM-8802 replaced the original break-out boxes, and the X-Bridge provided a CobraNet Audio Bridge for the X-Frame, which itself was upgraded to the X-Frame 88.

2002

Under Bill Xavier's leadership, there was a proliferation of new instruments and amps in 2002. Working closely with Eddie Van Halen, the Peavey Custom Shop was established to offer a custom-order service for the Wolfgang project. A wide range of paint jobs, hardware, inlay, and wood options was set up for customer selection and price quotation online. At the other end of the scale, the Wolfgang Special QT guitar began to be produced offshore, making ownership of the basic design concept affordable for many more players.

▼ *V-Type electric guitar*

Renewed interest in the pointy-headstock heavy metal guitar designs of the '80s spawned the new V-Type, a Vandenberg-based guitar offered in string-through and tremolo options. For bass players, there was a new Grind Bass. Both instruments were offered in American-made and EXP versions. A revised line of Briarwood acoustics replaced the Delta Series.

The new EFX versions of the TransTube guitar amps had onboard digital effects, and the XXL head was a TransTube solid-state version of the Triple XXX. As with its tube counterpart, matching enclosures and combos would follow. The ProBass 500 amp—with its tube preamp, full three-band parametric EQ, 500 watts of power, and matching enclosures—signaled a strong return to the professional bass equipment market.

In PA, the XR-800F+ powered console mixer and the XR-684F and XR-696F mixers addressed the increasing demand for more power output in small portable systems. A new assault on the DJ equipment market saw the introduction of two new mixers, the Battle Axe and Club Mix, and the DJS subwoofer speaker enclosure.

Recognition of the rapidly increasing power of computing and its relative decline in cost manifested itself in the release of the latest Architectural Acoustics device, the Digitool.

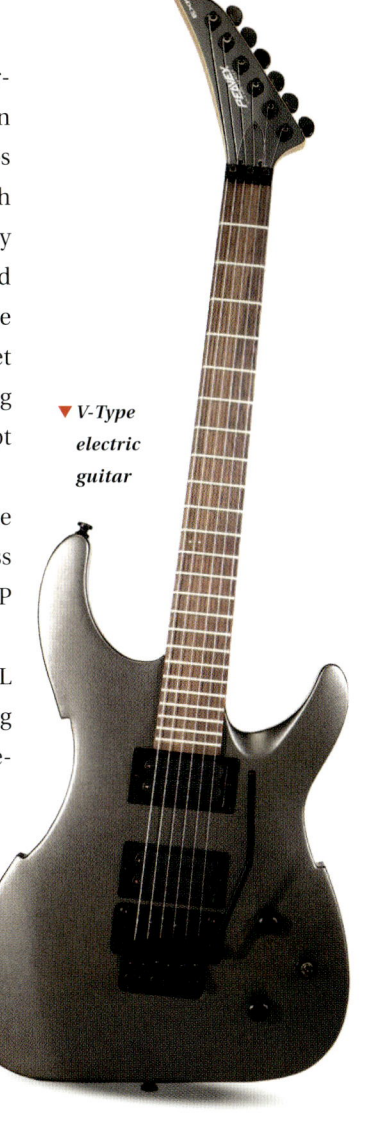

CHAPTER 15 • RENAISSANCE 159

▶ *Architectural Acoustics Digitool MX*

▲ *Hartley and Mary relaxing in the Bahamas*

This rackmount eight-in/eight-out fixed-configuration DSP system finally brought the power of control to small systems at an affordable cost.

The distribution of Generalmusic keyboards, begun with such high hopes, had required a big investment in resources, but the mutual benefits of the relationship had not materialized. With regret, the parties decided to abandon their collaboration.

2003

At the January 2003 NAMM show, Peavey added significantly to its trophy case with a clutch of industry accolades, including Manufacturer of the Year, awarded by retailers via the Music & Sound Awards. It was plain for all to see that Hartley was once again at the top of his game—and in June the City of Meridian named a stretch of Highway 493 running past the Plant 17 headquarters

▶ *Hartley and Mary Peavey at the inauguration of Hartley Peavey Drive — photograph courtesy of* **The Meridian Star**

160 THE PEAVEY REVOLUTION • **PART SIX** • AFTER MELIA

Hartley Peavey Drive in honor of his achievements.

The Italian market, located as it was on the periphery of Peavey's pan-European distribution, had always been too far away from the Corby warehouse for efficient service to customers. So, following the dissolution of the relationship with Generalmusic, Peavey Italia was formed as a joint-venture enterprise with an established Italian distributor, Syncro Srl. With this new arrangement, a warehouse facility was now available in the eastern sector of the European Union, opening up possibilities for business development in the expanding E.U. as it incorporates many of the former communist-bloc countries.

The discoveries coming from Peavey's R&D in synthesis and digital signal processing have spun off numerous new ideas and projects. One manifestation of this was seen in the return of the Generation name on guitars featuring circuitry for acoustic guitar emulation. The patented Analog Acoustic Modeling (ACM) featured on the new Generation models allows them to be played as either an electric guitar, an electro-acoustic, or a blend of both. While the regular Generation is a standard electric guitar, the ACM version has additional piezo pickups and the acoustic modeling module. The quilt-top ACM Custom features two humbuckers and a single-coil magnetic pickup, plus a piezo-bridge system that is augmented with a piezo pickup in the neck pocket. Acoustical information from the neck is captured by this additional pickup, refining the nuances of the guitar's natural resonance.

In other guitar developments, the V-Type series was augmented with a custom-bound neck-through-body version, and in Europe a single-pickup Raptor Junior and a full-body jazz guitar were developed to meet the needs of that market. The Rockingham, a cutaway archtop guitar, was developed with input from rockabilly specialist Darrel Higham; it was offered in a fixed-tailpiece jazz version or equipped with a tremolo tailpiece for retro rockers.

▲ *Rockingham semi-acoustic electric guitar*

Two new solid-state guitar amp heads were introduced in 2003. The TransTube 100 EFX embraced the full range of Peavey's solid-state technology in one amp, with WYSIWYG controls, programmability, T. Dynamics, and more. The Supreme XL, on the other hand, offered a 120-watt two-channel alternative to the three-channel XXL. For acoustic guitarists, the Ecoustic 110 EFX and 112 EFX featured digital effects (independent on each channel) and Feedback Ferret circuitry. Bass players got three new heads in the MAX series, and for keyboardists there was a complete new line of KB combos featuring revised electronics and styling.

The brand-new line of CS-H amps represented a celebration of all Peavey had learned about building power amplifiers since the first CS-800 in the 1970s. Over the years, the CS-800 had become one of the world's biggest-selling power amps, and these new models were designed to carry on that tradition. Variable crossovers and low-pass filters were built into both channels of each model, along with separate two-speed fans for reliability and quiet operation.

There was considerable activity in the transducer division, both in the U.S. and Europe. In America the PR series of lightweight molded enclosures was released, while in Europe the entire line was redefined and redesigned. The new Messenger series offered a "good, better, best" approach with the ST, Pro, and Ultra ranges, respectively. A unique transparent molded enclosure named the TransLite (available in clear, red, and blue) was another first from the European team.

The transducer team was also busy putting the finishing touches on a line of enclosures specifically tailored for houses of worship. Since the 1980s, when Peavey introduced furniture-finished speaker

▲ *Mary Peavey beaming during another successful NAMM trade show*

CHAPTER 15 • RENAISSANCE 161

enclosures, this had been an important niche market for the company, and Peavey sound reinforcement equipment had made its way into many churches and religious centers. A new line of products called the Sanctuary Series was launched to futher solidify this market position; the initial offerings were three mixers and seven speaker systems in three optional finishes.

2004

Early in 2004, Mary Peavey's son, Courtland Gray, was appointed executive vice president. A graduate of Southern Methodist University, he had completed the Advanced Management Program at the Harvard Business School and previously managed the PVF finance operation for three years. "Peavey Electronics is a company that has achieved a great deal in the music industry," he says, "and it is a company that has the potential for achieving much more. There are many opportunities for this company to be even more to the music industry, and to become a more recognized brand beyond just music aficionados. As our market changes, we must take advantage of the opportunities available and change with them. Increasing global brand awareness and developing applications outside the music industry for the 100-plus patents the company holds are opportunities we are only now beginning to develop."

The highlight of the January 2004 NAMM show was the announcement that guitar hero Joe Satriani had been working with Peavey to produce a signature amplifier. Based on the Triple XXX, the new JSX all-tube amp was created to deliver the tone and feel that Joe wanted—the latest in a long line of product developments resulting from close cooperation between Peavey and its endorsing artists.

In keeping with the "back to basics" philosophy that Hartley has emphasized since reasserting control, in recent years premium products have emerged that reflect the sum of what the company has learned over the years—not surprisingly, since Hartley himself is once more driving the product development effort. New amplifier products like the JSX, TransTube 100 EFX, Wiggy, BAM, and ProBass are good examples of how the company's past has provided a solid foundation for current and future development of gear that will satisfy the most discerning players.

The same holds true for the guitar program, as evidenced by the advent of the HP Signature series. "I wanted to bring to the market a guitar that encompassed everything I've learned during my many years of designing and making guitars," Hartley said at their introduction. "We pioneered a lot of technologies that are now industry standards, including shaping guitars with CNC router

▲ *Courtland Gray,*
Peavey's Executive
Vice President

▼ *Crest Audio*
HP-Eight console

162 THE PEAVEY REVOLUTION • PART SIX • AFTER MELIA

2004

technology. We build each HP Signature guitar on that solid foundation, using the finest selected woods, hardware, and pickups for brilliant tone as well as a distinctive, unmistakable appearance."

The HP guitars are fitted with two patented humbucking pickups. "The patent is for 'dual wind' technology," says Mike Powers. "This allows us to wind two bobbins as if they were four different coils of wire, and when you tap into the coils, you will get the same sound output as a single-coil device, with about the same tone—and no hum."

Never losing sight of Hartley's pledge to always make the best equipment and sell it at a fair

● *Joe Satriani live onstage and with the JSX amplifier*

CHAPTER 15 • RENAISSANCE **163**

▲ *Mike Kroeger of Nickelback endorsing ProBass Series amplifiers and a Proximity Effect-themed Rotor ad*

▲ *Hartley Peavey stresses the importance of "stickability" to graduates at his alma mater*

▲ *MAX bass amplifiers*

and reasonable price, the company also offered the HP Signature guitars in EXP and EX versions, making them accessible to many more players. The EXP range was further expanded with the semi-hollow double-cut JF-1 guitar and the Rotor EXP. In an unusual example of product placement, the all-mahogany "retro look" Rotor was selected to be featured in a Top Cow comic called *Proximity* Effect. In the new comic, the main character, Lisa, is featured with her Peavey Rotor guitar.

In May 2004, Hartley was awarded an honorary doctor of creative and performing arts degree by Mississippi State University. Speaking to the graduates at his alma mater, he said, "Thirty-nine years ago I left here with a diploma and a dream. In those 39 years, much of that dream has been realized in ways I never knew. I had faith that if I tried hard enough and if I worked hard enough that somehow I might succeed." Hartley told the students that he defined success as "feeling good about what you're doing," adding, "I don't care how smart you are, how talented you are—if you don't have the quality of 'stickability,' you will never be as successful as you

2004

▲ *NION, the next-generation MediaMatrix audio processing node, redefines the power of MediaMatrix for the new millennium*

▲ *Custom Shop Generation USA Custom electric guitar*

▼ *Jack Daniel's acoustic guitar*

should be or could be. . . . God knows, I didn't have the money or the experience that some of my competitors had, but I did have 'stickability.' Life is a test to see how much BS you can take, and I am as serious as a heart attack. I am not kidding you. It's a test, as you will find out, that whoever you're competing with, if you keep up, nine times out of ten they'll quit. Of the people I started out competing with years ago, many of them are not around—but not because I put them out of business. They simply surrendered."

As Peavey reaches the end of its fourth decade of innovation and technological advancement, it is appropriate that the latest incarnation of MediaMatrix is ready to stand the world of sound system engineering on its head. The original MediaMatrix designs were based on industrial PC hardware, but the cost of memory has declined and the capabilities of DSPs have increased greatly since then, enabling huge systems to be controlled by distributed processing. Networkable Input Output Node or NION (pronounced *nee-on*) is the new platform on which MediaMatrix will be delivered in the future. With an embedded LINUX operating system, NION can stand alone as a centralized system or be distributed within a network. It will set the pace in the new millennium just as the original MediaMatrix led the way in the 1990s.

During the 2004 Summer NAMM show in Nashville, Peavey announced an array of new products that will carry the company into its fifth decade. Notably, these included an extensive collection of inexpensive PV Series products designed to meet the needs of the mass market: mixers, power amps, crossovers, equalizers, and enclosures—and, perhaps most exciting, a complete new line of MAX bass amps. The company's well-received Sanctuary Series—launched at the preceding Winter NAMM show and featuring exclusive Peavey technologies aimed at making church audio easy for both professionals and novices alike—was extended with the S-4 and S-24 mixers and SA-4200 power amplifier. For the professional end of the instrument market, Peavey announced an extension of its Custom Shop program to incorporate the Cirrus basses. A Custom Shop version of the Generation ACM guitar was also introduced, sporting a pearloid top and triple soapbar pickups.

CHAPTER 15 • RENAISSANCE **165**

Perhaps the most exciting news—especially since the show was in Tennessee—was the announcement that Peavey and Jack Daniel's had forged a marketing alliance. Peavey would be the exclusive licensee of the Jack Daniel's brand for musical instruments and amplifiers, and the show floor buzzed with the news about a Jack Daniel's amplifier, acoustic guitar, and several electric guitar models. The Jack Daniel distillery is the oldest in America, dating back almost 140 years, and Jack Daniel's Tennessee Whiskey has become an American institution. "Bringing together two powerful brands like Jack Daniel's and Peavey is a tremendous opportunity," Hartley announced. "We're excited to distill Peavey's 39-year legacy of quality and craftsmanship with the rich history and tradition of Jack Daniel's into a line of custom-designed guitars and amplifiers that celebrates our common American ancestry."

▲ *The Nashville launch party for the partnership with Jack Daniel's. L to R: Christy Stanfield, Tara Bova, Hartley Peavey, Courtland Gray, Susan Buckmaster, Jack Kennard and Mary Peavey.*

▼ *Jack Daniel's USA electric guitar in whiskey*

▼ *Cirrus-4 bass guitar in redwood*

166 THE PEAVEY REVOLUTION • **PART SIX** • AFTER MELIA

A Maverick Looks to the Future

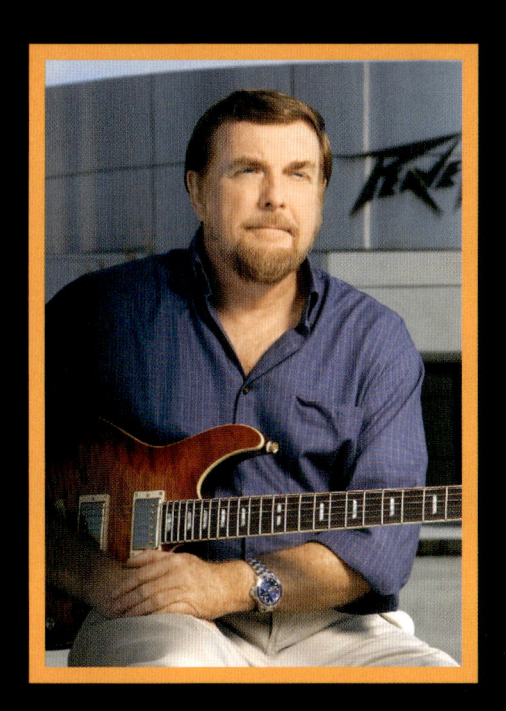

▲ *Hartley in 2005*

"Whether you think you can, or whether you think you can't, you're absolutely right." — HENRY FORD

▲ *Signature Series ad*

▶ *HP Signature USA Custom guitar in sunburst*

This chronicle of the life of a remarkable man, the company he founded, and some of the innovative products subsequently brought to market by that company is, of necessity, little more than a snapshot of a long, successful, and enduring career—one that is nowhere near over. It celebrates the power of an individual to achieve success through hard work, commitment, passion, and—above all else—persistence. Or, as Hartley would call it, "stickability." It is the story of a man who has eschewed convention in his relentless search to find a better

Guitar Player editor in chief Michael Molenda presents Hartley Peavey with its first-ever Lifetime Achievement Award given to a manufacturer

The 6505 halfstack continues the evolution of the 5150 line of amplifiers

way. "It's crazy people like me who are prepared to swim upriver, who do the things 'normal' folks won't do," Hartley once said. "It takes a certain amount of a rebellious nature to change things—to make a difference."

The place and the time in which Hartley grew up and the influences on his development notwithstanding, one is left with the feeling that there is some special motivating power at work inside this man. He is, quite rightly, proud of his achievements thus far, although not satiated—and he never will be. Hartley is also quick to point out, however, that it does not get any easier. "My greatest rationalization is that next year will be easier, but the fact is every year gets harder. There are always new frontiers to explore, and each day brings its own challenges."

Hartley's positive ethos has carried over to his family. His sons Joe and Marc came to live with Melia and their father soon after their wedding, and the boys say that one thing they remember clearly about their childhood is that Hartley was out of town a lot—and even when he was home, the business competed heavily for their time. Hartley's parents were regular babysitters, and just as Hartley was influenced by his grandfather, so his sons acknowledge the influence of Mutt Peavey on them—a legacy of the work ethic, manners, morals, and a positive attitude about life. Not surprisingly, they have grown up to be independent, although they both work for Peavey. Joe plays a central role in the MediaMatrix division, where his passion for computers has found a productive niche, while Marc oversees the advertising department. Although they were both encouraged to join the company, Marc is quick to note that "we've been taught to work for everything—that's the way Dad did it, and that's the way we're going to do it." For all his dedication to his work, Hartley has been the consummate father to his sons, encouraging them to excel in their studies while also cultivating real-world business acumen.

When outsiders visit the factories and facilities of Peavey Electronics, they come away with a strong sense of family. This can be traced back to the beginning, when Mutt Peavey was there to help his son build his fledgling enterprise. It was further nurtured by their belief in the Golden Rule and commitment to employee welfare. Even though the few has grown into many, the feeling of family is sustained not only by the employees but by customers and vendors, too. And today, Hartley has Mary as company president and Courtland on his management team, helping to maintain the family ties even as they steer the business in new directions.

Boating has continually provided Hartley with an important release from business pressures. He has owned an extensive collection of water craft, from a ski boat on Dalewood Lake when Joe and Marc were kids through a 44-foot sailboat, a 48-foot motor yacht, the 45-foot Sea Ray, and on up to a 112-foot Westship. His latest acquisition is a steel-hulled ocean-going 81-foot trawler specially designed and built in Canada. The "High Note" bristles with sophisticated equipment and luxury that will enable Hartley and Mary to ply the seven seas in safety and comfort.

It's doubtful they will spend too much time on that boat, however, as Hartley

2005

clearly revels in his work. "Peavey continues to look in new directions," he declares. "From my perspective, I see no end in sight. The truth is that product development is my first love, and I put up with all of the paperwork and business stuff in order to do my thing—which is to innovate, create, and, I hope, change the marketplace for the better." That includes approaching that ever-changing market in new and innovative ways. Peavey doesn't so much adapt itself to the market as it *adapts the market* to its own philosophy, especially when it comes to the retail sales structure. For example, Peavey carefully watched the burgeoning Internet sales industry in the late '90s, but refused to offer its products online until it discovered a way to make such an endeavor benefit its loyal retailer network. The resulting program, Peavey MAGNET (Music And Gear Network), allows customers to shop online at Peavey.com while its local retailers are responsible for shipping the orders. They get the profit for each MAGNET sale, just as they would if the customer walked into their store. It's a sign of the respect that Hartley extends to his retailers; raised in a music store, he understands the role that salespeople play in ensuring his own success, and fairness—never at the exclusion of responsibility—is a mantra. Retailers returned the favor in 2005 by voting Peavey a *Music Inc.* Supplier's Excellence Award for creating a level playing field for its retailers and continuing its DealerWise education and training programs. In the first half of 2005, MAGNET sales had increased by 80% over the same period in 2004.

Peavey has also been at work expanding the Peavey and Crest Audio product lines into new markets. The Crest Performance line distills that company's three decades of tour, studio, and installation technology into products for the MI market, and the PVDJ division extends Peavey's commitment to the DJ market with loudspeakers, processors, power amplifiers, and more designed to meet its specific needs. The DAI (Digital Audio Interface) continues the integration of computer technology, with a truly stable hardware/software package that allows DJs to remix .WAV, .CDA, .MP3, and other audio formats in real time on a laptop—eliminating the need to drag crates of vinyl or CDs to DJ gigs.

The pro audio market is also experiencing an influx of new Peavey innovations: the FX Series of mixers introduces dual USB ports and built-in .MP3 coding, which allows sound engineers

▲ *Hartley Peavey at the helm, charting the company's future. Photograph by Scott Pearson, courtesy of Yachting magazine*

▲ *logo for the Crest Performance audio line*

◀ *Peavey Sanctuary Series S-24 mixing console*

CHAPTER 16 • A MAVERICK LOOKS TO THE FUTURE **169**

and musicians to record live performances directly into a computer. From there, they can upload songs to the Internet or produce their own CD recordings instantly—yet another extension of Peavey's dedication to forward-thinking technologies. Peavey has also developed the VSX loudspeaker managers and Architectural Acoustics Digitool, essentially mini-MediaMatrix systems for use in live audio and event production or conference rooms. The all-purpose Messenger is a self-contained sound system the size of a briefcase that packs a solid 100 watts with five channels, plus exclusive technologies such as FLS and Split-Track Mix. Small enough to fit into an overhead airline compartment and weighing a mere 25 lbs., the Messenger is poised to become an essential tool for hotel events, press conferences, business presentations, and coffeehouse-style intimate music performances, just as the larger Escort and TriFlex systems before it.

Manufacturing in the U.S. and U.K., meanwhile, has become increasingly difficult as the Far East has emerged as the "workshop of the world." It's astounding that an electronics manufacturer can even exist in the U.S. these days, let alone thrive; just look at any consumer electronics, from stereos and televisions to laptops, and you're hard-pressed to find the words "Made in U.S.A." This has been tough for Hartley to accept, but Courtland Gray takes the long view. "Our decision to move certain products offshore has been flagging in comparison to competitors who never made, or were unable to make, as substantial a domestic investment as Peavey," he says. "We're as strong as ever financially, and we still utilize our talents and capital domestically where it makes sense. When necessary, we do look offshore to give the consumers what they expect from Peavey—a quality product at a fair and reasonable price. Every single Peavey product is still designed and tested in the U.S., even those lines manufactured offshore, and they all bear UL and CE certifications. We don't import off-the-shelf products. That's a major Peavey difference; Hartley insists upon maintaining the 'uniqueness' factor of the Peavey brand legacy. Every Peavey product is unique, compelling, and defensible."

Tony Moscal, Senior Manager of Marketing and Product Development, concurs. "It doesn't matter if it's a commodity or a U.S.A. custom piece—all products that bear a Peavey logo must meet those criteria," he says. "When Hartley started this company, he completely undercut the market with quality, U.S.A.-made products. Peavey dominated that category for decades, but then drifted into the middle of the market, price-wise, during the '90s. What we're doing now is going both down-market and up-market, which has given us a remarkable balance and allowed us to

▼ *The PVDJ division extends Peavey's commitment to the DJ market. Below is the DAI (Digital Audio Interface)*

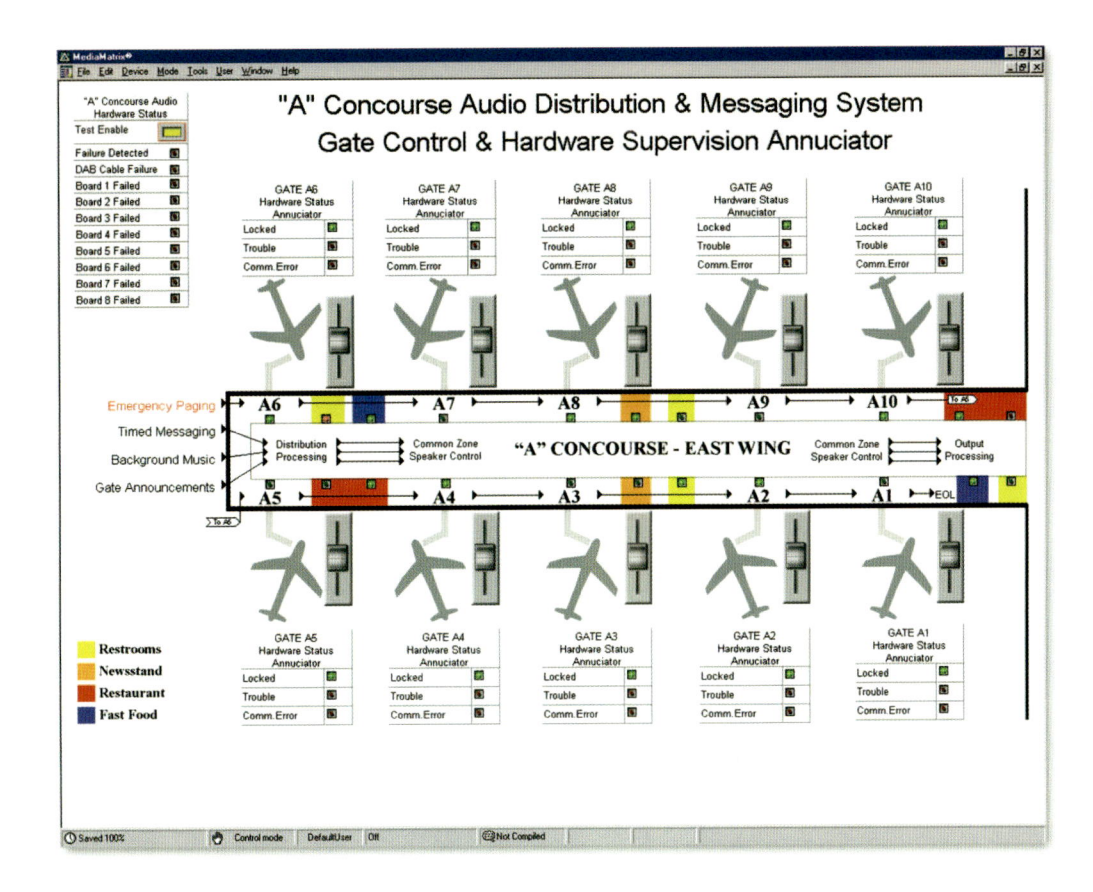

With more than 3,000 installations worldwide, Media-Matrix continues to expand the possibilities of audio and communications

maintain our U.S. manufacturing. In 2004, for example, the offshore-sourced, $79 Backstage was our best-selling guitar amp in volume, but the U.S.A.-made, $1500 JSX guitar amp was our dollar leader. Both segments of the market are vital to Peavey."

Always prescient, Hartley—who has been vocal against the outsourcing trend for many years and was appointed to the ISAC 4 committee (Industry Sector Advisory Committee on Consumer Goods for Trade Policy Matters) by the U.S. Secretary of Commerce from 1987 to 1998—weighed in after receiving the "Peace Through Trade" award from the Mississippi World Trade Center in 2003. "The challenge [of keeping U.S. manufacturers competitive] has been significant in the past, but it will be even greater in the future. Today our competitors are China and Indonesia. We're not just competing with companies any longer, but with countries." For all his experience in global trade matters, the reality of appropriate sourcing has not derailed the stalwart CEO. "It's a battle we can win. There's an old song that goes, 'You can make it if you try.' Peavey Electronics is an example of the truth of those words."

The Penta half-stack

Adaptability is synonymous with "stickability" in our global economy, and while Peavey maintains more U.S. manufacturing than its competitors, no company is immune to outsourcing's effects. Thus, it began restructuring its 27 active facilities during the early part of the millennium. This included returning its large-frame loudspeaker manufacturing to Meridian from Foley, Ala., and converting several lines of Plant 3 to accommodate them. Plant 2 is now home to the Peavey Custom Shop, where a team of luthiers makes the company's high-end USA Custom musical instruments—the popular Cirrus basses and HP Signature guitars among them. In 2005, Peavey

CHAPTER 16 • A MAVERICK LOOKS TO THE FUTURE

consolidated the Crest Audio facility from Fair Lawn, N.J., to Meridian and Decatur, where it had begun manufacturing its consoles and power amplifiers. In the process, it combined the best production methods from each to make the operation as efficient as possible while ensuring that the legacy of quality control shared by Peavey and Crest Audio flourishes. Further to that end, the engineering and design teams of both remain autonomous even though the brands share manufacturing space, and with more than 150 new jobs added in Mississippi since 2004, a strengthened employee force is keeping production standards high. Also in 2005, Peavey acquired the North American distribution rights to the Trace Elliot brand, a well respected U.K. maker of high-end bass and acoustic guitar amplifiers.

Peavey is also transforming itself into a marketing force both within the music industry and in mainstream channels. Tour sponsorships and event marketing with Jägermeister Music Tour, Zippo Hot Tour, and Hard Rock Café are ensuring Peavey is connecting with young music fans and musicians. The Artist Relations department—now under the wing of longtime Peavey endorser David Ellefson—is firmly established with "mainstream" rock acts as well as underground music scenes of all genres, and the company has reaffirmed its presence among Nashville's elite players. Web-based promotions with entities such as Sony, Apple, and Epic Records are a constant at Peavey.com, which is drawing a half-million visits each month. The public relations effort is earning Peavey pages in trade, national, and international media, while print advertising and direct mail campaigns are driving the message. And the aforementioned licensing deal with Jack Daniel's is putting Peavey products in front of people who may never encounter the brand otherwise.

By staunchly retaining sole ownership of his company and not owing creditors, Hartley Peavey has avoided the pitfalls to which many of his competitors succumbed. Reinvesting profits back into Peavey Electronics has fuelled research and development and expansions, all the while building an immense manufacturing and marketing juggernaut with which to engage Hartley's imagination. That, in our age of corporate buyouts and massive conglomerations, was Hartley's first revolutionary idea. It is one that continues to inspire awe today.

▲ *A fine representative of the Trace Elliot product line*

"Innovation" is a term bandied by many in any industry; "revolution" is yet another. But with more than 130 patents registered during its history and more in process at all times, Peavey has been more prolific in its innovation than most companies—in any industry—could ever dream. Hartley Peavey indeed started a revolution in the music industry, one founded upon tireless innovation and one which knows no bounds. Hartley, his company and its products have received literally countless awards and honors during its first forty years, and the trend continues: Peavey has been named Manufacturer of the Year by industry journal *Music & Sound Retailer* in 2002, 2003 and 2005, and retailers have bestowed a *Musical Merchandise Review* Dealers' Choice Award upon the company every year since 2000, with still many more preceding those. Hartley Peavey was voted into the *Vintage Guitar* Hall of Fame in April 2005 by

▲ *Mary Peavey with her mother, Mary Love, and "Montana"*

a margin nearly doubling his closest competitor, and *The Music Trades* named him Person of the Year for 2005. *Guitar Player*, a major consumer trade magazine, honored Hartley with its first-ever manufacturer's Lifetime Achievement Award. To many, these accolades would be a natural conclusion to an illustrious career; a chance to "go out on top." For Hartley Peavey, they are merely milestones indicating he's still on the right track.

Surveying his company's position after forty years, Hartley says: "We've seen companies come and we've seen companies go. We've seen competitors' ownership and management change, and in many ways I think that is unfortunate for the audio and music industry at large. A lot of times the companies we compete with have never had the opportunity to evolve. Evolution is a constant—industries evolve, companies evolve. It takes a considerable amount of time, but most companies never get above the level where their prime objective is to sell the maximum amount of product. Though selling 'tonnage' is important, what really makes a company important to the retailer, contractor, and system integrator is helping him make a profit. If doing business with a particular company makes you feel good, if it puts money in your pocket—then you feel good about them. If doing business with people is painful, you tend not to do it."

And even after all this time, Hartley Peavey marvels at what he has been able to accomplish since he started building amps in the attic. "This idealized corporate environment where everybody is on a first-name basis, this totally improbable industrial Camelot, should probably never have succeeded—but in fact it did, and it still does. It succeeds because a lot of people were given an opportunity, and they rose to the challenge. And if I ever hang up my rock 'n' roll shoes, what I would like people to say is, 'Well, that old boy did it right.' I suppose that the very best we human beings can ever expect to do on this earth is to make a difference. The world is a better place in some small way, I hope, because I am a part of something as special as Peavey Electronics."

▲ *Courtland and Hartley in Key West, Florida.*

▲ *Changes in latitude: Hartley and sons Joe and Marc recharging at Pete's Pub in Abaco, Bahamas*

▲ *Hartley and Mary Peavey, Christmas 2002*

The Peavey Mission Statement

Peavey is a family of diverse individuals growing together and achieving excellence in a unique and exciting environment.

At Peavey we believe:

It is the combination of traditional values, continuing education, and advanced technology that assures long-term success for our customers, suppliers, and ourselves.

People who care count.

Doing the impossible is within our reach.

APPENDIX A

Product Chronology
E. & O.E.

In the 40 years between 1965 and 2005, Peavey has developed and launched hundreds of products, to say nothing of the thousands of accessories brought to market during this period. In this book it has been possible only to skim over a selection of them, notably those that were most significant or tracked diversification and continuing improvements. This appendix has been compiled to provide a chronological history of Peavey's output. Because products were routinely launched at prototype stage and further developed pre-production, there was often a time lag between launch and availability. For this reason and because dating information has been collated from diverse historical sources such as price lists and marketing literature, actual dates of production are not definitive.

Some units (†) were released at prototype stage but did not go into production. The AMR prefix indicates products in the Audio Media Research line. The AA prefix indicates products from the Architectural Acoustics division. The MM prefix denotes a MediaMatrix product. The EURO prefix indicates products manufactured in the facility at Corby, England, and/or distributed specifically for the European market.

1965
Musician 212 35W single unit
Dyna-Bass 115 35W single unit
N.B. Numerous redesigns and power upgrades occurred in the first couple of years.

1968
The Musician and Dyna-Bass were now 120-watt heads available with various speaker enclosures.
PA-3 PA system with reverb

1969
Concert 115 single-unit bass amp
VTA-300 and VTB-300 amps

1969-72
Between 1969 and 1972 there was a frenzy of activity and growth such that it is difficult to pinpoint dates. The products included:
PA-300 PA system
PA-6
PA-9
8-, 12-, and 16-channel Festival Mixers
Deuce guitar amp
Standard 240 head 120 W
Bass head 150 W
Musician head 150 W
Dyna-Bass head 250 W
Vulcan head 250 W
VTA-400 Head 200 W (tube)
412 speaker enclosure (E-V SRO option)
412S speaker enclosure (E-V SRO option)
612H speaker enclosure (E-V SRO option)
115FH
215 speaker enclosure (E-V SRO option)
215H speaker enclosure (E-V SRO option)
315 speaker enclosure (E-V SRO option)
118FH

1972
Musician 210 W head
Bass 210 W head
F-800G Festival head
F-800B Festival head
Standard head 130 W
Vintage 212 guitar amp
Vintage 410 guitar amp
Vintage 610 guitar amp
215S (slot-ported) speaker enclosure
610 speaker enclosure
412 speaker enclosure
118S speaker enclosure (Vega)
PA-120 PA system
Standard PA head
PA-400 PA head
PA-6A powered console
210 PA enclosure
410 PA enclosure
412 PA enclosure
212H PA enclosure
412H PA enclosure
215H PA enclosure
612H PA enclosure
Festival System (215+212+horn)

1973
Classic 212 guitar amp
Classic 410 guitar amp
212 speaker enclosure
118S speaker enclosure
Monitor system
24-channel Festival Mixer

1974
Pacer 45W guitar amp
TNT 45W bass amp
Deuce II 212 guitar amp
Deuce II 410 guitar amp
Deuce II 412 guitar amp
Session 115 (JBL) steel amp
Session (212E-V) steel amp
Century 60W head
Festival head with strips 110W 2-channel
Roadmaster 200W (with Automix) head
810 speaker enclosure
800 mixer
Split Festival Projector (separate horn) option
PA-600 powered console
PA-900 powered console
260 Booster slave amp
800 Booster slave amp
Monitor system
CSP sound reinforcement speaker
PML microphone
PMH microphone
PM 1000† microphone
PM 2000† microphone
PM 3000† microphone

1975
Artist guitar amp
Mace guitar amp
LTD 115 (JBL) steel amp
412F speaker enclosure
Century and PA-120 boosted to 100W
1200 mixer
1210TS PA enclosure
1210T PA enclosure
1510T PA enclosure
115HT Vocal Projector PA enclosure
215HT Vocal Projector PA enclosure
Monitor head
112T monitor enclosure
112TS monitor enclosure
HF radial horn
T-12 tweeter bank
EQ-10 graphic equalizer
PBH microphone
PBL microphones

1976
Mace head
Session head
SP-1 sound reinforcement enclosure

174 THE PEAVEY REVOLUTION • **APPENDICES**

APPENDIX A

MF1-X horn
T-300 tweeter bank
PA-700 (stereo) powered console
600 mixer
900 mixer
1200 mixer
600S stereo mixer
800S stereo mixer
1200S stereo mixer
12ch Festival Mixer
24ch Festival Mixer
400 Booster slave amp
260S stereo booster slave amp
CS-800 power amp
Snake 15 line 100' multicore cable
22 Driver horn driver
Diaphragm kit for 22 Driver
A-1 adapter for 22 Driver
A-2 adapter for 22 Driver
A-3 adapter for 22 Driver

1977
T-60 electric guitar
T-40 bass guitar
Black Widow speakers
IP-1 instrument preamp
Backstage-30 guitar amp
Artist 112BW guitar amp
Artist 115BW guitar amp
Deuce 212BW guitar amp
Mace 212BW guitar amp
Session 400 (115BW)
LTD-400 (115BW)
212 BW speaker enclosure
412 BW speaker enclosure
412S BW speaker enclosure
412F BW speaker enclosure
115 BW speaker enclosure
215 BW speaker enclosure
PA-100 45W PA system
PA-200 PA head
XR-600 PA head
XR-600 FC PA head
PA 1000S powered console
MR-7 mixer
MC-8 mixer
MC-12 mixer
MC-16 mixer
MC-24 mixer
112PT PA enclosure
112TS BW monitor enclosure
212TS monitor enclosure
212TS BW monitor enclosure
CS-200 power amp
CS-400 power amp
CS-800 plug-in modules
CS-X2 crossover
KM-4 keyboard mixer
FH-1 sub enclosure

1978
Classic VT guitar amp
Artist VT guitar amp
Deuce VT guitar amp
TKO 40W bass amp
Combo 130W bass amp
Centurion bass head

Musician Mark III head
Bass Mark III head
Standard Mark III head
118D speaker enclosure
118FH BW speaker enclosure
Mark II Series mixers
EQ-27 graphic equalizer
210 Stereo EQ equalizer
SP-2 PA enclosure
Continental 115BW PA enclosure
International 115BW PA enclosure
RM-600 mixer
SA-1 stand adapter

1979
Session 500 steel amp
TNT upgrade to 50W with paramid
XC-400 top-box power amp
Sunburst T-60 and T-40
DDT emerges on CS amps
MP-4 PA head
XR-400 PA head
XR-500 PA head
XR-1200 powered console
110PT PA enclosure
SP-3 PA enclosure
112 International PA enclosure
118 International PA enclosure
1245 monitor enclosure
2445 monitor enclosure
FH-1BW subwoofer enclosure
M400 Monitor package
Mark III 260 Monitor with graphic EQ
801 mixer
1201 mixer

1980
T-60 & T-40 rosewood fingerboard options
T-25† "Sustanite" electric guitar
Decade guitar amp
Backstage 30 guitar amp upgrade to 18W
Studio Pro guitar amp
Bandit guitar amp
Outlaw† guitar amp
Rebel† guitar amp
XR-800 powered console
ECM crossover mainframe
Mark III-8 mixer
Mark III-12 mixer
Mark III-16 mixer
Mark III-24 mixer
FH-2 subwoofer enclosure
MB-1 mid-bass horn
CH-4C HF horn
MiniMonitor packaged monitor enclosures
Electric Pillow plug-in module
BW speakers available "over the counter"

1981
T-15 electric guitar
Electric Case guitar amp
Special 112 guitar amp
Renown 212 guitar amp

Scorpion speakers
Mark IV-12 mixer
Mark IV-16 mixer
Mark IV-24 mixer
1601 mixer
MB-2 mid-bass horn
1810 speaker enclosure
1210H PA enclosure
112FC International PA enclosure
115FC International PA enclosure
118FC International PA enclosure
115TS monitor enclosure
1545 monitor enclosure
M-2000 power amp

1982
T-30 electric guitar
T-25 electric guitar
T-25 Special electric guitar
T-26 electric guitar
T-27 electric guitar
T-27 Limited electric guitar
T-20 bass guitar
T-40 Fretless bass guitar
T-45 bass guitar
Decade guitar amp
Backstage guitar amp to 20W
Studio Pro 40 guitar amp to 40W
Bandit 65 guitar amp to 65W
Vegas 400 guitar amp
Nashville 400 guitar amp
Classic 212 VTX guitar amp
MX 112BW VTX guitar amp
Heritage 212 VTX guitar amp
Heritage 212BW VTX guitar amp
Basic 30 bass amp
TKO 65 bass amp to 65W
TNT 130 bass amp to 130W
Combo 300 bass amp to 300W
Citation head
210SX speaker enclosure
212SX speaker enclosure
212SX BW speaker enclosure
215C speaker enclosure
3620 speaker enclosure
410FC speaker enclosure
XR-600B PA head
MD-8 mixer
MD-12 mixer
MD-16 mixer
801 mixer
1201 mixer
Mark IV 16 x 8 monitor mixer
Mark IV 24 x 8 monitor mixer
MD 8 x 6 monitor mixer
MD 12 x 6 monitor mixer
MD 16 x 6 monitor mixer
601R mixer
701R mixer
R6M mixer
M-2600 power amp
M-3000 power amp
112HS monitor enclosure
112HS BW monitor enclosure
115HS monitor enclosure
112H PA enclosure
1201H PA enclosure

1201HS PA enclosure
2420H PA enclosure
210W PA enclosure
Project 4 sound reinforcement enclosure
Tri-Flex speaker system
Concept II sound reinforcement system
T-1000 CDH horn
FH-2 BW sub enclosure
Acoustic Wave
CoAxial BW speaker

1983
Horizon electric guitar
Mystic electric guitar
Razor electric guitar
Fury bass guitar
Fury FL bass guitar
Foundation bass guitar
Austin 400 guitar amp
Reno 400 guitar amp
LA 400 guitar amp
Rhythm Master 400 amp
Encore 65 guitar amp
Basic-40 bass amp
Roadmaster head
MX-FC head
Mark IV Bass head
MAX Bass head
210 powered enclosure
412FC speaker enclosure
KB-100 keyboard amp
KB-300 keyboard amp
KB-400 head
Flex Monitor enclosure
110 Criterion PA enclosure
112 Criterion PA enclosure
CD-20 microphone
CD-30 microphone
HD-40 microphone

1984
Mantis electric guitar
Patriot electric guitar
Milestone Custom electric guitar
Milestone LH electric guitar
Horizon II electric guitar
Horizon II Custom electric guitar
Hydra doubleneck electric guitar
Foundation Custom bass guitar
Foundation LH bass guitar
Patriot Bass bass guitar
Audition guitar amp
Backstage Plus guitar amp
KB-300BW keyboard amp
DECA-700 power amp
112CX monitor enclosure
115CX monitor enclosure
112 International NAT PA enclosure
115 International NAT PA enclosure
Project 5 sound reinforcement enclosure
EC-10 microphone
EC-15 microphone
EC-18 microphone
DEP-800 effects processor

DEP-1300 effects processor
EDI direct box

1985
Impact 1 electric guitar
Impact 2 electric guitar
Vortex 1 electric guitar
Vortex 2 electric guitar
Jeff Cook Hydra electric guitar
Dyna-Bass bass guitar
Dyna-Bass w/T bass guitar
Classic Chorus guitar amp
Studio Chorus guitar amp
Programmax-10 guitar amp
Butcher head
412-M speaker enclosure
412-MS speaker enclosure
XM-4 PA head
XM-6 PA head
XR-500C PA head
MDII-8 mixer
MDII-12 mixer
MDII-16 mixer
MDII-12B mixer
MDII-16B mixer
MS-1221 mixer
MS-1621 mixer
DPM-12 mixer
DPM-16 mixer
DECA-1200 power amp
CS1200 power amp
112 International III PA enclosure
115 International III PA enclosure
118 International III PA enclosure
118-SUB subwoofer enclosure
1510-HT PA enclosure
115H PA enclosure
CL-1 PA enclosure
GP-115 PA enclosure
1522-C PA enclosure
210-HP powered enclosure
1545 PM powered monitor
HT-94 super tweeter
PS-2B phantom power
PS-4AC phantom power
ED100 electronic drum amp
ED300 electronic drum amp
PEP-1310 effects processor
PEP-4000 effects processor
RMC-2000 MIDI controller
Scorpion Plus speakers

1986
Predator electric guitar
Nitro I electric guitar
Nitro III electric guitar
Nitro III Custom electric guitar
Foundation-S bass guitar
Stereo Chorus 400 guitar amp
Classic Chorus 130 guitar amp
Jazz Chorus guitar amp
Companion-15 guitar amp
Audition-20 guitar amp
Studio Pro-50 guitar amp
Basic-50 bass amp
KB-10 keyboard amp
ProBass 1000 bass pre-amp

MegaBass rack amp
KB-115 speaker enclosure
115PM powered monitor
115M monitor enclosure
CL-2 PA enclosure
115-HD PA enclosure
115-SC subwoofer enclosure
215D subwoofer enclosure
415 SUB subwoofer enclosure
V4-X crossover
EQ-31 equalizer
EQ-215 equalizer
XR-400B PA head
PVM-38 microphone
PVM-45 microphone
110PE Euro PA enclosure
112HE Euro PA enclosure
115HE Euro PA enclosure
315E Euro PA enclosure

1987
Falcon electric guitar
Falcon Classic electric guitar
Falcon Custom electric guitar
Nitro II electric guitar
Dyna-Bass 5 bass guitar
Rage guitar amp
Audition Chorus guitar amp
Triumph 60 guitar amp
Triumph 120 guitar amp
VTM-60 head
VTM-120 head
Minx bass amp
1516 speaker enclosure
Euro Megabox speaker enclosure
PGP-20 guitar preamp
KB-15 keyboard amp
Solo portable PA
HFD-1 effects pedal
AOD-2 effects pedal
CSR-2 effects pedal
CMC-1 effects pedal
BAC-2 effects pedal
DSC-4 effects pedal
DDL-3 effects pedal
SRP-16 effects pedal
DEP-16 effects pedal
PFC-5 effects pedal case
MFP-2128 MIDI controller
XR-700C powered console
XR-800C powered console
XR-1200C powered console
XR-1600C powered console
Monitor 300 head
DECA-424 power amp
DECA-724 power amp
M-2600 Mark V power amp
M-3000 Mark V power amp
M-4000 power amp
M-7000 power amp
CS900 power amp
MD-421/16 mixer
MS-2421 mixer
112PS PA enclosure
SP-4 PA enclosure
HDH-1 sound reinforcement enclosure
HDH Processor

PCS speaker processor
1245M monitor enclosure
1545M monitor enclosure
Euro ES-10 PA enclosure
Euro ES-12 PA enclosure
Euro ES-15 PA enclosure
Euro ES-315 PA enclosure
Euro Bassflex subwoofer enclosure 1245
PV microphone
PVM-48 microphone
Wireless Performer microphones
Univerb effects processor
Addverb effects processor
DEP-3.2S effects processor
PEP-4530 effects processor
IDL-655 delay line
AMR MCR-4 tape recorder
AMR MCR-4 Overdubber remote control
AMR 42 mixer
AMR 64 mixer
AMR PMA-200 power amp
AMR PMA-70+ power amp
AMR PRM-312 studio monitor
AMR PRM-310 studio monitor
AMR PRM-308 studio monitor
AMR PRM-298 studio monitor
AMR PRM-205 studio monitor
AMR DM-12 microphone
AMR DM-14 microphone
AMR ERO-10 microphone
AMR ERC-12 microphone
AMR PD-4 headphone box
AMR APS-4 phantom power
AMR BPS-2 phantom power
AMR EDB-1 direct box
AMR IA-10/4 interface amp
AMR PME-4 parametric EQ
AMR CDS-2 compressor/limiter
AMR NGT-2 noise gate
AMR DSR-100 digital reverb
AMR MIDI Manager remote controller
AMR MIDI Commander controller

1988
Tracer electric guitar
Tracer Deluxe electric guitar
Tracer Custom electric guitar
Falcon Active electric guitar
Generation I electric guitar
Generation II electric guitar
Generation Standard electric guitar
Generation Custom electric guitar
Nitro I Custom electric guitar
Nitro III Custom electric guitar
Nitro Limited electric guitar
Impact 1 Unity electric guitar
Vandenberg Signature electric guitar
Foundation S Active bass guitar
Dyna-Bass Unity bass guitar
Dyna-Bass Limited bass guitar
TL-5 bass guitar
Audition Plus guitar amp
Backstage 50 guitar amp
Studio Pro 60 guitar amp
Bandit 75 guitar amp
Special 150 guitar amp

Special 150 Wedge guitar amp
Session 400LTD steel amp
Session 400LTD Wedge steel amp
Stereo Chorus head
Triumph 60 head
Triumph 120 head
VSS-20 guitar amp
Microbass bass amp
Basic 60 bass amp
TKO-75 bass amp
TNT-150 bass amp
TNT-150 Wedge bass amp
Databass bass amp
Mark III Bass head
Mark VI Bass head
Mark VIII Bass head
Alpha Bass bass amp
Euro Mini-Bi 208 powered enclosure
Euro Megaten speaker enclosure
Euro Megasub speaker enclosure
212 MC speaker enclosure
212 MS speaker enclosure
RBS-1 speaker enclosure
KB-60 keyboard amp
Euro ES-50K keyboard amp
HKS-8 keyboard amp
HKS-12 keyboard amp
Euro EPA-100 slave amp
DECA-528 power amp
XR-600C PA head
Linemix-8 mixer
PLM-8128 mixer
PLM-8128E mixer expander
Production Mixer 502 DJ mixer
Production Mixer 902 DJ mixer
SRC-421-16 mixer
SRC-421-24 mixer
Mark VIII-36 mixing console
Euro CC-10 PA enclosure
Euro ES-12PM powered monitor
ES-12M monitor enclosure
Impulse I molded enclosure
Impulse II molded enclosure
ProSys-10 PA enclosure
ProSys-12 PA enclosure
ProSys-15 PA enclosure
Dynamic Systems Processor
HDH-2 sound reinforcement enclosure
HDH-3 sound reinforcement enclosure
HDH-4 sound reinforcement enclosure
HDH-M sound reinforcement enclosure
DSC-HDH speaker processor
PVM-380N microphone
MTB-2x4 MIDI switch box
Ultraverb effects processor
Autograph digital equalizer
Gatekeeper noise gate
AMR MCR-4/S tape recorder
AMR Syncontroller
AMR MIDI Director controller
AMR PME-8 parametric equalizer
AMR AEQ-2800 digital equalizer
AMR QFX 4x4 effects processor
AMR Q-Factor noise reduction
AMR MDB 2x4 MIDI switch box
AMR EAC-8 event controller

AMR MAP 8x4 audio patch bay

1989

DPM-3 workstation synthesizer
Tracer LH electric guitar
Destiny electric guitar
Destiny Custom electric guitar
Odyssey electric guitar
Vandenberg Custom Signature electric guitar
Rudy Sarzo Signature bass guitar
TL-6 bass guitar
Rage 108 guitar amp
Envoy guitar amp
Backstage 110 guitar amp
Studio Pro 112 guitar amp
Bandit 112 guitar amp
Special 112 guitar amp
Bravo guitar amp
Minx 110 bass amp
T.G.Raxx preamp
T.B.Raxx preamp
Rock Master preamp
Classic 60 tube power amp
Classic 120 tube power amp
Classic 60/60 tube power amp
KB-300 Wedge keyboard amp
HKS-15 keyboard amp
KBX-15 keyboard enclosure
DSC-KBX system processor
Futura 12" speaker enclosure
Futura 15" speaker enclosure
CS-1000 power amp
Unity 1000-8 mixer
Unity 1000-12 mixer
Unity 2000-12 mixer
Unity 2000-16 mixer
MD III-12 mixer
MD III-16 mixer
MD-16 x 6 monitor mixer
Mark VIII-24 mixing console
Stadia molded enclosure
PVM-520TN microphone
PVM-580TN microphone
PVR-1 microphone
PEL-20 microphone
PEL-25 microphone
PM-16 microphone
Audiolink multicore cables
PV Lite System 2400
Multifex effects processor
Automate digital EQ expander
MIDI Librarian MIDI-file storage
Impulse white molded enclosure
Stadia white molded enclosure
112 Powered Prosys PA enclosure
112 Criterion Bleached PA enclosure
1115 TF PA enclosure
Euro EN-305 PA enclosure
Euro HP400 PA enclosure
Euro EN-325 PA enclosure
DSC-12 speaker system processor
DSC-23 speaker system processor
12M monitor enclosure
BW Superstructure speakers
AMR 1242 mixer
AMR APB-32 audio patch bay

AMR PME-4000 parametric equalizer
AMR SDM-5200 microphone
AMR PRM 312A studio monitor
AMR PRM 310A studio monitor
AMR PRM 308A studio monitor
AMR PRM 208A studio monitor
AMR PRM 205A studio monitor
AMR Production Series 800 consoles
AMR Production Series 1600 consoles
AMR Production Series 2400 consoles
AA UA-5 utility amp
AA UA-12 utility amp
AA UA-35 utility amp
AA UMA-12 utility amp
AA UMA-35 utility amp
AA UMA-75 utility amp
AA UMA-150 utility amp
AA WFM-1 utility amp
AA IPA-75 power amp
AA IPA-150 power amp
AA IPA-300 power amp
AA IPS-400 power amp
AA IPS-800 power amp
AA CEX-4 crossover
AA CEQ-28 digital equalizer
AA CEQ-28R digital equalizer
AA RTD-215 graphic equalizer
AA RTD-31 graphic equalizer
AA PR-600 molded enclosure
AA PR-1000 molded enclosure
AA PR-1200 install enclosure
AA PR-1500 install enclosure
AA HV-1200 install enclosure
AA HV-1500 install enclosure
AA PAA-250 microphone
AA PAA-350 microphone

1990

G-90 electric guitar
G-90 LH electric guitar
Odyssey 25th Anniversary LE electric guitar
Express 112 guitar amp
Backstage Chorus 208 guitar amp
Studio Chorus 210 guitar amp
Classic Chorus 212 guitar amp
Stereo Chorus 212 guitar amp
SP-2A PA enclosure
388S PA enclosure
Euro EN-118 subwoofer enclosure
DSC-Subwoofer system processor
PVM-535N microphone
Univerb II effects processor
Addverb II effects processor
22T Driver horn driver
AMR PDR-16 power distribution
AA CEX-4L crossover
AA Performance Series 2480 console
AA Performance Series 3680 console

1991

DPM-2 synthesizer
DPM-3SE sampling workstation
DPM-V2 rack synthesizer
DPM-V3 rack synthesizer
DPM-SX sampling module
DPM-SP sample player

Predator electric guitar
Tracer LT electric guitar
Generation S-3 electric guitar
Ecoustic semi-acoustic electric guitar
B-90 bass guitar
B-90 LH bass guitar
Palaedium bass guitar
RSB-4 bass guitar
Renown 112 guitar amp
Renown 212 guitar amp
Classic 50/212 guitar amp
Classic 50/410 guitar amp
TKO-80 bass amp
TKO-80BW bass amp
TNT-160 bass amp
TNT-160BW bass amp
Supreme 160 head
Revolution head
Ultra 60 head
Ultra 120 head
ProFex effects preamp
ProFex FC controller
Classic 120/120 tube power amp
Rack Sentinel power distribution
410T speaker enclosure
DPC-750 power amp
Unity 1000SM mixer
Unity 2000SM mixer
XR-680C PA head
XR-800D powered console
XR-1200D powered console
XR-1600D powered console
Impulse III molded enclosure
Impulse Stereo Subwoofer
SP-2Ti PA enclosure
SP-3Ti PA enclosure
SP-4Ti PA enclosure
SP-5Ti PA enclosure
115 International HC PA enclosure
118 International HC PA enclosure
118-SUB HC subwoofer enclosure
RBS-2 sub enclosure
UDH sub enclosure
UDH-2† subwoofer enclosure
DS-1502 DJ enclosure
DS01803 DJ enclosure
DS-3003 DJ enclosure
Euro ES-15PE powered PA enclosure
Euro ES-15 '92 PA enclosure
Euro ES-315 '92 PA enclosure
Euro ES-10M monitor enclosure
VCM-1 microphone
PSM-1 microphone
SRC-1600 mixer
SRC-2400 mixer
CD Mix 7032 DJ mixer
CD Mix 9072 DJ mixer
Ultraverb II effects processor
PC-4XL equalizer
Protégé karaoke
PVM Lite System 3000
1:1 Interface impedance converter
BLS-3 balanced line splitter
44T compression horn driver
Sheffield stamped-frame speakers
Black Widow Kevlar-impregnated cones
AMR PRM-225 studio monitor

AMR PRM-308SL studio monitor
AA PZS-80 zone amp
AA MA-212 modular amp
AA MA-635 modular amp
AA MA-675 modular amp
AA MA-6150 modular amp
AA MPA-700 modular amp
AA PSX crossover
AA PR-603 molded enclosure
AA PR-603 stereo subwoofer
AA TZ-205 speaker enclosure
AA TZ-208 speaker enclosure
AA DSC-A system processor
AA ACM-1 microphone
AA ALM-16 microphone
AA ASM-1 microphone
AA LX-20 microphone
AA LX-25 microphone

1992

DPM-3SE+ sampling workstation
DPM-Si performance keyboard
DPM-C8 MIDI controller keyboard
DPM-SX II sampling module
DPM-Spectrum Bass module
DPM-Spectrum Synth module
Celeste II† digital piano
Celeste IV† digital piano
Falcon Custom electric guitar
Foundation 5 bass guitar
Resolite† bass guitar
B-90 Active bass guitar
Unity Passive bass guitar
RJB bass guitar
Midibase MIDI-controller bass guitar
Midibase module
Blazer 158 guitar amp
Classic 20 guitar amp
Classic 50 head
Classic 115E speaker enclosure
Classic 410E speaker enclosure
Classic 410ES speaker enclosure
Classic 50/50 tube power amp
EVH 5150 head
EVH 5150 Straight speaker enclosure
EVH 5150 Slant speaker enclosure
PT-3† preamp
Bassist preamp
ProFex II effects preamp
BassFex effects preamp
Valverb retro tube reverb
Valvex retro tube preamp
412 M speaker enclosure
412 MS speaker enclosure
210TX speaker enclosure
410TX speaker enclosure
115 BX speaker enclosure
115BW BX speaker enclosure
Protégé RM karaoke
Illuminator 600 lighting
CS-150† power amp
CS-1500† power amp
VSX crossover
Max Mix mixer
Six Mix mixer
RSM-1662 mixer
PC-1600 MIDI controller

RMC-2010 MIDI controller
MIDI-Streamer
XRD-680 PA head
HDH-244T sound reinforcement enclosure
DTH-1 sound reinforcement enclosure
DTH-SUB subwoofer enclosure
ProSys 112HC PA enclosure
ProSys-115HC PA enclosure
DJS-1000 DJ speaker system
1545Ti monitor enclosure
Mini Monitor II monitor enclosures
Euro EuroSys-1 PA enclosure
Euro EuroSys-2 PA enclosure
Euro EuroSys-3 PA enclosure
Euro EuroSys-4 PA enclosure
Euro EuroSys-Bassflex subwoofer enclosure
Euro EuroSys-1PM monitor enclosure
Euro EuroSys-1M monitor enclosure
Euro HiSys-1 PA enclosure
Euro HiSys-2 PA enclosure
Euro HiSys-3 PA enclosure
Euro HiSys-4 PA enclosure
Euro HiSys-SUB sub enclosure
PVM-480 microphone
AMR-Series 2482 consoles
AMR SRD-20/20 effects processor
AMR Delta-VU meter bridge
AMR PRM-308SV studio monitor
AA DL-1500 install enclosure
AA SMR-6 mixer
AA IDL-1000 delay line
AA PZS-80 Mixer
AA UA-12T utility amp
AA UA-35T utility amp
AA UMA-12T utility amp
AA UMA-35T utility amp
AA UMA-75T utility amp
AA UMA-150T utility amp
AA AMA-1200 powered mixer
AA IPA-75T power amp
AA IPA-150T power amp
AA IPA-300T power amp
AA IPS-150
AA PR-503 molded enclosure
AA PR-605 molded enclosure
AA PR-1003 molded speaker
AA ERW-1500 install enclosure
AA WS-502 install speaker
AA WS-802 install speaker

1993
DPM-4 sampling workstation
DPM-488 sampling workstation
DPM-SX II sampling module
PCX-6† keyboard
PCX-688† keyboard
Millennium DK-20 digital piano
Predator AX electric guitar
Reactor electric guitar
Axcelerator electric guitar
Axcelerator F electric guitar
Axcelerator Bass bass guitar
Axcelerator Bass FL fretless bass guitar
Axcelerator S Bass bass guitar
Forum bass guitar

B-Quad 4 bass guitar
Classic 30 guitar amp
Blues Classic guitar amp
Delta Blues guitar amp
Bandit w/Sheffield guitar amp
Duel 212 guitar amp
Classic 100 head
TKO115 bass amp
TNT115 bass amp
Combo 115 bass amp
Combo 210TX bass amp
Tubemaster pre-amp
MAX preamp
Classic 100
810TX speaker enclosure
PV-4C power amp
PV-8.5C power amp
PV-1.3K power amp
CS-200X power amp
CS-400X power amp
CS-1000X power amp
CS-1200X power amp
DPC-1000 power amp
CMX-602† mixer
Versamix mixer
RSM-2462 mixer
DSM-752 DJ mixer
CD Mix 7032A DJ mixer
CD Mix 9072 DJ mixer
Impulse V molded enclosure
Subcompact 15 subwoofer enclosure
Subcompact 18 subwoofer enclosure
DTH-2 sound reinforcement enclosure
DTH-2 sound reinforcement enclosure
DTH-3 sound reinforcement enclosure
DTH-4 sound reinforcement enclosure
DTH-M monitor enclosure
112Ti monitor enclosure
115Ti monitor enclosure
Euro EuroSys-1 8Ω PA enclosure
Euro EuroSys-5 PA enclosure
Euro EuroSys-1PM powered monitor
Euro EuroSys-2PM powered monitor
Euro HiSys-1 8Ω PA enclosure
Euro HiSys-2 8Ω PA enclosure
Euro HiSys-115 sub enclosure
Euro HiSys-118 sub enclosure
Euro HiSys-2M monitor enclosure
PVM-520i microphone
PVM-535i microphone
PVM-580i microphone
PVM-357 microphone
Q-215 equalizer
MIDI Master II controller
RhythmLite 1200 lighting
LB 1200 lighting
PV Lite 3008 lighting
PV Lite 4008 lighting
22XT horn driver
AMR PMA-250 power amp
AMR APB-8000 patch bay
AMR VMP-2 tube preamp
AA PRM-26i studio monitor
AA PRM-28i studio monitor
AA PRM-308Si studio monitor
MM Mainframe 900
MM Mainframe 700

MM-8830 break-out box
MM-8840 break-out box

1994
Radial Pro drum set
DPM- Spectrum Analog Filter module
Falcon I† international series electric guitar
Falcon II† international series electric guitar
Milestone I international series bass guitar
Detonator electric guitar
Detonator F electric guitar
Impact Firenza electric guitar
Impact Milano electric guitar
Impact Torino electric guitar
Ecoustic ATS electro-acoustic guitar
SD-9P acoustic guitar
SD-11P acoustic guitar
DD-21P acoustic guitar
SD-112PCE acoustic guitar
CJ-33PE acoustic guitar
CD-3312PE acoustic guitar
CD-37PE acoustic guitar
CD-3712PE acoustic guitar
CyberBass MIDI-controller bass guitar
Ultra Plus head
Mark III XP head
Mark VI XP head
Mark VIII XP head
DPB-115 bass amp
DPB bass amp
T-MAX bass amp
T-MAX 115 bass amp
Kilobass bass amp
XR-600E PA head
XR-680E PA head
XRD-680RM powered PA
XRD-680S PA head
XRD-680S RM powered PA
VX-1.5K power amp
VX-3.0K power amp
Unity 500 mixer
LM-8S mixer
LM-16S mixer
SP-2XT PA enclosure
SP-4XT PA enclosure
DTH-5 sound reinforcement enclosure
DTH-Concert Sub enclosure
112-Ti monitor enclosure
Euro HiSys-215 Sub enclosure
Euro AeroSys-1 PA enclosure
Euro AeroSys-2 PA enclosure
Euro AeroSys-3 PA enclosure
Euro AeroSys-4 PA enclosure
Euro AeroSys-5 PA enclosure
Euro AeroSys-Sub enclosure
Euro AeroSys-2PM monitor enclosure
MIDI Pro controller
XG-5 noise gate
ShowFex effects processor
Q-131 equalizer
Q-231 equalizer
PM-16S microphone
PVM-835 Diamond microphone
PVM-880 Diamond microphone

PVM-T9000 tube microphone

1995
DPM-C8p MIDI-controller keyboard
DPM-SP+ sample player
DPM-Spectrum Organ module
Millennium DK-40† digital piano
Raptor I international series electric guitar
Raptor II international series electric guitar
Raptor III international series electric guitar
Reactor AX electric guitar
Detonator JX electric guitar
Detonator AX electric guitar
Impact Firenza AX electric guitar
Cropper Classic electric guitar
Milestone II international series bass guitar
Axcelerator Plus bass guitar
Forum AX bass guitar
Forum 5 bass guitar
B-Quad 5 bass guitar
CyberBass 5 MIDI-controller bass guitar
Rage 158 Transtube guitar amp
Blazer 158 Transtube guitar amp
Audition 110 Transtube guitar amp
Envoy 110 Transtube guitar amp
Studio Pro 110 Transtube guitar amp
Express 112 Transtube guitar amp
Bandit 112 S Transtube guitar amp
Special 212 S Transtube guitar amp
5150 212 Combo guitar amp
TubeRex effects processor
Classic-400 head
TKO-115S bass amp
TKO-115S BW bass amp
TNT-115S bass amp
TNT-115S BW bass amp
T-Max 210 bass amp
Nashville-112E speaker enclosure
Nashville-115E speaker enclosure
Classic 412E speaker enclosure
Classic 412ES speaker enclosure
Classic 410TX speaker enclosure
Classic 810TX speaker enclosure
Classic 115E speaker enclosure
PV-2.6C power amp
MP-4+ PA head
XRD-680+ PA head
Unity 1002-8 mixer
Unity 1002-12 mixer
Unity 2002-12 mixer
Unity 2002-16 mixer
Unity 2002-24 mixer
Unity-4032 mixer
112SE PA enclosure
212SE PA enclosure
312SE PA enclosure
Impulse 6 molded enclosure
Impulse 652S molded enclosure
SP118P powered subwoofer enclosure
Q-Factor 2212 sound reinforcement enclosure
Q-Factor 218 sound reinforcement enclosure

APPENDIX A

Euro HiSys-1XT PA enclosure
Euro HiSys-1XT 8Ω PA enclosure
Euro HiSys-2XT PA enclosure
Euro HiSys-2XT 8Ω PA enclosure
Euro HiSys-3XT PA enclosure
Euro HiSys-4XT PA enclosure
Euro HiSys-5XT PA enclosure
Euro HiSys-215XT subwoofer enclosure
Euro HiSys-115XT subwoofer enclosure
Euro HiSys-118XT subwoofer enclosure
Euro HiSys-2MXT monitor enclosure
Euro HiSys-1XTF PA enclosure
Euro HiSys-2XTF PA enclosure
Euro HiSys-215XTF sub enclosure
MDJ-1150 DJ enclosure
MDJ-2150 DJ enclosure
DJS-1500 DJ speaker system
DJS-1800 DJ speaker system
XD-3/4 crossover
Q-431 equalizer
Q-431F equalizer
Q-431FM equalizer
PVi microphone
AMR PS-2482 console
AMR RSM-2462 mixer
AMR IA-84/10 interface amp
AMR SDR-20/20+ effects processor
AMR PMA-70+ power amp
AMR RP-500 power amp
AA CEX-4La crossover
AA CEX-5 crossover
AA AUTOMIX
AA AAM-150 microphone
AA AAN0535 microphone
AA AAM-580 microphone
AA AAM-835 microphone
AA AAM-880 microphone
AA PR-2652 speaker enclosure
AA PR-652S speaker enclosure
AA PR-1580 speaker enclosure
AA HV-1580 speaker enclosure
AA HV-1580 speaker enclosure
AA SC-8 system controller
AA IRM-8150 mixer
AA UM-10 utility amp
AA MMA-800T modular amp
AA MMA-825T modular amp
AA MMA-875T modular amp
AA MMA-8150T modular amp
AA UMA-35T II utility amp
AA UMA-75T II utility amp
AA UMA-150T II utility amp
AA IPA-75 T II power amp
AA IPA-150 T II power amp
AA IPA-300 T II power amp
AA IDC-150T safety amplifier
AA IA-200 power amp
AA IA-400 power amp
AA IA-800 power amp
MM Miniframe 200
MM Miniframe 100
MM-AC8 amp control
MM-A8P preamp

1996
EVH Wolfgang electric guitar
Predator '96 electric guitar
Axcelerator 2-T bass guitar
RSB II bass guitar
Backstage FX 208 guitar amp
Studio FX 210 guitar amp
Stereo TransFex 212 guitar amp
Ecoustic 112 acoustic amp
Microbass '96 bass amp
Minx '96 bass amp
Basic 112 bass amp
Combo 115 '96 bass amp
Combo 210TX '96 bass amp
Sessionbass bass amp
Classic 400 carpet-covered head
KB/A-100 keyboard amp
KB/A-300 keyboard amp
PFC-10 ProFex controller
RP-500 Radial Pro drum set
RP-750 Radial Pro drum set
RP-1000 Radial Pro drum set
XRD-680S+ PA head
CS-1800G power amp
CS-3000G power amp
LMS mixer
Unity 1002-8RM mixer
Unity 4024 mixer
Unity 4024-FC mixer
Unity 4032-FC mixer
SRC-6024 mixer
SRC-6032 mixer
Production Mixer 1000 DJ mixer
MAQ-300 monitor amp
MAQ-600 monitor amp
110DL PA speaker enclosure
112DC PA speaker enclosure
112DL PA speaker enclosure
1210DL PA speaker enclosure
115DL PA speaker enclosure
112M monitor enclosure
112DLM monitor enclosure
115DLM monitor enclosure
SP-2G PA speaker enclosure
SP-4G PA speaker enclosure
SP-5G PA speaker enclosure
SP-112M monitor enclosure
SP-115M monitor enclosure
Impulse 200 molded enclosure
Impulse 200P powered molded enclosure
Impulse 2652 install enclosure
HV-1280 install enclosure
HV-1580 install enclosure
DTH-S2 sound reinforcement enclosure
DTH-S4 sound reinforcement enclosure
DTH-S5 sound reinforcement enclosure
DTH-SF2 sound reinforcement enclosure
DTH-SF4 sound reinforcement enclosure
DTH-SF5 sound reinforcement enclosure
DTH-118 sound reinforcement subwoofer
DTH-218 sound reinforcement subwoofer
DTH-Concert Sub II sound reinforcement subwoofer
DTH-SML monitor enclosure
DTH-SMR monitor enclosure
Euro EuroSys-1 '96 PA enclosure
Euro EuroSys-2 '96 PA enclosure
Euro EuroSys-3 '96 PA enclosure
Euro EuroSys-4 '96 PA enclosure
Euro EuroSys-6 '96 PA enclosure
Euro EuroSys-SUB '96 subwoofer enclosure
Euro EuroSys-1PM '96 monitor enclosure
Euro EuroSys-1M '96 powered monitor
Euro HuSys-1XT '96 PA enclosure
Euro HuSys-1XT '96 PA enclosure
Euro HuSys-2XT '96 PA enclosure
Euro HuSys-2XT '96 PA enclosure
Euro HuSys-3XT '96 PA enclosure
Euro HuSys-4XT '96 PA enclosure
Euro HuSys-5XT '96 PA enclosure
Euro HuSys-115XT '96 subwoofer enclosure
Euro HuSys-215XT '96 subwoofer enclosure
Euro HuSys-118XT '96 subwoofer enclosure
Euro HuSys-2MXT '96 monitor enclosure
Q-231F equalizer
PC4-XLA crossover
DeltaFex effects processor
Addverb III effects processor
Univerb III effects processor
AMR PR-308SV-L studio monitor
AMR PR-308SV-R studio monitor
MM Mainframe-950
MM Mainframe-940
MM Mainframe-740
MM Miniframe-208
MM Miniframe-108

1997
EVH Wolfgang stop-tail electric guitar
Firenza electric guitar
Firenza JX electric guitar
Firenza AX electric guitar
Axcelerator 6 bass guitar
Cirrus-4 bass guitar
Cirrus-5 bass guitar
Cirrus-6 bass guitar
Ultra-112 guitar amp
TransFex 208s guitar amp
TransFex Pro 212s guitar amp
TransFex Pro head
MAX-100 preamp
TranstubeFex effects preamp
Combo 115TX bass amp
Combo 210TX bass amp
112MB speaker enclosure
210TXR speaker enclosure
115TXR speaker enclosure
KB/A-15 keyboard amp
KB/A-60 keyboard amp
XR-560 PA head
XR-886 powered console
PV-2000 power amp
CS0800S power amp
DPC-1200X power amp
Unit-300RQ mixer
Unity-3014RQ mixer
SRC-4026 mixer
SRC-4034 mixer
Euro HiSys-6XT PA enclosure
Euro HiSys-6XTF PA enclosure
Euro HiSys-112XT subwoofer enclosure
Euro HiSys-1MXT monitor enclosure
Euro MaxSys-1 PA enclosure
Euro MaxSys-SUB subwoofer enclosure
110-TL PA enclosure
112-TC PA enclosure
112-TL PA enclosure
115-TL PA enclosure
SP-1G PA enclosure
SP-3G PA enclosure
SP-6G PA enclosure
Mentor feedback locator
DeltaFex Twin effects processor
PVM-22 microphone
MM Mainframe-950
MM Mainframe-940
MM Mainframe-740
MM Miniframe-208
MM Miniframe-108
MM X-Frame

1998
Wolfgang flame-top electric guitar
Wolfgang Special electric guitar
G-Bass bass guitar
Ultra-212 guitar amp
Ultra-410 guitar amp
112SX speaker enclosure
115BX speaker enclosure
115BX BW speaker enclosure
MAQ-150 monitor amp
RQ-3014 mixer
Euro MaxSys-1 '98 PA enclosure
Euro MaxSys-2 PA enclosure
Euro MaxSys-115 subwoofer enclosure
Euro MaxSys-215 subwoofer enclosure
Euro MaxSys-312 subwoofer enclosure
HV-1282 install enclosure
HV-1582 install enclosure
PC-1600X MIDI controller
AMR VPM-2 tube microphone preamp
AMR VC/L-1 tube compressor/limiter
MM PageMatrix Station 4W
MM PageMatrix Station 4
MM PageMatrix Station 10
MM Paging Controller

1999
Wolfgang Special Flame Top electric guitar
Predator Plus guitar
Milestone III bass guitar
Milestone IV bass guitar
Euro C-4NT bass guitar
Euro C-4BN bass guitar
Euro C-5NT bass guitar
Fury II bass guitar
G-5 bass guitar
Clarksdale acoustic guitar
Tupelo acoustic guitar
Tupelo AE acoustic guitar
Indianola acoustic guitar

Indianola AE acoustic guitar
Classic 30BT guitar amp
Classic 50/212BT guitar amp
Delta Blues 210 guitar amp
Prowler guitar amp
Ranger 212 guitar amp
Revolution 112 guitar amp
TransChorus 210 guitar amp
EVH-5150 II head
Firebass 700 head
210-TXF speaker enclosure
410-TXF speaker enclosure
419-TXF speaker enclosure
412-TXF speaker enclosure
KB/A-30 keyboard amp
Dirty Dog effects pedal
Delta Stomp effects pedal
Vocal 100 effects pedal
DPM-C8X MIDI-controller keyboard
XR-600F PA head
XR-1204 powered console
PV-260 power amp
DPC-1400X power amp
RQ-200 mixer
RQ-1606M monitor mixer
RQ-880FX mixer
SRM-2410 monitor mixer
3D Mix Pro DJ mixer
CD-Mix Seven DJ mixer
CD-Mix Nine DJ mixer
XR-684 PA head
XR-1204 powered console
XR-2012 powered console
Impulse 200 subwoofer enclosure
Impulse 500 subwoofer enclosure
Impulse 200P subwoofer powered enclosure
112-TLS PA enclosure
115-TLS PA enclosure
115-TLS SUB PA enclosure
1522-TLS PA enclosure
SP-218 subwoofer enclosure
SP-Subcompact-18 subwoofer enclosure
112PM powered monitor
Euro EuroSys-500XT PA enclosure
Euro EuroSys-500XT SUB enclosure
Eiro EiroSys-500MXT monitor enclosure
Euro EuroSys-10PM powered monitor
Euro EuroSys-15PM powered monitor
DTH-118B subwoofer enclosure
DTH0218B sound reinforcement subwoofer
DTH-215B sound reinforcement subwoofer
DTH-4115 sound reinforcement enclosure
DTH-4215 sound reinforcement enclosure
DTH-4210 sound reinforcement enclosure
DTH-4115F sound reinforcement enclosure
DTH-4215F sound reinforcement enclosure
DTH-4210F sound reinforcement enclosure

EQ031FX equalizer
EQ-215FX equalizer
Q-215FX equalizer
Q-231FX equalizer
Q-431FX equalizer
TubeSweetner tube processor
CEL-2 compressor/limiter
StudioMix computer recording mixer
AA PZS-140
MM CAB-8o
MM CAB-8i
MM MM-DSP-AES
MM AmpWare 2.0

2000

Limited FT electric guitar
Limited QT electric guitar
Predator Plus 7 electric guitar
Predator Plus LH electric guitar
Predator Plus HB electric guitar
Raptor Plus electric guitar
Raptor Plus LH electric guitar
Raptor Plus TK electric guitar
Millennium-4 bass guitar
Millennium-4 Plus bass guitar
Millennium-5 bass guitar
Millennium-5 Plus bass guitar
Foundation 2K-4 bass guitar
Foundation 2K-5 bass guitar
Fury II Active bass guitar
Fury II LH bass guitar
Aberdeen acoustic guitar
Route-61 acoustic guitar
Glendora acoustic guitar
Glendora-12 acoustic guitar
McComb acoustic guitar
Euro PVi-705 acoustic guitar
Euro PVi-706 acoustic guitar
Euro EC-135 electro-acoustic guitar
Euro EC-108S electro-acoustic guitar
Euro EC-100 electro-acoustic guitar
Transformer 112 guitar amp
Transformer 212 guitar amp
Nitrobass head
Deltabass head
810TV speaker enclosure
Radial Pro 751 Kit 4 drum set
Radial Pro 751 Kit 5 drum set
Radial Pro 501 Kit 4 drum set
Radial Pro 501 Kit 5 drum set
Euro Pro-5 drum set
Euro Pro-5 Plus drum set
Euro PVi Rock-5 drum set
GPS-900 power amp
GPS-1500 power amp
GPS-1600 power amp
GPS-3500 (3400 export) power amp
RSM-4062 mixer
RQ-2310 mixer
RQ-2314 mixer
RQ-2318 mixer
MP-400 PA system
MP-4 PLUS PA head
MP-5 PLUS PA head
MP-600 PA head
XR-684 PLUS PA head
XR-560 PA head

XR-600F PA head
XR-800F powered console
Impulse-100 molded enclosure
Impulse 500P Subwoofer powered enclosure
SP-7G sound reinforcement enclosure
Euro HuSys-7XT sound reinforcement enclosure
3D-MIX DJ mixer
PM-1 DJ mixer
DJS-4 DJ enclosure
XD-2/3/4 crossover
ProComm wireless microphones
AA ILS-1564H4
AA ACi-485V amp control
AA SMR-821 mixer

2001

Limited VT electric guitar
Limited ST electric guitar
Limited HB electric guitar
Limited EXP HB electric guitar
Limited EXP ST electric guitar
Limited EXP LH electric guitar
Milestone-5 bass guitar
Grind Bass-4 bass guitar
Grind Bass-5 bass guitar
Fury 4QT Active bass guitar
Fury 5QT Active bass guitar
Fury 6QT Active bass guitar
Euro Dynabass-4QT bass guitar
Euro Dynabass-5QT bass guitar
Euro Dynabass-4FT bass guitar
Transtube 12 EFX guitar amp
Briarwood acoustic guitar
Euro Aberdeen Bass acoustic guitar
Transtube 212 EFX guitar amp
Transtube 258 EFX guitar amp
Transtube Supreme head
Triple XXX head
Triple XXX 412 speaker enclosure
Triple XXX 412S speaker enclosure
Wiggy head
Wiggy 212 speaker enclosure
Euro 212J speaker enclosure
Euro 412J speaker enclosure
Euro 412JS speaker enclosure
BAM 210 bass amp
PVi International drum set
Escort 2000 PA system
XR-696F PA head
XR-1600F powered console
RQ-4324 mixer
RQ-4332 mixer
PV-900 power amp
PV-1500 power amp
PV-2600 power amp
Impulse-1012 molded enclosure
Impulse-1015 molded enclosure
Impulse-1012|P powered enclosure
SP-1X PA enclosure
SP-2X PA enclosure
SP-3X PA enclosure
SP-4X PA enclosure
SP-5X PA enclosure
SP-6X PA enclosure
SP-7X PA enclosure

SP-118X subwoofer enclosure
SP-118X 8Ω subwoofer enclosure
SP-218X subwoofer enclosure
SP-Subcompact-18X subwoofer enclosure
SP-112MX monitor enclosure
SP-115MX monitor enclosure
Euro HiSys 1-RX PA enclosure
Euro HiSys 1-RX 8ΩPA enclosure
Euro HiSys 2-RX PA enclosure
Euro HiSys 2-RX 8Ω PA enclosure
Euro HiSys 3-RX PA enclosure
Euro HiSys 4-RX PA enclosure
Euro HiSys 5-RX PA enclosure
Euro HiSys 6-RX PA enclosure
Euro HiSys 7-RX PA enclosure
Euro HiSys 112-RX subwoofer enclosure
Euro HiSys 115-RX subwoofer enclosure
Euro HiSys 118-RX subwoofer enclosure
Euro HiSys 215-RX subwoofer enclosure
Euro HiSys 2-MRX monitor enclosure
Euro ClubSys 10 PA enclosure
Euro ClubSys 12 PA enclosure
Euro ClubSys 15 PA enclosure
Euro ClubSys 10F PA enclosure
Euro ClubSys 12F PA enclosure
Euro ClubSys 15F PA enclosure
Euro ClubSys 118 subwoofer enclosure
22RX horn driver
KOSMOS processor
Feedback Ferret processor
TMP-1 tube microphone preamp
Studio Pro M1 studio microphone
Studio Pro M2 studio microphone
MM Mainframe 980nt
MM Mainframe 960nt
MM Mainframe 760nt
MM Miniframe 280
MM Miniframe 180
MM Miniframe II 208
MM Miniframe II 108
MM MM-8802
MM X Bridge
MM CAB-4n
MM 16XT
MM MM-DSP-RJ
MM MM-DSP-CN
MM MM-DSP-AES
MM X-Frame 88
MM XControl
MM Octopower
MM Telephone Hybrid
MM AEC-4

2002

EVH Wolfgang Custom Shop
EVH Wolfgang QT Special electric guitar
V-Type electric guitar
V-Type EXP electric guitar
V-Type EXP Stop Tail electric guitar
Raptor Plus EXP electric guitar
Grind Bass-4 BXP bass guitar
Grind Bass-5 BXP bass guitar
Euro AC-D1 acoustic guitar
Euro AC-CS acoustic guitar
XXL head
Triple XXX 212 guitar amp

APPENDIX A

Classic 30 LTD guitar amp
Firebass II head
BAM Head
PRO 500 Bass head
PRO 115 speaker enclosures
PRO 210 speaker enclosures
PRO 410 speaker enclosures
KB/A 50 keyboard amp
XR-800F Plus powered console
Impulse 100P powered enclosure
Impulse 1012P powered enclosure
Impulse 1015P powered enclosure
Euro ClubSys-118X subwoofer
    enclosure
Euro Lowrider subwoofer enclosure
QW 2 sound reinforcement enclosure
QW 3 sound reinforcement enclosure
QW 4 sound reinforcement enclosure
QW 118 sound reinforcement enclosure
QW 218 sound reinforcement enclosure
QW ML sound reinforcement enclosure
QW MR sound reinforcement enclosure
PVM 321 drum microphone
PVM 325 drum microphone
PVM 328 drum microphone
DMS-5 drum microphone system
Battle Axe DJ mixer
Club Mix DJ mixer
DJS SUB enclosure
Q-215B equalizer
QF-131 equalizer
QF-215 equalizer
AA Digitool

2003

Wolfgang Custom Deluxe guitar
Wolfgang Custom guitar
Wolfgang Special Custom Deluxe guitar
Wolfgang Special Custom guitar
V-Type Set Neck TR electric guitar
V-Type Set Neck Baritone electric guitar
V-Type NTB Tremolo electric guitar
V-Type NTB Stop Tail electric guitar
Generation EXP electric guitar
Generation EXP ACM electric guitar
Generation Custom EXP ACM
    electric guitar
Predator Plus EXP FR electric guitar
Euro Raptor Junior electric guitar
Euro Rockingham semi-acoustic
    electric guitar
Raptor Plus Stage Pack
Millennium 4 bass guitar
Millennium 5 bass guitar
Millennium J-Style bass guitar
Millennium Standard bass guitar
Millennium Plus-4 bass guitar
Millennium Plus-5 bass guitar
Millennium Plus J-Style bass guitar
Millennium BXP bass guitar
Briarwood DR-1 acoustic guitar
Briarwood CL-1 acoustic guitar
Briarwood FL-1 acoustic guitar
Briarwood DR-2ER acoustic guitar
Briarwood DR-3ERS acoustic guitar
Briarwood DR-4CA EQ acoustic guitar
Briarwood DR-5CA EQ acoustic guitar

Triple XXX 112 guitar amp
Triple XXX Super 40 guitar amp
XXL 212 guitar amp
Supreme XL head
Nashville 1000 steel amp
MAX 700 head
MAX 450 head
MAX 160 head
PRO 810 speaker enclosure
Ecoustic 110 EFX acoustic amp
Ecoustic 112 EFX acoustic amp
KB 5 keyboard amp
KB 4 keyboard amp
KB 3 keyboard amp
KB 2 keyboard amp
KB 1 keyboard amp
XXL 212 speaker enclosure
XXL 412 speaker enclosure
CS 3000H power amp
CS 2000H power amp
CS 1200H power amp
CS 800H power amp
RQ 4324C mixer
RQ 4332C mixer
RQ 2326 mixer
RQ-2310FX mixer
16LM mixer
XR 600G PA head
QW 1 sound reinforcement enclosure
QW 2 sound reinforcement enclosure
QW 3 sound reinforcement enclosure
QW 4 sound reinforcement enclosure
QW 118 subwoofer enclosure
QW 218 subwoofer enclosure
QW Monitor enclosure
Impulse 115 subwoofer enclosure
Impulse 115P powered subwoofer
    enclosure
PR 110 molded enclosure
PR 112 molded enclosure
PR 115 molded enclosure
PR Sub molded enclosure
Euro TransLite CL-10 PA enclosure
Euro TransLite BL-10 PA enclosure
Euro TransLite RE-10 PA enclosure
Euro Messenger Line:
Euro UL-10 PA enclosure
Euro UL-12 PA enclosure
Euro UL-15 PA enclosure
Euro UL-215H PA enclosure
Euro UL-112 subwoofer enclosure
Euro UL-115 subwoofer enclosure
Euro UL-118 subwoofer enclosure
Euro UL-118S subwoofer enclosure
Euro UL-215S subwoofer enclosure
Euro PRO-12 PA enclosure
Euro PRO-15 PA enclosure
Euro PRO-SUB enclosure
Euro PRO-15PM powered monitor
Euro PRO-12PM powered monitor
Euro PRO-12M monitor enclosure
Euro ST-12 PA enclosure
Euro ST-15 PA enclosure
PVi Series II drum set
PVM-46 microphone
Feedback Ferret II processor
KOSMOS PRO effects processor

CEL-2A compressor/limiter
Q 2151 equalizer
Q 1311 equalizer
Sanctuary Series
Sanctuary Series S-14 mixer
Sanctuary Series S-14P mixer
Sanctuary Series S-24 mixer
Sanctuary Series SSE-10 enclosure
Sanctuary Series SSE-12 enclosure
Sanctuary Series SSE-15 enclosure
Sanctuary Series SSe-26 enclosure
Sanctuary Series SSE-6 enclosure
Sanctuary Series SSE-10M monitor
Sanctuary Series SSE-12M monitor

2004

Jack Daniel's acoustic guitar
Jack Daniel's electric guitars
Jack Daniel's ACM electric guitars
Jack Daniel's amplifier
HP Signature USA Custom electric
    guitar
HP Signature EXP electric guitar
HP Signature EX electric guitar
Generation USA Custom electric guitar
Rotor EXP electric guitar
Proximity Effect Rotor electric guitar
Mark Silvestri Cover Rotor electric guitar
Predator Plus EXP LH electric guitar
Acoustic Pack guitar and accessories
Stage Pack electric guitar and amp
JF-1 EXP semi-acoustic electric guitar
Millennium 4 BXP LH bass guitar
Millennium 4 BXP AC bass guitar
Millennium 5 BXP LH bass guitar
Millennium 5 BXP AC bass guitar
Cirrus Custom Shop
Cirrus 4 BXP bass guitar
Cirrus 5 BXP bass guitar
Grind Bass 4 NTB bass guitar
Grind Bass 5 NTB bass guitar
Grind Bass 6 NYB bass guitar
Briarwood DR-112 acoustic guitar
JSX Joe Satriani Signature 212 combo
Triple XXX Super 40 EFX guitar amp
Backstage guitar amp
X300L head
Pro 1600 head
BAM 110 bass amp
MAX 126 bass amp
MAX 158 bass amp
MAX 110 bass amp
MAX 112 bass amp
MAX 115 bass amp
QW 118P powered subwoofer enclosure
PVi International III PA enclosure
SP 2 PA enclosure
SP 3 PA enclosure
SP 4 PA enclosure
SP 5 PA enclosure
SP 112M monitor enclosure
SP 115M monitor enclosure
SP 118 subwoofer enclosure
SP 218 subwoofer enclosure
TriFlex PA speaker system
PR 10P powered enclosure
PR 12P powered enclosure

PR 15P powered enclosure
PV 115 PA enclosure
PV 215 PA enclosure
PV 900 Turbo-V power amp
PV 1500 Turbo-V power amp
PV 2600 Turbo-V power amp
PV 6 mixer
PV 8 mixer
PV 10 mixer
PV 14 mixer
PV 215EQ equalizer
PV 231EQ equalizer
PV 23XO crossover
PV 35XO crossover
Escort PA system
Dual DeltaFex effects processor
VSX 26 speaker management system
VSX 48 speaker management system
Studio Pro CM1 microphone
Pro Comm100-channel PCX U1002
    wireless system
PVi single-channel wireless microphone
Sanctuary Series S-4 mixer
Sanctuary Series SA-4200 power amp
MM NION n6
MM NION n3

2005

HP Signature Special electric guitar
HP Signature Special CT electric guitar
Omniac JD electric guitar
Rotor EX electric guitar
JSX Signature Head
6505 Head
6505 Plus Head
6505 212 Combo
6050 412 Straight enclosure
6050 412 Slant enclosure
Valve King Head
Valve King 212 Combo
Valve King 112 Combo
Valve King 412 enclosure
Penta Head
Penta 412
Cirrus Bolt-on Neck bass guitar
Cirrus Colored Alder bass guitar
Zodiak USA 4-string bass guitar
Zodiak USA 5-string bass guitar
PV Junior Drumkit
16PFX powered mixer
16FX mixer
24FX mixer
32FX mixer
CS 1400 power amp
CS 2000 power amp
CS 3000 power amp
CS 4000 power amp
CS 4080HZ power amp
CS 800X4 power amp
TriFlex speaker system
Messenger Lite PA system
PV-MSP1 microphone
PVi-100 microphone
PVi II microphone

APPENDICES • THE PEAVEY REVOLUTION 181

ACKNOWLEDGMENTS

I could not and would not have written this book without the support and blessing of Hartley Peavey. It was a challenge to overcome his modesty and his reticence to have his unique story recounted, and I thank him for agreeing to share it with all of us. Without access to his archived material and without his gracious agreement to devote his valuable time to reviewing and correcting the manuscript, this book would have been far more difficult to prepare. I am grateful to him for his friendship over the years, for a unique commercial education, and for the opportunities he has afforded me.

For their wonderful Southern hospitality during our research trip to Meridian in March 2004, Lin and I thank Hartley and Mary Peavey and Courtland Gray.

For their encouragement and willingness to share their intimate understanding of the early years of the company's development, I am indebted to my good friend Willie Hatcher and his son Greg. They have been a gold mine of information and have patiently endured my incessant e-mails. Together with Willie's wife, Faye, the Hatcher family graciously entertained us and drove us around Mississippi on an unforgettable day of discovery. Special thanks also to Dick Wiggins Jr. and his wife for their hospitality on that day.

I first got to know Joe and Marc Peavey when their parents brought these two "Dr. Who" fanatics to visit us in England when they were children. I thank them for their willingness to share with me insights about their father and their family life during my last visit to Meridian. I am especially obliged to Marc for locating old photos and illustrations in the Peavey archives and providing them for this book. He has tolerated my pestering with forbearance and has invariably come up trumps.

I am grateful for the many good friends I have met through my association with Peavey Electronics over the years, especially Melia Peavey, whose belief in the Golden Rule continues to inspire me. To those who agreed to help with the preparation of this book, I am especially beholden. These include past employees Jim and Jack Wilson, Frank Morris, Hal Aiken, Betty Holcombe, Chip Todd, Allan Sharp, Mike O'Neill, Kevin O'Brien, Rick Grigsby, Ernie Lansford, and John Roberts. Special thanks to long-serving Meridian employees and greatly valued friends Marty McCann, Mike Powers, Hollis Calvert, Grant Brown, and Monte Lamb for their input and assistance. Thank you also to the Peavey team in Corby, England—of whom I am immensely proud—and in Meridian to Beth Martin, Heidi France, Tonya Thompson, Dave Ellefson, Sharon Truelove, Amy Davis, and Brenda Slayton. In addition, Hartley and Mary Peavey would like to acknowledge Jim Beaugez for all of his work and dedication on assisting with the creation of this book.

Thank you Bjarne Christensen and Larry Linkin for sharing your memories, and thanks to veteran Peavey dealers Bill Everitt, Alan Levin, Reese Marin, and Don Wehr for your anecdotes—even though some of them were unprintable.

To all those at CMP Media and Backbeat Books involved in the publishing of this book, thank you for making it happen. Special thanks to Matt Kelsey and Richard Johnston for allowing me to work with them and for their encouragement. Huge gratitude goes to James Roberts, the highly respected and talented journalist who edited the manuscript and colonialized my "Queen's English" so well! Thank you, Jim. Then thanks to Richard Leeds for laying out the book so handsomely, and to all the others who made it happen behind the scenes, especially Nancy Tabor and Amy Miller.

Last, but absolutely by no means least, thank you Lin for your support, your help, and your patience (as ever). I love you more than anything.

INDEX

22 driver, 53–54
22A driver, 94
22T driver, 110
22XT driver, 128, 140
600S mixer, 59
800 mixer, 47
800S mixer, 60
801 mixer, 69
900S mixer, 59
1200 mixer, 52
1200S mixer, 59
1201 mixer, 69
5150 amps. *See* EVH 5150 amps
6505 head, 168

A

Addverb effects processor, 96
Adrian Vandenberg guitar, 98–99, 102, 103
AeroSys series, 128
Aiken, Hal, 54–55, 73
AlphaBass preamp, 102
AMR product line, 79, 81, 89–90, 93, 94, 116, 136
Architectural Acoustics line, 95, 97–98, 102, 103, 113, 137, 140
Artist guitar amp, 50, 63
Audition Chorus guitar amp, 94
Austin 400 guitar amp, 82, 83
Autograph digital equalizer, 96–97
Axcelerator guitars and basses, 123, 142
Axcess product line, 73–74, 94, 109

B

B-90 bass, 114
Backstage guitar amps, 61, 72, 83, 91, 97, 110, 139
BAM bass amp, 158
Bandit guitar amp, 72, 97, 121, 132–33
Basic bass amp, 78, 91
Bass amp, 34, 63
BassFex preamp, 118
Bassist preamp, 118
Battle Axe mixer, 160
Belfield, Don and Bob, 24, 34
Berlin, Jeff, 69, 114
Black Widow speakers, 54, 55, 58, 61, 71, 75, 110, 116, 117
Blakely, Larry, 81, 89
Blazer guitar amp, 118, 155
Bos, Rick, 129, 133, 135
Boutwell, Martha, 28, 49
B-Quad basses, 128, 129
Bravo guitar amp, 102
Briarwood Series, 159
Brown, Don, 49
Bush, George H.W. and Barbara, 112–13, 115
Butcher head, 88

C

Calvert, Hollis, 34, 35–36, 48, 73
Carter, Mike, 63
CD-Mix mixers, 115, 150
Centurion bass head, 63
Century head, 47, 52
Chick, Steve, 119
Christensen, Bjarne, 42, 47, 151
CinemAcoustics line, 141
Cirrus basses, 142, 165, 166, 172
City Series, 82, 83
Clarksdale guitar, 152
Class power amps, 129
Classic Series, 43, 63, 77, 88, 94, 107, 110, 113, 117, 118, 121–22, 128, 149
Club Mix mixer, 160
Combo bass amp, 63, 78, 122
Commercial Sound Projector (CSP), 43, 44, 53
Companion-15 guitar amp, 91
Concert bass amp, 29
Cook, Jeff, 83
Covington, Denzel, 23
Crest Audio, 151, 169
Cropper, Steve, 69, 133–34, 152
Cropper Classic guitar, 133–34
CS power amp series, 51, 58–59, 61, 67, 68, 85, 87–88, 96, 102, 122, 140, 143, 161, 170
CyberBass, 128

D

DAI (Digital Audio Interface), 169-170
DataBass, 97
DECA power amps, 82, 88, 93, 97
Decade guitar amp, 72
Deep Purple, 69, 88
Delta Series, 152
DeltaFex Twin effects processor, 143
DEP series, 82, 97
Destiny guitar, 102
Deuce guitar amps, 41, 47, 53, 63
Diddley, Bo, 4, 11, 12, 13
DJS systems, 136, 160
Douglas, George, 125
DPB bass amp, 128
DPC power amps, 122, 143, 150
DPM product line, 101, 102, 103, 114, 119–20, 123, 125, 135–36
DTH enclosures, 148, 150
Duel guitar amp, 122
DynaBass basses, 88, 158
DynaBass head, 22, 28, 29, 41, 43

E

Ecoustic line, 118–19, 128, 139, 161
ED electronic drum amps, 89
Ellefson, David, 152
Envoy guitar amp, 102
EQ equalizers, 52, 53, 150
Escort 2000 system, 158
EuroNational series, 102
EuroSys (ES) model line, 90, 115, 118, 122, 150
Everitt, Bill, 24–25, 49, 58, 59
EVH 5150 amps, 107, 120–21, 131, 134–35
EVH 5150 II amps, 152, 153
EVH Wolfgang guitars. *See* Wolfgang guitars
Express 112 guitar amp, 110

F

Falcon guitars, 93, 99
Feedback Ferret, 158
Feedback Locating System (FLS), 133
Fender, Leo, 13, 14, 18, 56, 64
Festival series, 41, 42, 50, 52, 59
Firebass head, 150
Firenza guitars, 142
Forum bass, 123
Foundation Bass, 88, 92, 155
Fury basses, 152, 155, 158

G

G-5 bass, 152
G-90 guitar, 114
Generalmusic (GEM), 153, 160
Generation guitars, 102–3, 134, 161, 165
Gilliom, John, 49, 53
Gray, Courtland, 162, 170, 173
Grigsby, Rick, 64, 70–71
Grind Bass, 159

H

Haggard, Merle, 29
Hamm, Stuart, 162
Hand, Larry, 91
Hatcher, Willie, 25, 34–35, 47, 76, 86, 110–11
HDH Series, 98, 102
Heritage guitar amp, 77–78
Hiatt, John, 107
HiSys series, 122
HKS series, 97
Holcombe, Becky, 36, 84
Horizon Custom guitar, 83
HP Signature guitars, 157, 164, 167
HRQ Series mixers, 149
Hydra doubleneck guitar, 83

I

IDL-655, 97
Impact guitars, 91–92, 123, 128
Impulse speakers, 98, 136, 140, 150, 158
Indianola guitar, 152
International Series, 62–63, 75
International Series III, 89, 92
Iommi, Tony, 135
IP-1 instrument preamp, 61

J

Jack Daniel's line, 165–66
Jackson, Randy, 88, 107, 114
Jazz Classic guitar amp, 83
JF-1 EXP guitar, 163
JSX amp, 162, 163, 171

K

KB series, 83, 94, 97, 102, 139, 142, 150, 161
Keel, 93
Kilobass amp, 128
KM-4 keyboard mixer, 61
KOSMOS, 157
Kroeger, Mike, 159
Kuchenrither, Mark, 154

L

LA 400 guitar amp, 83
Lamb, Monte, 102
Landers, Tim, 69, 70, 88, 99, 103
Lansford, Ernie, 92–93, 108
Lewis, Sonny, 23, 28, 34
Limited guitars, 158
LTD-400 guitar amp, 59, 61
Lynyrd Skynyrd, 60, 98

M

M-2000 and -7000 power amps, 76, 96
Mace guitar amp, 50, 63
MAQ power amps, 140
Mark I-VIII series, 61, 63, 73, 75–76, 88, 93, 97
MAX series, 88, 142, 161, 165
McCann, Marty, 40, 48, 53, 60, 62
MD series, 78, 79, 102, 115
MDG systems, 136
MediaMatrix, 124–25, 136, 137, 140–41, 143–44, 151, 153, 156, 159, 160, 165, 171
MegaBass amp, 91
Mendel, Nate, 152
Mentor, 143
Messenger series, 161
Microbass amp, 97
Midibase bass, 119, 128
MIDIMaster, 114
Milestone guitars and basses, 83, 84, 92, 128
Millennium basses, 155
Mini-Monitor package, 72
Minx bass amp, 94
Molly Hatchet, 67, 69
Monitor magazine, 82, 85, 92, 93, 108
Monitor system, 42, 43–44, 52
Morris, Frank, 28, 30
MS series, 92

INDEX

Multifex effects processor, 103
Musician head, 20, 22, 23, 28, 29, 34, 41, 43, 63
MX guitar amp, 77

N

Nashville amps, 83, 150
Nitro guitars, 85, 92, 93, 99

O

O'Brien, Kevin, 63, 76
Odyssey guitar, 102
O'Neill, Mike, 62, 68, 75, 127, 128
Outlaw guitar amp, 72

P

PA series, 25, 29, 35, 41, 42, 43, 45, 47, 52, 59–60, 61, 63
Pacer guitar amp, 47
PageMatrix, 151, 156
Palaedium bass, 114
Palmer, Ray, 28, 29, 30
Patriot guitars and basses, 83, 92
PC-1600, 120, 143
PCS speaker processor, 94
Peak Audio, 123–24, 153
Peavey, Anna Burleson, 8
Peavey, Bob, 7, 63
Peavey, Dawn, 31, 48, 50
Peavey, Hartley Davis. *See also* Peavey Electronics
  birth of, 5, 9
  childhood of, 4, 5–8, 9–13
  in high school, 14
  in college, 15, 16–18
  first patent of, 15, 17
  starts business, 18, 20–23
  marries and divorces Dawn, 31, 48, 50
  meets and marries Melia, 50, 60
  awards given to, 64, 70, 80, 81, 86, 94, 101, 106, 115, 125–26, 129, 164
  humanitarian efforts of, 106, 108, 121
  on Melia's death, 144–46, 150
  meets and marries Mary Gray, 153–54, 156
Peavey, Joe, 31, 167, 168–70, 173
Peavey, Joseph Burleson "Mutt," 4, 5, 9–13, 18, 22, 31, 49, 151, 168
Peavey, Joseph Lane "Pop," 7, 8
Peavey, Marc, 31, 167, 168, 173
Peavey, Mary Gray, 153–54, 156, 160, 172, 173
Peavey, Melia McRae
  begins working at Peavey Electronics, 42–43, 48
  marries Hartley, 60
  takes on bigger role in company, 73–74, 79–80, 81, 86
  awards given to, 106, 115

  humanitarian efforts of, 106, 108, 121
  declining health of, 129, 137, 138, 144–46
  death of, 146
Peavey, Sarah Davis, 5, 9, 151
Peavey Electronics. *See also individual products*
  founding of, 22
  logos of, 14, 16, 116–17
  mission statement of, 173
Peavey Factory Seminar program, 46, 49, 59–60
Peavey Finance (PVF), 76–77, 90
Peavey House, 108, 121, 159
Peavey Museum, 11, 108
PEP effects processors, 91, 93
Perkins, Carl, 74, 75
PGP-20 guitar preamp, 94
Phillips, Sam, 12
PLM-8128 mixer, 94
PMH and PML mics, 47–48
Powers, Mike, 74–75, 78, 99, 102–3, 128–29, 142, 163
PR series, 161
Predator guitars, 83, 123, 152, 155, 156
Pro 1600 head, 162–63
ProBass series, 91, 160
ProFex preamp, 114
Programmax-10, 85, 91
Project systems, 71, 75, 76, 78–79
Protégé, 120
Prowler guitar amp, 152
PV Lite System 2400, 103
PV series, 122, 143, 158, 165
PVDJ division, 169-170
PVI (Peavey International Series), 128
PVM mics, 93, 127–28, 143

Q

QW speakers, 158

R

Radial Pro drums, 127, 139
Rage guitar amp, 97, 155
Randy Jackson Signature model, 107
Ranger guitar amp, 150
Raptor guitars, 128, 155, 161
Reactor guitar, 123
Rebel guitar amp, 72
Reno 400 guitar amp, 82, 83
Renown guitar amp, 78
Resolite bass, 82, 118, 119
Revolution guitar amp, 118, 152
RJB-4 bass, 114
RMC-2000 MIDI controller, 91
Roadmaster head, 47
Roberts, John, 82, 89–90, 93, 98, 133, 154

Rock Master head, 83
Rockingham guitar, 161
Rotor EXP guitar, 163
RQ series, 150, 152, 156
RSB bass, 123
RSM-2462 mixer, 123, 136
Rudy Sarzo Signature bass, 99

S

Sabo, Snake, 134, 135
Sanctuary Series, 162, 165, 169
Sarzo, Rudy, 98–99
Satriani, Joe, 162, 163
Saturation circuit, 71–72, 77
Scorpion speakers, 70, 71, 75, 89, 116, 117
Session amps, 47, 59, 61, 62, 68, 97, 150
Sessionbass bass amp, 139
Sessions, Otho, 28, 30–31
Sharp, Allan, 36, 71, 76
Sheffield speakers, 116, 117, 121, 136
Smith, Dennis "Preacher," 29
Solo portable amp, 91, 94
Sondermeyer, Jack, 38, 40, 41, 53, 66, 71, 87, 97, 122, 133, 154
SP series, 53, 58, 59, 63, 68, 94, 136, 143
Special guitar amp, 97
Spectrum series, 135
SRC mixers, 139, 143, 150
SRM monitor board, 150
Standard system, 38, 41, 63
Stereo Chorus guitar amp, 88, 91, 110
Stereo TransFex guitar amp, 139
Studio Chorus guitar amp, 88, 91, 110
Studio Pro guitar amp, 72, 97
StudioFex guitar amp, 139
StudioMix, 153
SuperSat, 97

T

T series basses, 58, 63–64, 68, 75, 78
T series guitars, 51, 56–59, 63–64, 67, 68, 74–75
T-9000 mic, 128
Taylor, Skip, 91
T.B.Raxx and T.G.Raxxx preamps, 109
Tingle, Fred, 28, 30
TKO bass amp, 63, 78, 88, 97, 114
TL series, 99, 103, 143
T-Max bass amp, 128
TNT bass amp, 47, 68, 78, 88, 97, 114
Todd, Chip, 56–58, 74
TPA-9, 46
Tracer guitars, 99

TransChorus guitar amp, 152
TransFex series, 142
Transformer guitar amp, 155
TransTube line, 132–33, 156, 160, 161
Tri-Flex system, 78–79
Triple XXX head, 158, 159
Tube Fex preamp, 135
Tupelo guitar, 152

U

Ultra series, 114, 135, 142, 150
Ultraverb effects processor, 103
Unity series, 102, 139, 142, 150
Univerb effects processor, 96
Upchurch, Phil, 47

V

Van Halen, Edward, 120–21, 126, 138–39, 144, 152, 159
Vance, Tommy, 28, 30
Vandenberg, Adrian, 98–99, 102, 103
V-Cooling, 154
Vegas 400 amp, 83
Versamix mixer, 123
Vintage amp, 40, 41
Vocal Projectors, 52, 53
Volpp, Steven, 126–27, 142
Vortex guitars, 92, 93
VSS-20, 97
VT series, 63
VTA-400 head, 41, 52
VTB-300 amp, 33
VTM series, 94
VTX series, 77
V-Type guitars, 159, 161
Vulcan head, 29, 31, 33, 41
VX-1.5K power amp, 129

W

Webb, Jim, 29, 34
Whitesnake, 69, 98–99
Wiese, Bob, 86, 90, 136
Wiggins, Dick, 8–9
Wiggy amp, 157, 158
Wilson, Jack, 31–32, 80–81, 88, 101, 132, 138
Wilson, Jim, 31
Wolfgang guitars, 14, 126, 130, 138–39, 142, 149, 150, 155, 159
Wood, Pete, 45, 47, 64

X

Xavier, Bill, 155, 159
XC-400 power amp, 68
XR series, 61, 63, 68–69, 72–73, 98, 115, 139, 142, 150, 152, 160
XT-40 bass, 73

Z

Zappa, Dweezil, 158
Zaza, Neil, 133, 152